ARROGANCE AND ANXIETY

The Ambivalence of German Power, 1848–1914

L. L. Farrar, Jr.

UNIVERSITY OF IOWA PRESS

University of Iowa Press, Iowa City
© 1981 by The University of Iowa. All rights reserved
Printed in the United States of America

Library of Congress Cataloging in Publication Data

Farrar, L. L., Jr. (Lancelot L.), 1932–
    Arrogance and anxiety.

    (University of Iowa studies in history)
    Bibliography: p.
    1. Germany—Politics and government—1848–1870.
2. Germany—Politics and government—1871–1918.
I. Title. II. Series.
DD210.F37   943′.07   81–10374
ISBN 0–87745–112–5   AACR2

ARROGANCE
&
ANXIETY

University of Iowa Studies in History

To my daughter Shepard
on the occasion of her graduation
from Milton Academy, June 1981
"Dare To Be True"

CONTENTS

FOREWORD

The Department of History and the University of Iowa Press are pleased to present the first volume in the University of Iowa Studies in History. It is the hope of the department and the University to publish for the profession and the public books which, without being limited to any field or theme, have particular distinction and importance as original contributions to our knowledge and understanding of the past.

Dr. L. L. Farrar's work was judged by the department to fall without doubt into this category. The department found it a book based on monumental learning and research concerning an historical problem of obviously first-rate importance. At the same time it is clearly a work of great originality, both in its contribution to the understanding of German political behavior during the half-century of the Hohenzollern Empire and in its revolutionary break with many established traditions of professional historical writing. Dr. Farrar's huge and ramified substructure of erudition may be seen as a foundation, a sort of deep and multi-storied cellar, for a book whose text takes the form of an intricate and subtle argument that in some ways belongs to the intellectual tradition of Plato rather than that of Herodotus. He is concerned neither with the setting forth and verifying of facts nor with the writing of a narrative history revolving around personalities and anecdotes. The former have been done elsewhere, as is apparent from the book's massive and imposing body of footnotes, and a knowledge of the latter is assumed to be either known to the reader already or irrelevant to the book's purposes. What appears instead is an intricate but powerful argument concerning the evolution of ideas and their interplay with the realities, or perceived realities, of nationhood, economics, and politics.

As Dr. Farrar sees it, the coming of World War I can be explained in terms of the international system in which it occurred. Having analyzed the nature of this system, he proceeds to show how its properties and internal logic led, step by step, to the decisions for war. He reveals the illogic in much that has been written about "war guilt" and prewar diplomacy, especially by those focusing on the history of Germany; and he offers a novel base capable, he believes, of supporting a new and better understanding of these matters. The Department of History feels itself truly fortunate in having such an important and original work, controversial though it may be, as the first entry in its new series.

Department of History   Laurence Lafore
The University of Iowa

INTRODUCTION

Despite receding more than two-thirds of a century into the past, the First World War retains its fascination. This attraction is attributable in part to the war's historical importance as the overture of a revolutionary era ending in 1945 and comparable with previous tumultuous periods such as the French Revolution and Napoleonic wars. Indeed, the world war generation was the most significant of these revolutions since it effectively destroyed Europe's dominant role in the world. Equally important, though more difficult to measure, were the psychological and cultural responses to the First World War, which combined with the Second World War, atomic bomb, and Holocaust to create modern man's dominant myth, an amalgam of apocalypse, absurdity, and anxiety.[1]

It is, therefore, not surprising that the origins of World War I have drawn so much attention. During the interwar years studies were dominated by the desire to justify national policies—above all, to defend or condemn the Versailles treaty—and fed by a plethora of official published documents. A simultaneous current of thought—led by liberals such as Woodrow Wilson—sought to avoid future wars by isolating and abolishing the causes of the First World War. After World War II the question at first lost some of its immediacy because the second conflict seemed to validate the treaty's verdict of sole German guilt for the first. But interest revived with the opening of governmental archives. The devastation of the Second World War and threat of imminent destruction by atomic war, meanwhile, reinforced the impulse to find lessons in World War I which might prevent a Third World War.[2] Beyond these practical concerns, the war also offered the intellectual challenge of classic historical issues, above all, ascertainment of the relative influence of long-term causes (forces and institutions) and short-term causes (individual responsibility and chance events).[3]

Regardless of how the Versailles treaty's assertion of sole guilt is evaluated, the German role is central to interpretations of the war's origins, and the literature on prewar Germany has continued to expand. In being presented with yet another work on the subject, the reader is therefore justified in asking why this furrowed field should be plowed once again. The rationale lies precisely in the problem. The volume of new scholarship, the variety of interpretations, and the heat of the debate have created confusion. In fact, the debate is in danger of producing the paradox that the more historians know about prewar Germany, the less they understand. The present study is designed to isolate and evaluate the contending theses and is therefore interpretive and synthetic.

At the same time it offers a theory of German behavior. Understanding of Germany's role in the origins of World War I depends on how it is conceived. Some studies have conceptualized the problem in relatively narrow terms, concentrating on events immediately before the war and thus emphasizing the contribution of individual statesmen. Others have formulated the issue more broadly in tracing it back to German policy decisions of the previous decade or even to 1871. The present work perceives Germany in terms of the existing international system, whose fundamental premise was power; whose basic elements—the states—were defined by their power; whose ultimate test of power was war; whose most important issues were resolved by war; and whose pattern of periodic wars made World War I "due." The shift of power among the states and rapid rise of German power gradually became the system's central issues after German unification in 1871. This augmented power became the primary impulse for German policy and conditioned its policy making by restricting the choices available to its statesmen, their control over events, and the efficacy of their diplomacy.

Interpretations of prewar German behavior are multifaceted and varied but can be roughly divided into groups designated as arrogance and anxiety. The first sees German policy as motivated by aggressive aspirations for expansion, possibly culminating in European hegemony or even world power.[4] The second disagrees in claiming that German policy, however mistaken or erratic, was impelled by fear and sought to defend rather than increase what Germany had.[5] The present work questions this dichotomy by arguing that both elements were not only present—sometimes even simultaneously—but also essential to German policy. This ambivalence was caused by the ambiguity of German power, which appeared sufficient to warrant expansive aims but was insufficient to achieve them as extensively or expeditiously as many Germans wished.

Although it is the work's primary focus, German policy cannot be understood in isolation from the policies of the other powers. The policies of each conditioned the other when German moves produced reactions which in turn caused German responses. The growth of German power could be realistically measured only in relative terms, i.e., as this power compared with that of its contemporary rivals. German policy makers were deeply affected by their estimates of how German power would develop in the future relative to the power of other states. The power and behavior of Germany's contemporaries must consequently be studied if Germany's role in the war's origins is to be comprehensible.

German diplomatic policy must also be viewed in relation to German domestic politics. In traditional diplomatic studies politics was largely, though not entirely, excluded and diplomacy seen as determined primarily by foreign considerations, an approach aptly designated by German historians as *Primat der Aussenpolitik*. More recently the roles were reversed when some historians perceived it as the *Primat der Innenpolitik* because foreign policy was conditioned or even determined by domestic factors such as tariff policy, social questions, imperialist impulses, interest groups, and perhaps even by efforts to preclude revolution by foreign success. The present study examines these two extremes and suggests that they exaggerate the conflict between policy and politics.

German foreign policy is likewise incomprehensible without examination of German military strategy. The compulsion to apportion responsibility sometimes fostered the theory that the war had been consciously precipitated by a war party which was frequently identified with the military. War was sometimes seen as the unavoidable consequence of military plans and timetables, as when it is asserted that Schlieffen's "dead hand automatically pulled the trigger."[6] Some liberals perceived the prewar arms buildup as an important cause of war. The present work questions the notion that diplomacy and strategy were competitive and argues instead that they were complementary aspects of the same policy based on shared assumptions and aspirations.

Although it examines specifically the role of Germany and generally the roles of the other powers in the outbreak of World War I, the book has a number of broader implications. Its examination of the impasse in 1914 suggests some insights into the eventual breakdown of the European system during the following thirty years. Questions are raised about the relative importance of personality, forces, institutions, and, above all, power in the formulation of foreign policy. It examines the traditional distinctions drawn between policy, politics, and strategy. Most ominously it reflects serious doubts that permanent peace will be possible as long as international relations remain power politics.

Like states, authors seldom operate in isolation. It is a great pleasure to acknowledge the contributions of others. The loyal backing and gentle suggestions of James Joll have been not only essential but also gratifying. I am indebted for their support and advice to Laurence Lafore, Ellis W. Hawley, and the members of the University of Iowa Department of History Committee on Publications. The book was possible only because of the presence, counsel, and affection of my wife, Marjorie. It was pleasant because of the humor and *joie de vivre* of my daughter, Shepard, who embarks simultaneously into the world with this, her book.

"The Farriery"
Chestnut Hill
Massachusetts

5 June 1981

NOTES

1 For explorations of this myth of modernism, see: Paul Fussell, *The Great War and Modern Memory* (New York and London, 1975) and Eric J. Leed, *No Man's Land: Combat & Identity in World War I* (Cambridge, England, 1979).

2 See the bibliography for the works of Choucri and North, Hermann, Holsti, Kahler, Nomikos and North, and Sola Poole.

3 For a general examination of these issues, see: L. L. Farrar, Jr., "The Causes of World War I," in *War: A Historical, Political, and Social Study*, ed. L. L. Farrar, Jr. (Santa Barbara and Oxford, 1978), pp. 165–70.

4 See the bibliography for the works of Albertini, Bartels, Berghahn, Böhme, Burchardt, Calleo, Craig, Fischer, Fisher, Gasser, Geiss, Groh, Heidorn, Jarausch, Kehr, Klein, Marder, Rathmann, Renouvin, Röhl, Schmitt, Stenkewitz, Strandmann, Taylor, and Wernecke.

5 See the bibliography for the works of Barnes, Erdmann, Fay, Herzfeld, Mommsen, Ritter, Ropponen, Rosenberg, Stern, Vietsch, Zechlin, and Zmarzlik.

6 A. J. P. Taylor, *A History of the First World War* (New York, 1966), p. 20.

I / THE SYSTEM JEOPARDIZED:

The Implications of Industrialization,
Population Growth, and German
Unification (1848–90)

THE EUROPEAN SYSTEM: ASSUMPTIONS AND ASSERTIONS

Any effort to make sense of the past is founded consciously or unconsciously on a set of assumptions. It is both fair to the reader and helpful to the writer that these assumptions be clarified at the outset. The interpretation suggested here assumes that both the rise and decline of European power in the nineteenth and twentieth centuries were caused by forces set in motion during the period from 1848 to 1871 and developed during the period from 1871 to 1914. Both these forces and the system in which they developed must be defined if this analysis is to be convincing. It is assumed that the European state system can be defined in terms of its essential characteristics, as evidenced by its previous behavior. Thus, as long as these characteristics existed, the system persisted; when any or all desisted, the system ceased to exist.

Like other civilizations, European civilization was based on power. The distinguishing feature of modern European civilization was the division of power between states rather than centralization (as in Roman, Chinese, or North American civilizations) or dispersion (as in African or feudal European civilizations). This organization made power a more important element within European civilization than it was for civilizations in which power was either centralized or dispersed. When power is centralized, it is great but irrelevant and only politics or a coup d'état is possible. When power is dispersed, it is relevant but small, and only limited wars can occur. Power is significant within a civilization only when it is divided among units which are sufficiently strong to compete but not strong enough to centralize power. Thus, European civilization was dominated by a will to power.

This struggle for power determined the definition and behavior of the states. The state was the basic unit of power. States could exist and function as states only if they had the power to defend their independence. Thus, the state's basic objective was to accumulate power.

This competition for power also affected the perception of power. The nature of power was determined by the most powerful. Great power was defined as the ability not only to participate in the system but also to influence it significantly, not only to defend one's own independence but also to threaten the independence of others. Great power effectively erased the distinction between defensive and offensive impulses; great power survival implied the subordination of small states. Regardless of rights or claims to the contrary, the existence of power was assumed to constitute a threat. Not intentions but capabilities were the crucial consideration. In this sense, a state was not expected to control its own power since it neither could nor should. Instead, the other states had to control it by cooperating between themselves and containing the powerful. Thus, power was perceived as basically aggressive.

The competition between the states developed certain basic features which can be understood as a system. Like the states themselves, this system emerged only gradually and as a result of the interaction between the states rather than through any historical necessity or preconceived plan. It survived because of its ability to parry dangers from within (i.e., centralization or dispersion of power) and from without (i.e., foreign domination). Centralization proved the greatest threat. The successive attempts of Spain, Austria, and France to unify the system were, however, defeated by the cooperation of the other states. This preservation of European disunity and the division of power among states became known as the balance of power. The danger of dispersion of power in the sense of dissolution of all the European states proved less ominous. Although some states collapsed and others were threatened by revolution, there always remained sufficient states to perpetuate the system. The possibility of outside domination also was minimal. Occasionally, peripheral areas were lost to outside forces but the system as a whole was never threatened. As Europe's power increased, its independence, in fact, became more secure.

The competition among the states for power caused the system as a whole to amass greater power. Nonetheless, Europe's power remained compatible with the survival of the state system until the nineteenth century. This compatibility of power and system was due not to rational planning, perspicacity, or mutual agreement, but to technical, institutional, and political limitations. No state could limit its power for the general good without risking its own existence. Nor could the system as a whole limit its power without altering its basic character. Furthermore, Europe's success in resisting outside domination depended on its power: the greater its power, the greater its independence. Thus, the dangers of self-destruction and outside domination had contradictory implications for Europe. To survive, Europe had to navigate between the Scylla of too much power and the Charybdis of too little.

Not only the quantity but also the quality of power changed. Power was determined by economics, population, geography, political and social organization, military technology, and leadership. The nature of each of these elements varied according to circumstances. What was an advantage in one context became a detriment in another. The shifting basis of power affected the power of the individual states. Quite literally, many states in their time played many parts. Consequently, although the system as a whole survived, change in the relationships among the states became one of the system's salient features.

This change was frequently accompanied by violence. It was altogether appropriate that it should be in a system based on power. War both demonstrated how power had shifted and adjusted the system to accommodate shifts. In short, war was the most effective means of reconciling power and change. The permanent abolition of war would have required renunciation of either power or change. Since power and change were basic features of the system, war was not aberrational but normal and indeed necessary. The operative question was not whether but when and why war would occur.

Three basic types of wars occurred in the European system. Most important were hegemonic wars, which implicated the whole system. They were willing to risk war in order to maintain their independence (and by the other states as threats to their existence. The less powerful states were willing to risk war in order to maintain their independence (and thus the system) rather than renounce their independence in order to maintain peace. Such hegemonic wars recurred about once every century since the beginning of the system in the sixteenth century. Wars of succession were more frequent but somewhat less significant. They were caused by the resistance of a declining state to encroachment or even partition by its neighbors and recurred about twice every century since the beginning of the system. Finally, probing wars were most frequent but least important. They were caused by efforts to test the existing distribution of power, which proved to be sound, and recurred about every generation. The wars of the twentieth century were "due" in all three of these senses.[1]

Violence was recurrent but not continual. Peace indicated that the distribution of power corresponded with the status quo. Although the status quo was tested periodically by probing wars, it was more frequently examined by nonviolent means. Thus, diplomacy was developed as an alternative to war. It prevented some wars by improving communication and demonstrating that no real conflict of interest existed. It avoided others by arranging compromises where real conflicts existed. It averted still others by indicating that the disadvantages of war were greater than the advantages. Diplomacy also functioned during wartime to organize or disorganize coalitions. Finally, and most important, diplomacy was used to conclude wars, i.e., to adjust the system to the distribution of power as demonstrated by war. In short, diplomacy constituted an effort to rationalize power. But it was not a substitute for war. Like war, it was designed to serve the interest of the state, not the ideal of peace. Its appeal as an alternative to war was infrequently based on any consideration but self-interest. Diplomacy and pacifism were sometimes confused by pacifists but seldom by diplomatists. When its power was at stake, a state had to choose war over peace.

Power was distributed within the system in a discernible geographic pattern. Medieval civilization had been a central European phenomenon: power was concentrated at the middle of the continent. Modern Europe reversed this pattern: power gravitated to the periphery (England, France, Spain, Prussia, Austria, and Russia) and the center (Germany and Italy) became weak. This configuration helped to maintain the balance of power. The weak center acted as a buffer between the powers; served as an early warning system for attempts to dominate it; and provided an area for compensations which preserved the balance. This pattern also tended to reduce the concentration of power within the system by encouraging the peripheral powers to divert some of their energy outside the system into commercial-colonial activities. But the most important result of central European weakness was negative: it precluded a strong German state. Such a state would not only be strongest but also—because of its central position—unlikely to divert its power outside the system and therefore more likely to threaten the balance of power.

Expansion and involvement with the rest of the world were other salient characteristics of European civilization. They were results of the European drive for power and the best gauges of Europe's power relative to the rest of the world. European expansion was directly related to the shift of power from the center to periphery. European trade with the Orient shifted at the end of the Middle Ages from the central European-Mediterranean-Middle Eastern overland route to the coastal European-overseas route. This shift fundamentally altered the pattern of European relations with the rest of the world. The geographic and political barriers between Europe and the Orient were circumnavigated; Europe became, in effect, next door to the rest of the world. Direct contact allowed greater involvement, and power superiority eventually encouraged domination. This shift had far-reaching implications for the distribution of power in Europe. It reinforced the decline of central Europe and the rise of the periphery. It facilitated commercial activity, thus increased wealth, thus power within the system as a whole. It had contradictory effects on the balance of power. Whereas the continental imperial powers—Spain and France—used power gained overseas to dominate the continent, the maritime imperial powers—Britain and the

Netherlands—used theirs to maintain the balance. Since the maritime powers probably gained more power overseas, European involvement overseas may have had a net effect favorable to the balance. Furthermore, the existence of this extra-European power vacuum may have had beneficial effects for the balance analogous to those of the central European power vacuum. It provided flexibility for the European system, an area for compromises and concessions, and perhaps even a distraction for aggressions otherwise expressed within Europe. Whatever its net effect on the total and balance of power, extra-European involvement was an indication of the balance of power in Europe. Large-scale expansion occurred only when the system was stable and was reduced when the balance was threatened.

The nature of the state determined the character of European domestic politics. The state's primary goal was survival in a competitive system. The operative question was, therefore, the accumulation, rather than the distribution, of power. As a consequence, the outstanding feature of developments within the European states before the French Revolution was centralization rather than politics. Domestic politics had relatively little effect on international politics.

The character of the state also affected the conduct of foreign policy. Both the centralization of power and the need to preserve the state allowed rulers a high degree of control over policy. Consequently, foreign policy became flexible (within, for example, the limits of geography, state power, and the existing political configuration), secretive, non-ideological, and formalistic (i.e., involving special vocabulary, format, and rituals). These characteristics tended to reinforce the assumption that the state system was governed by immutable laws analogous to natural laws. The nature of the state and the conduct of foreign policy were related to the amount of state power. Eighteenth-century governments exercised only a small part of their states' potential power—as the French Revolution would demonstrate. Absolutist governments in effect imposed limits on their own power and the total power within the system by refusing to win greater support through sharing control. Foreign policy was, therefore, characterized by high control over limited power.

The basic features of European civilization at the end of the eighteenth century emerge. Its drive for power was striking. Power increased but remained limited relative to its potential and compatible with the survival of European civilization. Power was divided among states whose primary goal was survival. The competition of these states for power developed patterns which can be perceived as a system. The relative power of the states changed. These changes were usually accompanied by war. Power gravitated from the center to the periphery of the system. Europe's power allowed it not only to remain independent of foreign domination but also to become superior to other civilizations and impose dominion over them. Relations among states were typified by high control over limited power. If European civilization is defined in terms of these elements, it persists only as long as they exist.

The state system was jeopardized during the French Revolution and Napoleonic wars. The independence of individual states was threatened: Austria and Prussia approached extinction, Britain and Russia were sorely tried, while France was revolutionized and ultimately defeated. The system as a whole was endangered by French hegemony and thus by centralization. The Revolution and Napoleon accelerated change by dissolving anachronistic political institutions (e.g., the Holy Roman Empire) and by demonstrating that small states (e.g., the Netherlands, Switzerland, and the Italian and German states) were not viable in a hegemonic and revolutionary conflict. The most serious threat was the mobilization of the European (particularly French) masses since it radically augmented power and jeopardized the prevailing view of the state's purpose. The absolutist argument that the state's object was power was vulnerable to criticism from the democratic argument that the state's purpose was happiness. Paradoxically, democracy—in the form of democratic totalitarianism—released more power than had absolutism. The ideology of international stability which had dominated the eighteenth century was suddenly challenged by the myth of change: French revolutionaries claimed that the international system was as anachronistic and discriminatory as the domestic systems prevailing throughout Europe. Ideology became significant in international politics both because the masses took it more seriously than the absolutist governments and because it was revolutionary. As power increased, control declined, and the eighteenth-century relationship was reversed: state relations were characterized by less control over greater power. The state system was therefore threatened on the one hand by centralization under French hegemony and on the other by dissolution because of increased but undisciplined power. But there were counter forces at work to preserve the system. French success required not only French power but also dissension among France's rivals and passivity of their populations. When the other powers cooperated and mobilized anti-French nationalism, French hegemony became impractical and revolutionary mass power was directed into the traditional channel of state power. Thus, the state system was preserved.

The Vienna settlement was an attempt to reconstruct the state system in a form which would deter the dangers of French hegemony and mass power. To protect against French hegemony, the other powers pursued a policy of containment, compensation, and cooperation: they contained France with barriers, compensated for French power by strengthening the other powers, and promised to cooperate against future French aggression. To reduce the danger of mass power, the statesmen at Vienna followed a policy of conservatism and constraint: they discouraged mass movements by establishing conservative governments and by imposing constraints on German and Italian unification. The central European settlement was reinforced by giving Austria a mandate to police it. A contradiction existed, however, between the two purposes of the Vienna settlement. Whereas containment of France implied a strong central Europe, containment of central European nationalism implied a weak central Europe. Metternich managed to square this circle for a generation largely because of the quiescence of his rivals. The French made no attempt to conquer Europe, while central European nationalism proved insufficiently developed and its potential leaders (Prussia and Piedmont-Savoy) more afraid of revolution than anxious to exploit nationalism. Above all, the Vienna settlement survived because the powers which had established it—Austria, Britain, and Russia—cooperated to maintain it.

BEGINNING THE TRANSFORMATION (1848–71)

The Vienna settlement was shaken in the years from 1848 to 1860 by central European nationalism, French revisionism, and dissension among the founding powers. The revolutions of 1848 revealed the depth of central European popular opposition to the settlement. Although able to reestablish control, the Austrians alienated Russia and Britain by treating this control as an Austrian right rather than an Anglo-Russian mandate. The Crimean conflict seriously complicated Anglo-Russian cooperation in central Europe and further isolated Austria because it refused to join either side. In contrast to Austria, its rivals in Europe— France, Piedmont-Savoy and Prussia—won the sympathy of either Russia or Britain. Although it contributed to the Vienna settlement's collapse, France failed to profit from events because of the familiarity of the French hegemonic threat, the maladroitness of French leadership, and the growing conservatism of the French nation. But Piedmont-Savoy and Prussia, the losers of 1848, became the victors after 1858. The success of Piedmont-Savoy in expelling Austria and uniting Italy was due to French support, Austrian isolation, the adroitness of Italian diplomacy, perhaps the unfamiliarity of Italian initiative, and the fact that Italian unification did not threaten the balance of power. The Vienna settlement was shaken but nonetheless survived.

The settlement was destroyed in the years from 1866 to 1871 by German unification. The mid-nineteenth century Austro-Prussian conflict for primacy in Germany was the final act of their eighteenth-century struggle. Austrian primacy had been established at Vienna and maintained by Metternich's manipulation of the Prussian monarchy's fears of revolution. Perceiving Austria rather than revolution as the main enemy, Bismarck pursued a policy of dismantling the Vienna settlement and replacing Austrian with Prussian primacy. Yet while the Prussian victory over Austria in 1866 destroyed the settlement, it did not replace it with a new one since the question of south Germany remained unanswered. This issue was resolved in favor of Prussian domination (rather than neutralization or partition) when Prussia defeated France in 1870 and the Vienna settlement was replaced by the Berlin settlement.

Bismarck's success provides an insight not only into the state system and his subsequent policy but also into the failures of his successors. He succeeded primarily because of the isolation of Austria and France. He discouraged Anglo-Russian aid to Austria by playing on their alienation from Austria, by winning Russian gratitude (with aid against the Polish revolt), and by exploiting Anglo-Russian disinterest in central Europe and distraction by domestic and overseas problems. He rendered Anglo-Russian intervention unnecessary after Austrian defeat by neither destroying Austria nor otherwise threatening the balance of power. He prevented French assistance to Austria by encouraging French ambitions at Austrian expense. He then deterred Anglo-Russian aid to France by presenting French ambitions as a greater threat to the balance of power than were Prussia's. Bismarck discouraged Austrian aid to France by playing on Austrian bitterness toward France and on Hungarian opposition to a war against Prussia. Italian aid to either Austria or France was precluded by bribes. French isolation was critical not only to Prussian military but also diplomatic success. France concluded peace only when it could find no ally with which to continue the war. Control over policy was another factor in Bismarck's success. He might have increased Prussian power by exploiting German nationalism more extensively but did not because it would have threatened the Prussian political structure and European balance of power. He chose instead to increase Prussian power only slightly by the traditional means of limited expansion and improvement of military organization, transportation, and technology. Effectively, Bismarck opted for greater control over slightly greater power in preference to less control over vastly greater power. The wars of 1866 and 1870 were limited and resembled the wars of the eighteenth century more than they did the revolutionary and Napoleonic wars. Accordingly, isolated opponents, high control, and limited power were the keys to Bismarck's success.

The events of 1848–71 produced fundamental changes in the European state system. The relative power of the states shifted. Italy became a state. Prussia advanced from the weakest great power in 1848 to the front rank. Austria had been expelled from Italy and Germany. Characteristically, such changes had involved violence. All the powers went to war at least once, and three (Russia, Austria, and France) suffered serious defeats with profound political repercussions. The pattern of power for four centuries was altered when central European weakness was transformed into strength. The configuration of international conflict was reversed as a result. The peripheral powers had traditionally vied over the weak center, and relations had been conditioned by Anglo-French, Russo-French, Austro-Prussian, and Austro-French wars. When the central European object of these conflicts disappeared, the conflicts desisted. They would subsequently be replaced by wars between the center and periphery in which the peripheral powers would become allies instead of rivals.

The foundations for a radical increase and shift of material power were simultaneously laid during the period from 1848 to 1871. The nature of material power had altered during the history of the state system. Habsburg material power during the sixteenth century had been based largely on precious metals from South America, whereas the material power of France, Britain, and the Netherlands during the seventeenth and eighteenth centuries had been based largely on commerce. European material power during the nineteenth and twentieth centuries was based on industrialism. Industrialism not only altered the form but also increased the quantity of power. Despite the disruptions caused by war and revolution, the production of Europe as a whole increased during this period.[2] The pattern of industrialization was uneven. Although Britain and France were already industrialized by the mid-nineteenth century, the foundations of central and eastern European industrialization were only being laid during this period. Political and economic events in central Europe were interrelated: the desire to industrialize encouraged unification, and the impulse to unify facilitated industrialization. The military and diplomatic successes of Prussia were accompanied by economic success. In 1850, Britain's industrial power was dominant and contested only by France; between them, they controlled most industrial power. By 1870, Germany and Russia had begun to industrialize.[3] Thus, material power not only increased but shifted during the period from 1848 to 1871.

The foundations of a radical increase in human power were laid at this time. Human power is a function of mobilization and population. Throughout most of their history, the great powers had mobilized only a small portion of the available human power for military or nonagricultural economic purposes. Most wars had been fought with limited forces and without involving the masses. Mobilization of the French masses during the Revolution and Napoleonic wars departed sharply from this pattern and in large measure explains French military success for a generation. The diplomats at Vienna successfully reestablished the previous pattern of limited popular involvement by demobilizing French nationalism. Commercialism likewise involved a relatively small proportion of the population. Thus, before the mid-nineteenth century, human power remained largely unmobilized for military or nonagricultural economic purposes. This pattern began to change during the middle of the nineteenth century. For the first time, nationalism became pervasive (particularly in central Europe) and relations between the powers became genuinely "international" instead of "interstate." The masses began to be politicized by such disparate developments as democracy in France, universal suffrage in Germany, the expansion of suffrage in England, the popular press, and emancipation of the serfs in Russia. Industrialism would likewise involve far greater human power than commercialism. Consequently, the means for mobilizing increased human energy were emerging at mid-century. Meanwhile the human potential available for mobilization increased rapidly. The population of the great powers had risen gradually until the beginning of the nineteenth century, when its growth accelerated and then rose sharply during the period from 1848 to 1871 because of the unification of Germany and Italy.[4] In short, population and the means for mobilizing it augmented simultaneously.

These developments implied a new definition of state power. State power before the nineteenth century can be defined as commercial-elitist-limited and after the nineteenth century as industrial-mass-unlimited. This definition of post-nineteenth century power must be quantified to be useful. If industrial power is equated with manufacturing production and mass power is equated with population, a rough gauge of industrial-mass power is provided as a function of production and population. It indicates that the system's power increased by about 133 percent between 1848 and 1871. If it is assumed that a state's power within the system was relative, a rough gauge of state power can be calculated as a percentage of total industrial-mass power. It indicates that the new power was distributed inequitably. Britain's power dropped most but remained greatest. Germany gained most and displaced France as the second strongest power. French power declined significantly and had to share third place with Russia, which had risen notably. Not yet industrialized, Austria-Hungary and Italy had inconsequential power.[5] Power, therefore, shifted from west to east and corresponded with the diplomatic-military events of the period. But the unequal distribution of new power made the great powers more equal in 1870 than before or after.[6] Furthermore, Britain and Russia, the two traditional patrons of the balance of power, still held more than half of Europe's power.[7] The system, therefore, seemed more stable than ever.

Appearances were deceptive. Developments during the period from 1848 to 1871 had fundamentally altered the system. The pattern of peripheral strength and central weakness had been changed to one of general strength. Likewise, the pattern of limited power had been transformed into one of increased power and potential for even greater augmentation. Thus, two of the basic characteristics of the system had been changed.

POWER WITH RESTRAINT: GERMANY UNDER BISMARCK (1871–90)

The European great power system was confronted with some fundamental issues in 1871. How would it accommodate the changes of 1848 to 1871? Would the status quo of 1871 persist, revert, or evolve? Would European civilization generate ever more power or would it stabilize? Would the state system adjust to the new power or destroy itself? Would the balance of power in 1871 be retained, reinforced, or revised? Would the relationship between central and peripheral power stabilize at relative equality or would the old pattern of central weakness and peripheral strength be reversed to one of central strength and peripheral weakness? The answers to these questions would determine the future of European civilization.

The new situation posed specific questions in regard to Germany. Would it exploit its new power to revise the system further or be satisfied and practice restraint? Hypothetically, Bismarck could have elected to exploit his success. During the previous decade Germany had been the most revolutionary power in destroying the Vienna settlement as well as the patterns of French primacy and central European weakness. Bismarck might have sought to repeat 1866 or 1870. But either would have risked Anglo-Russian opposition, therefore a hegemonic struggle, therefore German unification. Alternatively, Germany might have sought to extend its power in eastern Europe at Russia's expense. Success would have required avoidance of a two-front war against France and Russia by reaching an agreement with France. But a *détente* with France would have demanded at least the return of Alsace-Lorraine. Even after a victory over Russia, Germany might have had to face the prospect of a revisionist Franco-Russian alliance. Finally, Germany might have cooperated with Russia and France against Britain in the colonial world. But Britain could always lure France away from Germany with the offer of Alsace-Lorraine, and Germany would then have to confront an Anglo-French alliance in Europe. To avoid Russia's joining such an alliance, Bismarck would have had to bribe Russia at Austro-Hungarian expense and thus risk Austro-Hungarian dissolution. Furthermore, Britain and France could outbid Germany, since they could afford Austro-Hungarian dissolution more than Germany. Thus, further German expansion implied serious international political dangers. It also involved domestic political disadvantages. Further expansion meant annexation of non-German populations which would create domestic problems. Another war would probably have required mobilizing the German masses and thus revolutionizing the domestic political structure of Germany. But even the power thus generated would not have insured victory against a coalition of the other great powers. Consequently, negative considerations were probably critical. The costs of success and the risk of failure outweighed the reward of success. Above all, the price of failure might be higher for Germany than for other powers seeking hegemony: while France had paid with border provinces, Germany risked dissolution.

Bismarck elected to preserve rather than exploit his gains and reversed his diplomatic role after 1871. The diplomatic revolutionary became the diplomatic conservative. Despite the change of objective, Bismarck's problems remained generally the same. He still had to isolate Austria-Hungary and France, the traditional rivals in central Europe, and placate Britain and Russia, the traditional patrons of the balance of power. Isolating Austria-Hungary and France was more difficult after defeat than before, when each had looked more like a threat to the balance of power than Prussia. Austria-Hungary proved to be the less difficult to isolate because it had renounced its hegemonic aspirations earlier, had serious domestic problems, was weaker, and had a substitute for central European domination in the Balkans. Bismarck took out the ultimate insurance against Austria-Hungary's joining an anti-German coalition by allying with it in 1879. This insurance was not without risk, however, since either dominating or supporting Austria-Hungary in the Balkans could precipitate an anti-German coalition.

Isolating France turned out to be more difficult. Its central European aspirations were more recent, its power larger, its bitterness deeper, and its willingness to use revolutionary means greater. Bismarck was assisted, however, by a fundamental contradiction between French aspirations and the policy necessary to fulfill them. France wanted to undo 1871. But it could not do so alone and therefore needed allies. Austria-Hungary became increasingly unlikely. Russia and Britain were interested in maintaining the balance of power in central Europe and would probably have joined France to defend it. But neither Russia nor Britain would help France reestablish its primacy in central Europe; on the contrary, they would probably oppose it. Here was the dilemma for France: it wanted an alliance to revive its power but could get an alliance only by demonstrating its weakness and German power. The French never escaped this dilemma during Bismarck's tenure in office. Their task was more difficult than his. Whereas Bismarck only wanted to maintain the status quo, the French wanted to undo it. Whereas Bismarck simply had to look pacific, the French had to force him to appear aggressive.

Bismarck's policy toward Russia and Britain was therefore clear. He had to avoid alienating either by threatening its interests or the balance of power in Europe. Consequently, he generally respected British sensitivities in the Low Countries, the Near East, the colonial world, and the naval question and Russian sensitivities in Poland, the Balkans, and the Near East. He likewise persuaded Britain and Russia that Germany was satiated and disinclined to threaten the balance of power. In short, to retain what he had, he renounced more.

Although generally successful during his period in office, Bismarck had no easy task. It was difficult to make both Russia and Austria-Hungary accept the status quo in 1871. Both expected to be paid in the Balkans for allowing German preponderance in central Europe. Acceding to Russia risked an Austro-Russian conflict in the Balkans and thus Austro-Hungarian defeat. Bismarck was, however, determined to preserve Austria-Hungary as the best alternative to either a large German state which risked an anti-German coalition or Russian domination in eastern Europe. In effect, he maintained Austria-Hungary for the reasons Russia and Britain had permitted Metternich's mandate over central Europe—as the least of evils. Next to accepting the status quo in 1871, preservation of Austria-Hungary was probably Bismarck's most important decision. It necessitated reconciling Austria-Hungary and Russia, which became both Bismarck's greatest diplomatic headache and accomplishment after 1871. He managed to do so by brilliant manipulation. Ultimately his success depended, however, on acceptance of the Balkan status quo by both Austria-Hungary and Russia. If Austria-Hungary and/or Russia sought change in the Balkans or if the Balkan status quo were changed from within to the detriment of either, it would be difficult to reconcile them. Furthermore, his success depended on German disinterest in the Balkans. If Germany became involved in the Balkans, it would be difficult to avoid Russian antipathy. Thus, Bismarck's policy required both Austro-Russian reconciliation and German restraint.

While the Balkans complicated Bismarck's task, colonial imperialism simplified it. Imperialism distracted the other powers from Europe and caused frictions between them which deterred an anti-German coalition. Consequently, Bismarck encouraged these rivalries and generally discouraged German imperialism which might drive the other powers together against Germany. Since the other powers' involvement outside Europe required security in Europe, Bismarck avoided threatening the balance of power both to encourage imperialism and to preclude a hegemonic struggle. As elsewhere, success necessitated German restraint.

German restraint depended on Bismarck's ability to resist pressures from within Germany for a more aggressive policy. He succeeded by pursuing a domestic policy analogous to his diplomatic policy, i.e., isolation and balance. He encouraged the monarchy, lesser royalty, and aristocracy to remain conservative by preserving their dominant position within the new Germany. He sought to reconcile the old liberals with the new Germany by satisfying their aspirations for a national state. To the bourgeoisie in general he offered the prospect of great wealth and minor privilege. The preservation of aristocratic power and rural society tended to keep the peasants quiescent. Bismarck chastened all these groups with the bogey of social revolution as the only alternative to the existing order. Meanwhile, he sought to defuse the revolution by luring the workers away from socialism with material security. By these devices Bismarck tried to distract the German people from pursuit of greater political power with the inducements of prosperity and peace. Generally he was successful. His domestic success both contributed to and depended on his control over foreign policy. He maintained control by insuring that foreign policy remained the prerogative of the monarch whom Bismarck—because of his personality, prestige, and political perspicacity—was able to dominate for a generation. This arrangement was accepted by most Germans largely because the Prussian ruling class had produced victory without making concessions in order to mobilize the masses. The liberals had been tarred with the brush of failure in 1848 and many renounced the ideal of political liberalism for the reality of national unification. Accordingly, Bismarck was able to restrain German power because his previous successes had reinforced the conservative system and his control over policy.

Like German diplomatic policy, German military strategy became conservative after 1871. In 1866 and 1870 German strategy had been offensive and sought victory to revolutionize the central European status quo. After 1871 it became defensive and sought to avoid defeat in order to preserve the new central European status quo. The nature of war also changed in 1871. Since a Prussian victory had not jeopardized the balance of power, Prussia had been able to fight Austria and France alone. Consequently, the government had been able to win with limited power and without making concessions to the masses. But, since a German victory after 1871 would jeopardize the balance, Germany would probably be met by a coalition of the other powers. The government would therefore probably have to make concessions in order to mobilize the power necessary for victory. War after 1871 would probably be total rather than limited and might threaten the domestic political structure even if Germany won. Diplomatic, military, and political considerations therefore tended to reinforce one another in making German strategy conservative.

When formulated in 1871, German diplomatic and military policies corresponded with German power. Since France might have been able to undo the settlement of 1871 with Russian or British help, it was critical for Bismarck to isolate France by placating Russia and Britain.[8] German policies were therefore consistent with German power and Bismarck lived within his power means. But the increase of German power after 1871 rendered Bismarck's fears increasingly baseless and his policy apparently anachronistic. Since it had more power in 1890, Germany seemed to have less reason for restraint.

The state system as a whole survived, but important changes occurred within it by 1890. The individual states remained constant. Bismarck's system of alliances was the most significant development and tended to preserve the status quo in 1871. But power relationships shifted radically among the powers. Germany displaced Britain as the greatest power, Russia remained third, while France's share of power dropped radically and Austria-Hungary's rose slightly.[9] Although these changes were significant, they took place without war. Power had not only shifted but increased sharply within the system as a whole.[10] The system was less balanced than it had been in 1871 but the balance was not threatened and no hegemonic power jeopardized the system.[11] The system maintained its cohesion; indeed, Bismarck's alliance system made it even more integrated and self-conscious than it had been during the previous generation. The pattern of power continued to reverse as German power grew but no reaction of the peripheral power had as yet begun.

Europe's power relative to the rest of the world altered paradoxically. European power allowed it to extend domination over a large part of the unmodernized world. Although it is difficult to estimate the effects of imperialism on the European system, some circumstantial observations can be made. Whereas the power of the two most committed colonial powers, Britain and France, dropped most, the power of the least committed imperialists, Germany and Austria-Hungary, rose most. The decline in Anglo-French power would continue during the 1890s, when their imperial commitment and competition reached its acme. Meanwhile, German power increased less rapidly during the 1890s, when it committed itself more resolutely to imperialism. Still uncommitted to colonial imperialism, Austria-Hungary's power continued to increase. Russia is the deviant: its power rose slowly before 1890, when it was less committed to imperialism, but rapidly after 1890, when it became more involved in imperialism. If a correlation exists, it suggests that imperialism may have reduced rather than increased a state's power. Bismarck may have been wise to discourage imperialism not only because of diplomatic but also power considerations. The money and energy diverted by the Anglo-French into their colonial empires and elsewhere was invested by the Germans in the German Empire. If imperialism caused a net loss of power, it may have had the beneficial effect of a safety valve which slowed the augmentation of European power. It also indicated that the state system was in balance since the powers could not afford imperialism if they were not secure in Europe. But, insofar as it reinforced the decline in Anglo-French power and rise in German power, imperialism contributed to the imbalance emerging by 1890. Whatever its effects, imperialism was a subordinate consideration for all the powers: despite frictions, no war between European powers occurred over colonial questions. While imperialism demonstrated that Europe's power had risen relative to the unmodernized world, European power fell relative to that of the United States.[12] Thus, Europe was more dominant but less independent in 1890 than it had been in 1871.

The human resources of the great powers had continued to increase.[13] The forms of political organization had, however, altered little, and the masses exerted only slightly more influence over foreign policy in 1890 than they had in 1871. Public opinion was occasionally mobilized, but more often to serve rather than to control foreign policy. What ideology crept into diplomacy was primarily conservative. Bismarck's control over foreign policy was perhaps greater than, but not incomparable with, that of his counterparts. Diplomacy was still conducted by cabinets.

The questions of 1871 had been answered. The system had accommodated the changes of 1848–71 without significant international or domestic violence. The diplomatic settlement of 1871 had persisted. Germany had preserved rather than exploited its new power. Although these adjustments were made, the forces set in motion during the period from 1848 to 1871 accelerated and caused further change. Europe generated ever more power, which was distributed inequitably. The revolution sown in the generation of 1848–71 germinated during the following generation.

NOTES

1 For a development of these ideas, see L. L. Farrar, Jr., "Cycles of War: Historical Speculation on Future International Violence," in *International Interactions* (1977), 3:161–80.

2 The increase in European coal production between 1850 and 1870 was 160 percent or 8 percent per annum (as compared with 6.5 percent per annum between 1870 and 1914). The increase in pig iron production was 257 percent or 12.5 percent per annum (as compared with 6.5 percent between 1870 and 1914). The increase of manufacturing production between 1860 and 1870 was 26.2 percent or 2.6 percent per annum (as compared with 7.68 percent between 1870 and 1914). The calculations presented in this chapter are based on statistics provided in, A. J. P. Taylor, *The Struggle for Mastery in Europe* (Oxford, 1960), pp. xxv–xxxi. The percentages have been calculated as precisely as the statistics allow. Since the statistics themselves are of course inexact, such calculations can be only approximate. It seemed preferable to indicate precise results rather than introduce yet another inexactitude by rounding them off.

3 In 1850, Britain produced 84.6 percent and France the other 15.4 percent of Europe's pig iron. Britain's share of manufacturing production was 41.5 percent in 1860, France's share was 31.7 percent. Thus, Britain and France produced all the pig iron in 1850 and 73.2 percent of manufactured goods in 1860. In 1870, Britain still produced 64.5 percent of pig iron, France 12 percent, Germany 14 percent, and Russia 4.3 percent. Britain produced 53.8 percent of the steel, while France and Germany shared the rest with 23.1 percent each. Britain produced 42.3 percent of the manufactured goods, France 29.8 percent, Germany 15.4 percent, and Russia 12.5 percent.

4 Part of this increase was due to the rise of population of the great powers existing in 1850 (Britain, France, Austria, Russia, and Prussia) which amounted to about 17 percent. The rate of increase (0.85 percent per annum) is slightly lower than the rate between 1870 and 1914 (1 percent per annum). A larger part of this increase was due to the incorporation of Germans and Italians into their national states and thus effectively into the great power system. This increased the great power populations by 27 percent. The great power populations therefore increased by about 80 million between 1850 and 1870 or about 48 percent. Thus, the great power populations increased at a faster rate during this period than between 1870 and 1914 (3.25 percent as compared to 1 percent per annum).

5 Britain's share of power in 1850 is estimated to be 50 percent of Europe's power. By 1870, it dropped to 34.7 percent. Germany's power rose from about 10 percent in 1850 to 25 percent in 1870. France's power fell from about 30 percent in 1850 to 20.3 percent in 1870, while Russia's power rose from about 10 percent in 1850 to 20 percent in 1870.

6 The difference between the strongest power in 1870, Britain, and the weakest of the major powers, France and Russia, was 14 percent. The spread would increase, until the difference between the strongest in 1910, Germany, and the weakest of the major powers, France, would become 27 percent.

7 Russia and Britain had a total of 54 percent in 1870.

8 If France had been joined by Russia in 1871, they would have had about 40 percent of European power as compared to Germany's 25 percent. In 1880, a Franco-Russian alliance would still have had 37 percent and Germany 27 percent. Britain still held the balance in both cases, with 34 percent in 1871 and 36 percent in 1880. If an Anglo-

French alliance had been formed against Germany, it would have had 55 percent in 1871 and 1880. If both Britain and Russia had joined France, they would have over-whelmed Germany with 75 percent in 1871 and 73 percent in 1880.

9   In 1871, Britain had been the strongest power, with 34.7 percent of European power, and Germany second with 25 percent. In 1890, Germany was strongest with 32 per-cent, Britain second with 29 percent. Russia was tied with France for third in 1871 with 20 percent each. In 1890, Russia had 19.7 percent and was third. France fell from tied-for-third to fourth in 1890 with 15.2 percent. Austria-Hungary had about 4 per-cent in 1890.

10   The amount of power had increased by 116 percent between 1871 and 1890.

11   The system had been most balanced in 1871. The difference between the largest pow-er's share (Britain's, at 34.7 percent) and the smallest (Russia and France's, at 20 per-cent) was smaller (14.7 percent) than at any time between 1871 and 1914. In 1890, it was 17 percent (between France at 15.2 percent and Germany at 32 percent), i.e., slightly larger but not significantly. The balance in central Europe was more equitable in 1871: Germany had 25 percent to France's 20.3 percent; in 1890, Germany had 32 percent to France's 15.2 percent. In 1871, the proportion of power held by the tradi-tional patrons of the balance of power, Russia and Britain, was larger (54 percent as compared with 48.8 percent), but they could still hold the balance in a struggle be-tween the central European powers.

12   American manufacturing production was 45.6 percent of Europe's in 1871, i.e., al-ready ahead of Britain's. By 1890, American manufacturing production was 74.7 per-cent of Europe's, i.e., larger than the total of Britain and Germany. American econom-ic power, however, continued to play an insignificant political role in Europe.

13   The population of the great powers increased by 18 percent between 1870 and 1890 or at a rate of slightly less than 1 percent per annum. During the period from 1848 to 1870, population had increased at a rate of 0.85 percent per annum.

II / ILLUSION OF STABILITY:
The Implications of German Power (1890–1912)

The answers of 1890 generated new questions. Would the state system accommodate the changes of 1871–90, as it had the events of the previous generation? Would change stop or continue? Would power increase or stabilize?

The situation of 1890 also implied a basic problem for Germany. Would Germany continue to pursue its policy of restraint or seek to enjoy, exploit, or even expand its new power? By 1890, Bismarck's policy had become a catalogue of contradictions. It had been appropriate to German power in 1871, and Bismarck had been successful in the sense that he had preserved the diplomatic and domestic settlements of 1871. But success became increasingly difficult. Like all institutions in a changing society, a policy—particularly an avowedly conservative policy like Bismarck's—becomes anachronistic as soon as it is promulgated. One price of Germany's increasing power was pressure for domestic political reform. The aristocrats and probably the peasants still supported Bismarck's domestic political system both because it served their interests and because they had benefited least from the social changes after 1871. But the new urban-industrial rich and poor had experienced great changes. They had radically increased in number; indeed, the rise in their number is a rough gauge of Germany's increased power.[1] They sought political power commensurate with their economic and numerical power—not least, in order to compete against one another. The patricianism inherent in Bismarck's system may also have been an impulse for change as the Germans became more self-confident. Bismarck himself recognized the conflict between institutions and nation at the beginning of the 1890s, when he advocated a forceful revision of the constitution as the only alternative to reform.[2]

Another price of Germany's rising power was pressure for the revision of diplomatic policy. Bismarck's conservative diplomacy no longer seemed relevant since Germany had become the strongest power and was no longer threatened by attack—if it ever had been. Nor did Bismarck's policy seem practical any longer. Russia had become less satisfied with monarchical solidarity as a substitute for Balkan gains, and Bismarck found it increasingly difficult to get other powers to oppose Russia for him. Domestic pressure had forced him to become a reluctant imperialist and thus into potential rivalry with the other powers, particularly Britain. These frictions with Britain and Russia jeopardized his policy of pacifying the peripheral powers in order to isolate France. Even his control over Austria-Hungary might be threatened if he could not influence Russian policy in the Balkans. In short, since the forces of 1890 could no longer be accommodated to the policies of 1871, the policies had to be adjusted to the forces.

A revolt against restraint occurred in Germany during the 1890s. Bismarck's evaluation of Germany's proper role in Europe no longer satisfied many Germans. This revolt may be attributable in part to a kind of generation gap. Almost half the Germans living in 1890 had not known preunification Germany and most leaders—like Bismarck—who had held significant power before 1871 had been replaced by men who had come to power after 1871.[3] The older generation was more aware of the status quo's tenuity, having known the status quo ante. The younger generation regarded unification more as historical necessity than fortuity. The older generation used a central European standard and compared Germany to France and Austria-Hungary. The younger generation used a world standard and compared Germany with Britain, Russia, and the United States. Another impulse to revolt against restraint may have been the effects of rapid urbanization and industrialization. Both tended to loosen the conservative bonds of traditional rural society, increase awareness of change and power, and generally augment the appeal of nationalism and imperialism. In brief, Germans at all levels of society were becoming increasingly aware of Germany's new power.

Whether because of generations, industrialization and urbanization, or power, Bismarck's conservative policy appealed to Germans less after 1890. They wanted the status quo reformed to conform with German power rather than German power restrained to conform with the status quo. This impulse was not uniquely German but typical of Europe and indeed a precondition for its characteristic vitality. Both diplomatic and domestic institutions were periodically adjusted to accommodate new forces. The international reform sought by the Germans was analogous to the domestic reform sought by the bourgeoisie and workers in Germany and elsewhere. The one was no more or less commendable than the other. Both applied prevailing intellectual theories of social evolution through struggle. In particular, the German response to new power conformed with the fundamental assumption of the state system that power would be used. Succinctly put, revolt against restraint was normal.

Bismarck's successors declared their independence from his policy with their announcement of a "new course." It had immediate effects in Europe. When Bismarck's policy of isolating France was jettisoned, the Franco-Russian alliance was concluded. The new policy also affected colonial events. Whereas Bismarck had been a reluctant imperialist, Kaiser William II and his advisers became enthusiasts. "World policy" became the German motto and participation in "the last division of the world" the German objective. Although earlier expansion in Asia and Africa continued to be encouraged, the major departure was in the Near East. In contrast to Bismarck, who had proclaimed his disinterest in the area in order to resolve Austro-Russian differences and encourage Anglo-Russian friction, William and his associates declared the Near East a primary interest. The new course was one of action in contrast to the old course of reaction.

The departures of German policy during the 1890s have frequently been criticized. Yet German imperialism was typical of prevailing attitudes and European civilization in general. One of the salient characteristics of modern Europe was its expansion and imposition of domination on other civilizations. In defense of William and his advisers, it can be argued that they changed the style but not the content of German policy, that they did not bankrupt Bismarck's policy but simply declared it bankrupt, and that the immediate practical effect of Germany's new policy was minor. Although concluded in the 1890s, the Franco-Russian alliance was largely ineffective until 1914. When Germany ceased to reconcile them, Austria-Hungary and Russia reconciled themselves in the Balkans during the 1890s. Even after "world policy" was proclaimed, colonial frictions among the other powers dwarfed problems involving Germany. Indeed, if imperialism diverted power from Europe, German imperialism can even be defended as a contribution to the balance of power and peace. Thus, the immediate effects of Germany's new policy were neither important nor ominous.

Germany's new policy was significant, however, as an indication of the change in German attitudes toward German power and the European system. Whereas Bismarck had regarded the status quo as essential to the preservation of German power, his successors perceived the status quo as a restriction on German power. The contradictions which would emerge later in German policy were already implicit. Germans wanted to alter the status quo both in and outside Europe. But changing the extra-European status quo required accepting the European status quo. Conversely, changing the European status quo required accepting the extra-European status quo in order to allow the other powers— especially Britain and Russia—to conflict and thereby give Germany a free hand in Europe. Had they pursued one goal consistently, the Ger-

mans might have succeeded, although it is doubtful that the other powers would have sacrificed the European balance for colonial gains. Instead the Germans sought both goals simultaneously and ultimately
achieved neither. In fact, the two objectives were linked together. By
adjusting their standards from continental to world power, the Germans
implied—perhaps unconsciously at first—a revision of the European
state system. Germany required a European power base incompatible
with the balance of power if it was to become a world power of American, British, or Russian magnitude. In these ways a German revolt
against Bismarck's restraint implicated the whole state system and
risked restraint by the other powers.

Just as the change in policy was a normal response to Germany's increased power, so the reactions of the other powers were also normal.
The German renunciation of cooperation in the Balkans caused Russia
to turn to France as a substitute. The alliance compensated for the radical decline in French power. Russian and French motives in allying were
conservative in Europe. The Russians were not anxious to undo the settlement of 1871 in order to win back Alsace-Lorraine for France or even
to fulfill their own Balkan aspirations. The French did not seriously
consider risking a war to satisfy Russian aspirations in the Balkans or
even to retrieve Alsace-Lorraine. Instead, both wanted security in Europe to pursue colonial ambitions, primarily against Britain. In effect,
the roles reversed in Europe after 1890. Previously the revisionists had
been France in Europe and Russia in the Balkans, while Germany had
been conservative. After 1890 the French and Russians became conservative and the Germans revisionist. Franco-Russian pressure in the colonial world might have caused a change in British behavior in Europe. It
seemed possible in the late 1890s that Britain might turn to Germany for
assistance. But an Anglo-German alliance was never concluded because
the price was too high for the British. They refused the Germans a free
hand in Europe (i.e., a promise of neutrality in a war with France and
Russia) in exchange for German pressure on the French and Russians. It
was preferable for the British to meet Franco-Russian challenges alone
and for the Germans to await a colonial conflict. Although the change in
German behavior was the most notable event during the 1890s, the
course of events depended more on relations between the other powers.
Since German power was insufficient to dominate an alliance of the
other powers, the central question was whether such an alliance would
be precluded by a colonial conflict. That this conflict did not occur indicates either that the other powers did not take their colonial aspirations
seriously enough for war or that they took the balance of power more

seriously. Imperialism was a luxury but European security was a necessity.

The increase in German power produced a new strategy as well as a new policy. Like the new policy, it had no immediate practical effects since it did not alter the course of diplomacy, cause a war, or produce even a significant increase in military expenditures.[4] Like the new policy, however, it reflected a change in German assumptions about the state system. Moltke had developed a strategy consistent with Bismarck's policy, i.e., designed to preserve the settlement of 1871. Schlieffen, Moltke's eventual successor, developed a strategy which was consistent with the new policy and implied a change in the settlement of 1871. Schlieffen has been charged with lack of political awareness. But if he reflected the prevailing mood, then the charge is either unjustified or must be levelled at the policymakers and indeed all politically articulate Germans. Schlieffen would have created an unacceptable contradiction between policy and strategy if he had retained Moltke's conservative strategy. Strategy, policy, and public opinion were in fact consistent.[5]

Schlieffen reversed many of Moltke's assumptions. Moltke assumed that quick military victories were no longer possible over modern, mass, industrialized states; wars would therefore be protracted. Schlieffen drew the opposite conclusion: precisely the complexity of modern states precluded a long war. Like Moltke, Schlieffen assumed that Germany would have to fight both Russia and France. Whereas Moltke concluded that a victory over one opponent was therefore impossible, Schlieffen regarded it as necessary. This conclusion compelled Schlieffen to reverse Moltke's assumption about modern war: because it was essential to defeat one opponent quickly, it had to be regarded as possible. The operative questions, therefore, became not whether one opponent could be defeated, but which, and how. Schlieffen agreed with Moltke that France was both more vulnerable and more dangerous than Russia. Both French strength and weakness were considerations for Schlieffen's strategy. After considering but rejecting a frontal attack on French eastern fortifications as likely to protract the war, Schlieffen decided that the French army could be defeated quickly only if it were encircled from the north by a German sweep through Belgium. Whereas Moltke wanted to immobilize the enemy, Schlieffen sought to keep the war mobile. Moltke could forfeit the initiative; Schlieffen had to grasp it. Moltke need not take chances; Schlieffen had to risk weakness in one place to concentrate in another. Schlieffen thereby reversed Moltke's strategy as Bismarck's successors reversed his policy.[6]

Schlieffen's strategy was, however, based on circular logic. Total and rapid victory was assumed to be possible because it was assumed to be necessary. It was assumed to be necessary because a separate peace with France was assumed to be necessary. A separate peace with France was assumed to be necessary because the avoidance of a two-front war was assumed to be required. But it was not essential to avoid a two-front war. Schlieffen could have stood on the defensive against both France and Russia with greater prospect of success than Moltke because Germany was stronger. It was necessary to avoid a two-front war only if Germany intended to revise the settlement of 1871. Intention was the mother of necessity. The logic cut both ways, however. A two-front war was probably necessary only if Germany were dissatisfied and probably unnecessary if Germany were satisfied. German aspirations rather than the Franco-Russian alliance made a two-front war likely and the Schlieffen plan necessary. Polarization of alternatives was characteristic of Schlieffen's strategy. Defense was equated with defeat, survival with victory. The status quo became untenable since the only alternatives perceived by Schlieffen—victory or defeat—would alter it in either eventuality. Schlieffen's strategy was symptomatic of the syndrome created by Germany's new power. But the strategy paradoxically cancelled the advantages of this power. German industrial power could be most effective in the long, total war Schlieffen sought to avoid, whereas the short, strictly military war he wanted would favor his two less industrialized continental opponents. Consequently, Schlieffen's strategy both reflected and neglected German power.[7]

The most serious fallacy of Schlieffen's strategy was, however, diplomatic rather than military. Like many German leaders of his generation (but not Bismarck or Moltke), Schlieffen misread 1871. Not only military defeat but also diplomatic isolation had caused France to surrender in 1871. Even if he could reproduce French military defeat, Schlieffen could not insure French isolation. On the contrary, the Franco-Russian alliance which seemed to necessitate his strategy also insured against French isolation. Therefore, the Schlieffen plan would be implemented only when it could not succeed. German diplomacy sought to produce the precondition for the plan's success by encouraging an Anglo-Russian colonial war which would leave France isolated in Europe. But an isolated France would probably have accepted diplomatic defeat rather than fight Germany alone. Accordingly, the Schlieffen plan would probably not be implemented when it could succeed. Thus, the plan was caught in a logical trap: it would probably be unsuccessful when necessary but successful when unnecessary. Neither Schlieffen nor his successors could ever escape this dilemma.

Germany instituted a new naval strategy analogous to its new diplomatic and military policies. Whereas Bismarck had opposed a large navy as well as imperialism, his successors proclaimed a naval policy along with their "world policy." Although it was argued that a colonial empire required a navy for protection, the navy was probably more explicable as another symptom of Germany's desire for prestige commensurate with its new power. The German navy is frequently criticized but was no less justified than the German colonial empire or the navies and empires of the other powers. Like the new German military strategy, the navy had no significant effect before 1900.[8] Although consistent in reflecting Germany's new power, the new military and naval strategies were inconsistent diplomatically. A German navy threatened primarily Britain and implied that Germnay should cooperate with Britain's colonial rivals, Russia and France. Schlieffen's strategy threatened primarily Russia and France and implied that Germany should cooperate with Britain. The German navy reduced the chances of German military success, while the Schlieffen plan reduced the chances of German naval success. The conditions for European and colonial revision were mutually exclusive: the realization of the one implied the renunciation (or at least postponement) of the other. But renunciation requires restraint and the Germans preferred to renounce restraint rather than European or colonial revision.

Bismarck's successors also proclaimed a new domestic political policy. Like his diplomatic policy, Bismarck's domestic policy had been conservative: he had imposed restraints and resisted reform. His successors sought to avoid fundamental reform by removing some restraints. Although it produced popularity which obscured the lack of genuine reform, this policy eventually backfired. The government hoped the minimal concessions would mark the end of reform, but the reformers regarded them as only the beginning. The removal of restraints (particularly on the Social Democrats) not only encouraged pressure for further reform but also augmented the means to achieve it. William's experience demonstrated that he could not be popular without genuinely sharing power. But he had sought popularity to preserve his power. The government was thereby confronted with a choice between popularity and power. One possible escape from this choice was to retain power and seek popularity through diplomatic success. International reform might obviate domestic reform. But pursuing international reform risked international unpopularity. Conversely, avoiding international unpopularity required renunciation of international reform and acceptance of either domestic reform or unpopularity. It turned out that the new domestic and diplomatic policies were interdependent.

German foreign policy was not determined, however, by domestic politics. Bismarck's successors seemed to sacrifice some of his control over foreign policy to the needs of domestic politics. They did so consciously in order to give the appearance of conducting a popular policy. The impression was deceptive, however, since William sought popularity to retain, not to reduce, control. The pressures for reform may have provided a further justification for an ambitious diplomatic policy, but the diplomatic policy would probably have been pursued even without domestic pressures. The contrast between Bismarck and his successors was, therefore, not so much in degree of control over foreign policy as in the desire to exercise control. Bismarck had to exert greater control because his policy was increasingly at odds with German power and public opinion. His successors exerted less because their policy was more consistent with the popular mood and German power. Whereas Bismarck sought to exclude public opinion, his successors sought to mobilize and exploit it. Therefore, domestic politics did not determine foreign policy any more than foreign policy determined domestic politics. Instead, both were determined by German power.

Germany had become the most powerful European state in the late 1880s. Although the rate of increase slowed during the 1890s, German power continued to grow. This power made it less necessary to fear a revision of the 1871 settlement. Indeed, if France were left to face Germany alone by an Anglo-Russian colonial struggle, Germany could probably improve upon the settlement. A challenge to British naval supremacy was justified in terms of relative power. German power was, however, insufficient as yet to challenge a Franco-Russian or Franco-Anglo-Russian alliance. Nonetheless, having become the greatest power, Germany began to act it.[9]

The European state system continued to change during the 1890s. The individual states had been able to maintain their independence, although two—France and Russia—had to ally to insure it. Like Bismarck's alliances of the previous generation, this alliance was conservative. Power relationships continued to shift. While Germany was tightening its grip on the position of most powerful, Britain and Russia exchanged places as second and third most powerful. In the sense that such reversals had frequently been accompanied by violence, there was a precedent for Anglo-Russian tension as well as actual colonial frictions. Meanwhile, France dropped further off the pace and Austria-Hungary reduced the gulf between itself and France. Despite the shifts in power, war had not occurred either inside or outside Europe between European states. The implications of a European war became more serious because Europe's total power continued to increase. Accordingly, Europe's power grew and shifted.[10]

The system managed to adjust to this new power. The distribution of new power continued to be inequitable and reinforced the distinction between great and greater powers. Nonetheless, the balance of power had been maintained by the conclusion of the Franco-Russian alliance. The most serious threat to the balance was the possibility that Germany would be left with a free hand in Európe by the distraction of the other powers to colonial questions. The other powers managed to evade this danger by settling their differences without violence. As long as they cooperated, Britain and Russia still had sufficient power to play their traditional roles as patrons of the balance. Because of German activism and imperial disagreements between the other powers, the system lost some of the cohesiveness and stability given it by Bismarck's alliances. But imperialism indicated that the powers still felt secure in Europe. Despite changes, the balance persisted.[11]

Europe's relationship with the rest of the world continued to evolve. The increase in European power allowed it to extend its dominion further over the unmodernized world, and the operative question was how, not whether, Europe would do so. If imperialism reduced European power, it lessened the seriousness of a European war. But, to the extent that it reduced European power, it contributed to the reduction of European industrial superiority over the United States. Thus, Europe's domination continued to increase, but its independence continued to decrease.[12]

Politicization of the masses continued. Popular participation in politics increased slightly. Although imperialism reinforced the appearance of popular involvement in foreign affairs, in actuality it demonstrated the propaganda skill of governments and interest groups more than it increased popular control over foreign policy. Governments in general sought to increase their power by making their policy popular rather than winning popularity by sharing power. As a result, styles changed, but power remained in the same hands: the classes which had ruled in 1871 still ruled in 1902. Ideology crept increasingly into foreign policy as governments sought popularity. It did not, however, increase European tension very noticeably. The ideology of imperialism in particular was used by governments more to arouse their own public at the expense of the colonial people than against the other European states. In the sense that this propaganda asserted European superiority, it tended to reinforce European solidarity and thus reduce tension. To the extent that imperialism did cause popular tension, it distracted attention from European problems and blurred the lines of European conflicts, such as Franco-German and Austro-Russian frictions. Thus, as the masses were mobilized, Europe's human power increased but popular influence on policy remained minimal.

The issues of 1890 had been resolved. The state system had adjusted to the radical changes of the previous generation. The shifts in power had been accommodated and the balance preserved. These adjustments had been made without violence either among or within the European states. Although significantly altered, the state system had not only survived but had also apparently prospered.

CONTAINMENT AND ENCIRCLEMENT:
GERMAN PROBES AND ENTENTE RESPONSES (1902–12)

The answers of 1902 created further questions. Would the state system stabilize or continue to change? Would its power increase? Would it be distributed inequitably and jeopardize the balance? Would Europe extend its power throughout the world? The events of the 1890s posed problems for Germany in particular. Would it pursue its new policies or draw back and sacrifice some of the pleasures of power to regain the advantages of restraint? Would the other powers resist or appease Germany?

A colonial war between the other European powers was the precondition of success for Germany's new policy. An Anglo-French war had seemed the most likely colonial conflict during the nineties and remained a possibility at the turn of the century. An Anglo-Russian colonial conflict had been possible during the nineties and seemed even more likely during the first decade of the twentieth century. Conversely, a colonial conflict involving Germany seemed unlikely and an Anglo-German colonial agreement even possible at the turn of the century. Designed in theory as insurance against Germany, the Franco-Russian alliance seemed to become a colonial alliance against Britain in practice. In brief, the prospects seemed propitious for Germany in 1902.

The situation altered abruptly during the next few years. In Japan, Britain found an ally against Russia to which Britain would not have to pay the price demanded by Germany. The Anglo-Japanese alliance reestablished the colonial balance as the Franco-Russian alliance had the continental balance. The difference lay in the fact that Germany held the balance in the colonial world, whereas Britain held it in Europe. The Anglo-Japanese alliance might have caused the war between the two colonial alliances for which Germany hoped. Such a war would have forced on France the awkward choice between Russia and Britain. The French avoided this dilemma by reconciling their colonial differences with the British in 1904 and thereby limiting their alliance with Russia to Europe. This solution was acceptable to Russia since it reduced the likelihood of British resistance in the Far East and allowed Russia to confront Japan alone. But Russian defeat and revolution rather than Far

Eastern domination resulted. The reduction in Russian power radically altered colonial and European relations. Britain was left predominant in the colonial world and Germany in Europe.

Although the Anglo-Russian war had not occurred, the situation suddenly seemed conducive to German success. Russian weakness rendered the Franco-Russian alliance ineffectual and thus upset the balance it had reestablished for a decade. In a superficial sense, the Bismarckian pattern reemerged, and France was again isolated. But the situation was fundamentally different because European power had continued to shift. In 1890 France could not match German power; by 1905, German superiority was even more marked. Russia was the stronger and increasingly strong partner in the Franco-Russian alliance.[13] It therefore seemed possible that Germany could win European and/or colonial concessions from France. The critical element for German success was French isolation. Defeat, revolution, and German amiability seemed to insure against Russian intervention. A generation of Anglo-French colonial friction and the opportunity to exploit Russian weakness in the colonial world made British support for France seem unlikely. German success against France would probably have invalidated the recent Anglo-French colonial agreement and perhaps would have even replaced it with a German-French agreement. By such a process, colonial cooperation between France, Germany, and Russia against Britain might have been the ultimate result. Germany would undoubtedly have dominated a Franco-German entente, and France would probably have slipped into the role of a second Austria-Hungary appropriate to its declining power. The Franco-Russian alliance would then have been superfluous. Germany would have established its predominance not only over Austria-Hungary but also over an isolated France and a weakened Russia. Germany would thereby have revised both the colonial and European situations in its favor.

The German policy proclaimed in the 1890s was tested against the French in 1905. The immediate objective was disruption of the recent Anglo-French Mediterranean agreement. The responses to German pressure were unexpected. Despite the unpromising prospects, the French might have defended their Mediterranean interests and their European independence. Instead, they recognized the risks of resistance and sought a colonial accommodation with Germany. This response was a step in the evolution of French policy, perhaps even more significant than the colonial agreement with the British. Theretofore the French had not completely renounced their hopes to undo 1871 and retrieve their lost primacy. The French, however, could not undo 1871 alone and needed at least Russian, if not also British, support. But neither Russia nor Britain was anxious to reestablish French primacy. Consequently, French dreams of past grandeur were a diplomatic weakness. The French, accordingly, made the decision in 1905 which had been implicit since 1871. They recognized that their independence, not primacy, was the critical issue and depended on the balance of power rather than on their own power. French weakness had paradoxically become a diplomatic strength, since France could now win British support by threatening a *détente* with Germany. Germany played into French hands when, instead of accepting an amicable accommodation as the first step toward an eventual Franco-German colonial entente, the Germans exploited their advantage to humiliate the French and justified a French request for British assistance.

The considerations which made British intervention seem unlikely indeed made it undesirable to the British. They would have preferred to exploit Russian colonial weakness and to allow Russia to support France against Germany. Defending French independence and colonial interests not only implied risks with little reward for Britain but also ran against the grain of a generation of Anglo-French colonial frictions. British domestic developments were likewise inconducive to intervention. But the considerations which made victory over France desirable to Germany made it undesirable to Britain. It would not only establish a new rival in the Mediterranean but would also jeopardize the Anglo-French agreement and possibly even British communication with India. But, if German penetration into the Mediterranean were undesirable to Britain, German domination of France was unacceptable. Indeed, British imperialism presupposed security in Europe, thus the balance of power, thus French independence. Supporting France consequently seemed an unavoidable, however undesirable, necessity.

British support for France confronted the Germans with an awkward choice. They could persist in the hope of a major diplomatic victory, but at the risk of diplomatic defeat or even war. Alternatively, they could desist in the hope of avoiding war and winning a minor diplomatic victory, but at the cost of renouncing a major diplomatic victory. They considered the option of diplomatic victory at the risk of war. Schlieffen produced the strategy for military victory. Circumstances had paradoxically adjusted to his strategy when he had not adjusted his strategy to circumstances. His initial object had been to defeat France in a two-front war against the Franco-Russian alliance. His strategy had revealed, however, that French defeat was possible only in a one-front war against an Anglo-French alliance. With the Russian defeat and revolution, this precondition for success was suddenly fulfilled. Consequently, Schlieffen and Holstein, the strong man in the Foreign Ministry, favored a hard line against the French and British. But Chancellor Bülow and the kaiser opted for a minor diplomatic victory rather than risk war to achieve a major diplomatic success.

Although Schlieffen and Holstein had to pay for their dissent with dismissal, their disappearance did not prove them wrong. On the contrary, if Germany were to revise the European and colonial status quo, Schlieffen and Holstein were probably correct that this was the most propitious moment. They were realistic in recognizing that genuine revision of the status quo would involve the risk, if not the necessity, of war with France and England. In short, if Germany wanted revision, it had to accept the risks; if it did not want the risks, it should renounce revision. Instead, Bülow and the kaiser wanted revision without risks. They dismissed the principal policy maker (Holstein) but retained the policy and dismissed the principal strategy maker (Schlieffen) but retained the strategy. Yet the Bülow-Kaiser policy of revision without risk was based on a fallacy. Germany could revise the system without risk only if the system had effectively desisted, i.e., if the other powers had already renounced the balance of power and accepted German domination. Germany could not revise the system without risk if the system persisted. In short, this policy could succeed only if it were unnecessary, but not if it were necessary.

Despite this contradiction, revision without risk remained German policy until the war. After 1905 German leaders sought to reduce the risks by isolating and threatening their opponents. This procedure was tested first against Britain. In order to make Britain amenable, Germany intensified its naval program. Although prestige, protection, pique (at British support for France), and public opinion were probably contributing factors, the navy's main purpose was probably diplomatic. Its rationale was found in Tirpitz's "risk theory" that Britain would make diplomatic concessions rather than risk its naval superiority in a confrontation with the German navy. The Tirpitz plan was based on assumptions similar to those of the Schlieffen plan. Both were blueprints for war only after diplomatic threats had failed. Both assumed enemy isolation as the precondition for success. Schlieffen assumed France would be isolated from Russia (though not from Britain) and Tirpitz assumed Britain would be completely isolated. But the naval threat would have been unnecessary if Britain had been isolated—i.e., if Britain had not supported France—and was necessary only when Britain was not isolated. Thus, the Tirpitz and Schlieffen plans were based on the same contradiction that they could be successful when unnecessary but not when necessary.[14]

The German threat proved unsuccessful. Instead of renouncing the

balance of power to preserve their naval superiority, the British reinforced their superiority by increased building to preserve the balance.
They also avoided isolation by patching up their quarrel with Russia in
Persia. Although it by no means resolved their differences, this agreement indicated that an Anglo-Russian conflict was less likely and that
both would probably make colonial in preference to European concessions. The agreement allowed each to confront Germany in Europe with
less concern that the other would seek colonial gains. But it was not a
military agreement against Germany and resembled the Anglo-French
entente more than the Franco-Russian alliance. German pressure, accordingly, produced Anglo-German tension and Anglo-Russian *détente*
rather than British concessions to Germany.

The Germans next sought to isolate Russia by threatening its Balkan
interests as they had sought to isolate Britain by threatening its naval
interests. The Balkans had been quiescent for a generation because of the
distraction of Russia with extra-European problems and of Austria-
Hungary with domestic problems. When Austria-Hungary broke the
Balkan truce by annexing Bosnia in 1908, Russia unsuccessfully sought
Anglo-French support in resisting the annexation. The French were
alienated by Russian nonsupport in the Mediterranean and nonconsul-
tation in the Balkans, while the British were disinclined to encourage
extension of Russian influence toward the straits. Russia was thereby
isolated and had to accept a minor diplomatic defeat. At this point, the
Germans intervened. Despite the Franco-Russian alliance, German policy toward Russia since the 1890s had been friendly, perhaps partially in
an effort to encourage an Anglo-Russian conflict; German gestures of
sympathy for Russian defeat and revolution had preserved amity and
Russian noninvolvement in the Franco-German crisis of 1905 had
avoided enmity. The pattern of relations suddenly reversed as harmony
was replaced by humiliation. German policy may have been motivated
in part by the compulsion to preserve Austro-Hungarian dependence on
Germany, since either a bilateral Austro-Russian agreement or a unilateral Austro-Hungarian success might have made Austria-Hungary less
reliant on Germany. But German policy was probably motivated primarily by a desire to demonstrate to Russia that the Anglo-Russian
agreement over Persia and the Franco-Russian alliance were inapplica-
ble to the Balkans: Russia's Balkan ambitions could be fulfilled only in
Berlin. In short, the Germans typically sought amity through the threat
of enmity.

The Germans turned back against the French in 1911. As in 1905,
France seemed isolated. Russia was embittered by French lack of support
during the Bosnian crisis, and Britain was unenthusiastic about acting

as protector of French colonial interests. The French government was again willing to make concessions and perhaps even more inclined toward a colonial agreement with Germany than in 1905. Although concessions were regarded by the Germans as the first of many but by the French as the last, a limited agreement might have been reached. But the disparity in strength between the two was probably an insurmountable barrier to a genuine Franco-German *détente*. A *rapprochement* was acceptable to France only if it prevented German domination and to Germany only if it facilitated domination. The Germans were again right about the Russians but wrong about the British. The unlikelihood of a Franco-German *détente* was not immediately clear to the British, who could afford it almost as little as a French defeat. Far from deterring British intervention, the German naval threat had demonstrated the necessity of avoiding isolation. Consequently, the British encouraged French resistance, and Anglo-French cooperation rather than a German-French *détente* was the result of German pressure.

Rather than isolating their opponents, the Germans had driven them together. The other powers had not yet formed a firm alliance and would not until after war had begun. They had, however, demonstrated a determination to defend their own independence, interests, and the balance of power. Their objective had become the containment of German power, which Germans claimed meant encirclement, i.e., a determination to weaken or even destroy Germany. Although they periodically exploited this notion to arouse public support, German statesmen probably did not take it seriously in this sense before 1914. They probably did believe, nonetheless, that encirclement existed in the sense of resistance to a revision of the colonial and European status quo which might seem justified by Germany's new power. Each side naturally regarded its own perception as objectively true and its opponents' as distorted by self-interest. The relative merits of containment and encirclement are debatable. German aspirations were neither more nor less selfish than those of their opponents. The rights of preponderant power and prior possession are both assertions which had long precedents in European relations. The resolution of such confrontations had usually been based on considerations of power rather than justice. But the tensions caused by these conflicting views of the situation were undebatable and produced an encirclement-containment syndrome by 1912.

This syndrome was not only normal for the system but also necessary to its survival. If no power exerted pressure, the status quo would become permanent and no change would occur. If Germany were not resisted, however, the balance of power would desist and the system would become centralized. The tension between encirclement and containment, therefore, reflected the system's basic characteristics of change and balance. It was also typical that a state with rising power should probe the status quo until it was contained; in this sense it had been unnatural for Bismarck to restrain Germany. If Germany had not used its power, power would have become irrelevant and the system would have been fundamentally altered. Although tension had increased, the danger of war was not yet imminent. It had been considered only infrequently and confidentially; the crises had remained diplomatic and the immediate issues relatively minor. But German probing had created an atmosphere of crisis which had a cumulative effect. Like other human behavior, diplomacy is partially retrospective: statesmen would alter their policies after 1912 as a result of what had happened before.

German strategy remained consistent with the objectives, though not with the practice, of German policy. German leaders were agreed that a revision of the status quo was desirable. Schlieffen and Bülow disagreed, however, as to whether revision was feasible without the risk of war. As a result of Bülow's victory over Schlieffen, German policy after 1905 sought revision without the risk of war. The Schlieffen plan was retained, however, by Schlieffen's successor, the younger Moltke. In fact, Moltke had little choice, not because no alternative strategy existed, but because the Schlieffen plan was logical in terms of German objectives. It would have been absurd for Germany to seek revision if Schlieffen's revisionist, aggressive strategy had been replaced by a conservative, defensive strategy. If the Schlieffen plan were unrealistic, not only the strategy but also the policy and its objective of revision should have been changed. Since German leaders did not want to renounce revision, Moltke's decision to retain the Schlieffen plan was not only consistent but also necessary.

Although Moltke accepted Schlieffen's plan, he altered Schlieffen's basic assumption. The precondition for success of the Schlieffen plan was a one-front war in the west. Schlieffen had, therefore, communicated little with the Austro-Hungarians, since it seemed both unwise and unnecessary. Russia might not intervene quickly if Germany did not encourage Austria-Hungary. If Germany defeated the Anglo-French quickly, Austro-Hungarian aid would not be required. But, since Moltke assumed that a two-front war was inevitable, Austro-Hungarian aid was necessary, and a German promise of support was essential to insure it. Moltke thereby reinforced Austro-Hungarian activism and increased the likelihood of Russian intervention. The vicious circle was closed: by assuming a two-front war was inevitable, Moltke made it more likely. By rejecting Schlieffen's assumption, Moltke sharpened the contradiction in German strategy. Whereas Schlieffen regarded a one-front war as essential for success, Moltke would implement the plan only in a two-front war when it was even less likely to succeed.

Like the new diplomatic policy, the government's domestic policy had been tried and had failed by 1912. William had not been able to conceal domestic problems behind monarchical popularity. This bankrupt policy was not replaced, however, by either Bismarckian restraint or genuine reform. Although he had a taste for politics, Bülow lacked character and substituted duplicity for direction. His successor, Bethmann Hollweg, lacked a taste for politics and preferred to sublimate rather than solve problems which were probably insoluble in any case within the existing structure. Meanwhile, the forces of change—industrialization, urbanization, and socialism—continued to grow.[15] The pressures for reform caused resistance and thus tension. These internal tensions could implicate foreign policy if the government were tempted to distract attention from them with foreign adventures. Whereas Germans were disagreed on domestic reform, they could be expected to agree that Germany should play a larger international role. These domestic considerations may have reinforced, but probably did not alter, German diplomatic policy. Power, not politics, remained the basic impulse behind German policy. Domestic tension did raise the cost of diplomatic failure, however, since it would probably cause demands for domestic reform. Thus, seeking international reform had domestic as well as international risks.

However unsuccessful, Germany's diplomatic policy was consistent with its rising power. Germany need not fear a Franco-Russian alliance but could not yet be certain to defeat it. The prospects in a one-front war against an Anglo-French alliance were considerably better. Against an Anglo-French-Russian alliance, an Austro-German alliance could probably defend itself but not prevail—a consideration which made Moltke's retention of the Schlieffen plan unjustifiable. In short, Germany had sufficient power to defend itself but not to dominate the system if the other powers cooperated.[16]

The system continued to change. The individual powers had maintained their independence by cooperation against Germany and reconciliation of colonial differences. Like Bismarck's alliances, this combination of cooperation and reconciliation was designed to preserve the colonial and European status quo. Although power shifted, the rank order remained constant and therefore did not increase tension. Tension rose instead because of German revisionism, Austro-Hungarian revival, and Anglo-French-Russian resistance. Despite greater tension, no war occurred in Europe. The implications of war became more serious, however, since European power increased. Characteristically this new power was dispersed inequitably and reinforced the disparity between great and greater powers. The balance of power was threatened by Germany but preserved by Anglo-French-Russian cooperation. This cooperation survived the threat of disruption because of a colonial conflict. It also survived the threat of weakness due to the Russian defeat and revolution when Germany let the opportunity pass. At best, the coalition against Germany was, however, erratic: the Franco-Russian alliance had proven surprisingly weak but the Anglo-French entente had been surprisingly durable. The system had become more cohesive in the sense that the powers were more concerned with Europe than the colonial world. It was a cohesiveness of crisis and conflict, however, not concord. Although the rise of European power suggested that it would maintain its colonial dominion, the threat of Japanese-American industrialization was confirmed by the Japanese defeat of Russia. Furthermore, rising European tension made it possible that the powers would vitiate their power against one another rather than impose it on non-Europeans. The old pattern of central European weakness and peripheral strength had been reversed by 1910: instead of competing for control over central Europe, the peripheral powers cooperated to contain it. The tendency toward popular participation in politics continued, and public opinion was mobilized increasingly during diplomatic crises. But popular influence over foreign policy did not increase, and governmental control remained high. The basic question of 1902 had accordingly been answered: new powers and policies had been accommodated by the system without violence, but not without increased tension.[17]

The European system had been fundamentally altered since 1850. Although all the powers had survived, Austria-Hungary and France had preserved their independence by such dependence on other powers that their great power status had become a question of semantics by 1912. The rank order of the powers had virtually reversed. Britain, the greatest power in 1850, had dropped to third by 1910. France, the second power in 1850, had slipped to fourth. Austria, the policeman of central Europe in 1850, had become least powerful. These trends were likely to continue, certainly in the cases of France and Britain. Prussia-Germany and Russia, the two sleeping giants of 1850, had become the most powerful. These drastic changes had typically been accompanied by violence, but the violence had occurred early during the process and was neither very destructive nor prolonged. This general absence of violence was fortunate for the system, since its capacity for destruction rose in proportion to its power. Europe's power in 1910 not only dwarfed most of the world but also its own power in 1850. Although the inequitable distribution of this new strength had made the powers more equal, the balance of power was less secure in 1910 than in 1850. Britain's overwhelming power in 1850 had been a sufficient guarantee in itself for the balance, whereas the balance in 1910 was dependent on the vicissitudes of Anglo-French-Russian cooperation. The implications of imperialism had come full circle between 1850 and 1910: not a threat to the balance in 1850, imperialism had threatened to distract the anti-German coalition around 1900 but did so less by 1910. Although Europe's dominion had extended greatly since 1850, its independence of outside power had decreased because of Japanese-American industrialization. The traditional pattern of high governmental control over low power was altered by the rise in power. Governmental control might have been jeopardized by the increase of popular participation in politics but was preserved by propaganda and publicity. The pattern had become high control over high power. Consequently, the European state system had seemed to accommodate the revolutionary changes since 1850, but the balance between revolution and accommodation was in fact delicate.[18]

NOTES

1   In 1871, Germany's population was 63.9 percent rural and 36.1 percent urban. By 1890, it had become 57.5 percent rural and 42.5 percent urban. It became equally rural-urban around 1895. The rural population had remained almost stable, while the urban population had increased by 74.3 percent since 1871.

2   Gerald D. Feldman, *Army, Industry and Labor in Germany, 1914–1918* (Princeton, 1966), p. 23. Egmont Zechlin, *Staatsstreichpläne Bismarcks und Wilhelms II, 1890 bis 1894* (Stuttgart, 1929), pp. 43–50.

3   The German population rose from 41 to 49 million between 1871 and 1890. If it is assumed that persons under the age of 15 are politically unaware and that one-third of Germans living in 1871 were under 15 years of age, then, by 1890, 21 of the 45 million Germans had not known pre-1871 Germany. If it is assumed that most leaders in positions of highest responsibility are over 45 years of age, then most would have been 65 years of age or older by 1890.

4   German army expenditures during the 1880s had risen by 33.5 percent, during the 1890s by 39 percent. Germany's increase and total expenditures were the largest in Europe although they were only slightly larger than those of France and Russia. The increase in German expenditures during the decade from 1900 to 1910 was, however, only 21.5 percent. Thus, expenditures rose more slowly after the Schlieffen plan had become German strategy.

5   Ritter attributes Schlieffen's change of strategy in part to "that overestimate of German power and German ability which was quite generally characteristic of the epoch of William II, in contrast to the epoch of Bismarck and the elder Moltke." Gerhard Ritter, radio lecture, 2 August 1964 (Bundeszentrale für politische Bildung, 1964), pp. 12–13. Moltke was succeeded by Waldersee (1888–91), who accepted Moltke's strategy in general. Waldersee was succeeded by Schlieffen (1891–1905). For criticism of Schlieffen's political insensitivity, see Gordon A. Craig, *The Politics of the Prussian Army, 1640–1945* (Oxford, 1955), p. 277.

6 For Schlieffen's view that a complete victory was necessary for Germany, see Craig, *Politics*, p. 278. For discussions of the Schlieffen plan, see Gerhard Ritter, *Der Schlieffenplan: Kritik eines Mythos* (Munich, 1956), passim; *Der Weltkrieg 1914–1918*, ed. Reichsarchiv (Berlin, 1925), 1:8–9, 51; Craig, *Politics*, p. 277.

7 In 1900, German power (34.3 percent) was notably superior to that of France (11.6 percent) and of Russia (27.4 percent). But, arms expenditures for the three were comparable: Germany 33.6 (million pounds), France 27.8, Russia 32.1. Thus, the ratio of German to Franco-Russian power was 34:39, of German to Franco-Russian military expenditures 34:60. Interested more in speed than size, Schlieffen did not mobilize the nation's total resources or even radically increase military expenditures.

8 Like German military expenditures, German naval expenditures did not increase radically during the 1890s. In fact, naval expenditures increased at a slower rate than under Bismarck. Between 1870 and 1880, German naval expenditures increased by 78.5 percent; between 1880 and 1890, by 91.5 percent; between 1890 and 1900, by 61 percent. The rate of increase under William was less than the increases of France, Britain, and Russia from 1890 to 1900. Germany's naval expenditures increased by 61 percent during this period, while Britain's rose by 112 percent (in large part, because of the Boer War). France's rose by 66 percent and Russia's by 91 percent. In 1900, Britain's expenditures were 3.95 times as large as those of Germany; France's were 1.97 times as large as Germany's; Russia's were 1.13 times as large as Germany's.

9 German power had increased by 5.3 percent during the 1880s and by 2.3 percent during the 1890s. In 1890, Germany had 32 percent, Britain had 29.1 percent, Russia had 19.7 percent, France had 15.2 percent, and Austria-Hungary had 4 percent of European power. In 1900, Germany had 34.3 percent, Britain had 20.9 percent, Russia had 27.4 percent, France had 11.6 percent, and Austria-Hungary had 5.8 percent of European power. In 1890, an Austro-German alliance had 36 percent and a Franco-Russian alliance had 34.9 percent of European power. In 1900, an Austro-German alliance had 40.1 percent and a Franco-Russian alliance had 39 percent of European power.

10 Ibid.

11 The spread between the strong powers (Germany, Russia, and Britain) and the weaker powers (France and Austria-Hungary) increased during the 1890s. In 1890, the gap between Russia (the weakest of the big three) and France was only 4.5 percent. By 1900, the gap between Britain (the weakest of the big three) and France had become 9.3 percent. In 1890, Germany was already twice as powerful as France; by 1900, it had become three times as powerful. Britain was almost twice as powerful as France in 1900. By 1900, French power was more comparable with Austro-Hungarian power than it was with British, Russian, or German power.

12 In 1890, American manufacturing production was 74 percent of Europe's. By 1900, it had risen to 77.5 percent.

13 In 1890, France had 15.2 percent to Germany's 32 percent, i.e., one-half of Germany's power. In 1905, France had 11.1 percent to Germany's 35.8 percent, i.e., less than one-third. (1905 is the average of 1900 and 1910 for each.) In 1890, Russia had 19.7 percent and France had 15.2 percent. But in 1905, Russia had 28.1 percent and France had only 11.1 percent. Thus, whereas they had been more or less equal partners in the 1890s, Russia dominated increasingly. (The figures for 1905 are the average of 1900 and 1910. Russia's share in 1905 was probably even higher since the 1910 figure reflects Russia's defeat.)

14 The German naval budget increased by 106 percent between 1900 and 1910. This was a larger increase than any decade since 1870, both in percentage or absolute terms. The increase fell off to 8.5 percent between 1910 and 1914, i.e., from 10.6 percent per annum (1900–10) to 2.1 percent per annum (1910–14).

15 In 1900 Germany was 45.6 percent rural and 54.4 percent urban. In 1910, it was 40 percent rural and 60 percent urban. Thus, during William's reign, the proportions had almost precisely reversed: in 1890, Germany had been 57.5 percent rural and 42.5 percent urban. Between 1900 and 1910 the rural population had remained stable (c. 25

million), while the urban population had increased radically (30.7 to 38.9 million, i.e., by 27 percent). Membership in the Socialist party increased from 0.38 million in 1906 to 1.09 million in 1914.

16 German power had increased from 34.3 percent to 37.2 percent between 1900 and 1910. Equally significant was the fact that Germany's lead over Russia, the second strongest power, had increased from 6.9 percent to 9.1 percent, in part because of the setback to Russian power caused by its defeat and revolution. The increase of German power between 1900 and 1910 was slightly higher than during the previous decade: 2.9 percent as compared with 2.3 percent. In 1910, the Austro-German alliance had 44.4 percent, the Franco-Russian alliance 38.7 percent. In 1905, Germany had 35.8 percent, the Anglo-French 30 percent. (1905 is the average of 1900 and 1910 figures). In 1910, Germany had 37.2 percent, the Anglo-French 27.5 percent. In 1910, the Austro-German alliance had 44.4 percent, the Anglo-French-Russian group 55.6 percent. Without Austria-Hungary, Germany would have had only 37.2 percent. Thus, Moltke's concern about insuring Austro-Hungarian participation.

17 The power order remained what it had been in 1900: Germany, Russia, Britain, France, and Austria-Hungary. Europe's total power had risen by 49 percent since 1900. This was less than during the 1890s (62.5 percent) or the 1880s (56.5 percent). In 1900, German power was 3 times French power, Russian power was 2.5 times French power, and British power was 1.8 times French power. In 1910, German power had risen to 3.5 times French power, and Russian power had grown to 2.8 times French power, while British power had dropped to 1.6 times French power. In 1900, French power had been 2 times Austro-Hungarian power; by 1910, it had dropped to 1.5 times Austro-Hungarian power. In 1910, the Anglo-French-Russian group had 55.6 percent, the Austro-German alliance 44.4 percent. This was a drop from 59.1 percent in 1900 for the Anglo-French-Russian group. In 1910, American manufacturing production was 86.25 percent of Europe's. If its rate of increase between 1900 and 1910 continued, American manufacturing production would equal Europe's by 1925.

18 In 1850, Britain had 50 percent, France 30 percent, Russia and Prussia 10 percent each of European power. In 1910, Britain had 16.9 percent, France 10.6 percent, Russia 28.1 percent, Germany 37.2 percent, and Austria-Hungary 7.2 percent of European power. If their rates of decline during the decade from 1900 to 1910 continued until 1920, Britain would have 12.9 percent and France 9.6 percent of European power. If their rates of increase during the decade from 1900 to 1910 continued until 1920, Germany would have 40.1 percent, Russia 28.8 percent, and Austria-Hungary 8.6 percent of European power. The Russian rise was deceptively small because of defeat and revolution. Europe's power in 1910 was 12 times greater than in 1850, 5 times greater than in 1870. In 1910, Germany had 4.5 times as much power as all of Europe in 1850. Even the weaker powers in 1910 could have dominated the Europe of 1850: France had 1.3 times and Austria-Hungary had 0.9 times Europe's power in 1850. In 1850, American manufacturing production was 27.7 percent of Europe's and Japan's was nil. In 1910, American production was 86.2 percent as large as Europe's, and Japan's was considerable.

III / THE SYSTEM IMPACTED:
Great Power Relations (January 1912–June 1914)

The answers of the previous decade generated new questions. Would power increase? Above all, would the trends of Anglo-French decline, and of German, Russian, and Austro-Hungarian increase in power continue? Would German probing persist or desist as a result of the other powers' response? In short, would new changes be accommodated without violence as they had been since 1871, or would they require war?

It was hypothetically possible that the system could adjust to the events of the previous decade without violence. Whether or not it did so depended in large measure on how the events of the previous decade were perceived. Germany had taken the initiative in all the crises since 1905 except the Bosnian crisis and had pursued an aggressive policy in all. But Germany had so far probed the status quo only by diplomacy and had not sought to change it by military means. German probing had caused a response from the other powers which indicated that they were determined to defend their independence. But they had not yet probed the status quo or taken the initiative against Germany and/or Austria-Hungary. It was possible that Germany might accept the other powers' response as sufficient warning and renounce its aspirations for colonial and European revision. It was also possible that the other powers might regard their responses to German probing as sufficient to defend their independence. Conceivably the events of the previous decade had established a new balance of power. Such a balance of power is only partially definable in terms of measurable power and depends on the perceptions of statesmen: it exists if they perceive it. Accordingly, whether the system was in balance depended in part on how great-power statesmen viewed the events of the previous decade.

The system's adjustment to the previous decade's events also depended on how statesmen expected power to shift in the future. If they expected it to be distributed in a manner favorable to themselves, they would contemplate the future with optimism. If they expected shifts unfavorable to themselves, however, they would be pessimistic and perhaps seek to alter or deter events. These anticipated shifts in power would affect their expectations regarding their opponents' policies and above all the likelihood of war. Statesmen's perceptions of the system in 1912, consequently, depended in part on how they expected it to develop.

Finally, accommodation depended in part on the existing status quo. If it remained secure, the system was more likely to adjust to the events of the previous decade. If the status quo were jeopardized, however, it would complicate adjustment to the previous decade's events.

As it turned out, the system was not able to adjust without violence. Only the British perceived the events of the previous decade as conducive to the balance of power, whereas the continental powers read them at once as a threat to themselves and as an impulse to alter the system in their own favor. The distribution of power during the previous decade was also perceived by the continental powers as inconducive to stability: German growth made France anxious, and Russian growth made Germany anxious. The status quo was threatened by events in the Balkans which not only created issues among the powers but also threatened the existence of Austria-Hungary. The increased anxieties were reflected in increased military expenditures which reached the proportions of an arms race. Public opinion became increasingly agitated by international questions. The system was, therefore, less adjusted than impacted, less at a balance than at an impasse.

Like all historical events, this impasse and its eventuating in war can be understood in chronological or problematical terms. It can be argued that the chronological approach is superior because the issues developed simultaneously and were interrelated. The chronological approach is, however, more conducive to description than analysis. Since the primary interest of this study is analysis, the problems approach is applied in the following chapters. The events of 1912–14 are interpreted in terms of four themes. The question of great-power policies and alliances is central. The threat to the status quo caused by the Balkan wars is a second issue. Another is the relationship between domestic and international politics. The fourth involves the implications of military strategy and expansion for diplomatic policies.

A PATTERN ALTERED: FRANCO-RUSSIAN REVIVAL, GERMAN ARMS, AND BRITISH DETACHMENT (1912)

The international events of the decade before 1912 had been characterized by Anglo-French-Russian response to German initiative. While Germany continued to be active—especially in military expenditures— after 1912, it became more cautious in diplomatic relations. By contrast, France and Russia, which had been relatively passive, now became more active. Austria-Hungary, which had taken an initiative during the Bosnian crisis, was forced to react to events after 1912. Britain, which had been an active participant in three of the four crises during the previous decade (two Moroccan and one naval), became more detached after 1912. The pattern of the previous decade was thereby reversed after 1912.

The French and Russians sought to make their alliance a more useful diplomatic tool after 1912. These efforts were stimulated by the alliance's ineffectuality during the previous decade. They were also justified in terms of power considerations which made the alliance necessary to both France and Russia if they were to insure their independence from Germany. Russian recovery from defeat and revolution made increased diplomatic activism possible. In addition to these largely defensive considerations, there were positive inducements as well. The Russians were anxious for greater French support in the Balkans, the French for greater Russian support in the Mediterranean which would liberate them from complete dependence on Britain. The imperatives of the alliance had gradually become clear as a result of the previous decade's experience. France could not expect Russian support against Germany unless France supported Russia in the Balkans. Conversely, Russia could not expect French support against Germany and Austria-Hungary in the Balkans unless it supported France against Germany. Consequently, the impulses for tightening the alliances came from both sides. The Russians repeated their promises of a rapid offensive against Germany in case of war. The activists Messimy and Joffre took charge of French strategy during the second Moroccan crisis and began to replace the traditional defensive strategy with an offensive one. The last attempt at a Franco-German *détente* backfired at the end of 1911, and Caillaux, the proponent of reconciliation, was replaced in January 1912 by Poincaré, the advocate of "national revival." In August and September 1912, Poincaré committed France to support Russia in a war against Germany, even if it were provoked by an Austro-Russian conflict in the Balkans.[1]

Revived Franco-Russian activism is usually interpreted as an important factor in the trend toward war, but evaluations of responsibility differ. The apologists argue that Franco-Russian motives were basically defensive, while critics condemn the French and Russians for irresponsibility and even aggressiveness.[2] A judgment of Franco-Russian policy depends, however, on an interpretation of German policy during the previous decade. If German policy is perceived as threatening, Franco-Russian response was justified and defensive; if German policy is interpreted as unthreatening, however, Franco-Russian activism becomes unjustified and aggressive. The interpretation presented in the foregoing chapter suggests that German policy during the previous decade jeopardized French and Russian security; in these terms Franco-Russian activism was therefore justified and basically defensive. However the motives are interpreted, revived Franco-Russian activism undeniably altered the previous pattern of German initiative and Anglo-French-Russian response. It also increased tensions between the continental powers. In fact, the ambivalence of the continental powers' motives tended to reinforce tensions, since each side perceived both opportunities and dangers in the situation. The appropriate response to both seemed to be action.

The German reaction to the second Moroccan crisis was as ominous as Franco-Russian activism. The German government's strong line during the crisis had aroused public opinion but had won no striking success and had thereby caused severe criticism of the government. This criticism and the crisis in general redounded to the advantage of those who advocated augmentation of German naval and military strength. After intensive Reichstag debate and involved maneuvering within the government, increased expenditures for both the army and navy were voted by the Reichstag in May 1912. The German increases altered another pattern of the previous decade. Despite diplomatic crises, military expenditures had not increased much more rapidly than they had before 1902. Military budgets suddenly rose in 1912, the Germans leading the way in both total expenditures and rate of increase, which reinforced diplomatic tension with an arms race.[3]

In contrast with those of the continental powers, Britain's relations became less difficult. This too was a departure from the Anglo-German naval rivalry and confrontations during the two Moroccan crises. The tensions of the second Moroccan crisis were followed by a moderate *détente*. Although no agreement was reached, Anglo-German naval discussions in early 1912 clarified the issues and thereby cleared the air. The British again refused to promise neutrality during a continental war in exchange for German naval concessions, and the Germans refused concessions without such a commitment. But the discussions marked a kind of tacit recognition of British naval superiority on the one hand and Germany's a right to have a major navy on the other. As it turned out, the talks corresponded with an even more important turning point: the high spending on naval expansion during the previous decade was now replaced by high spending on army expansion. Thus German naval competition with Britain was replaced by military competition with France and Russia. This tacit Anglo-German naval *détente* was accompanied by negotiations on colonial problems. The reduction of tension with Germany had the effect of allowing Britain a freer hand in dealing with Russian pressures in Persia. The British were hardly more amicably disposed toward the French. Once the second Moroccan crisis had passed, the British reverted from their active support of France to their characteristic diplomacy of contingency. The British demonstrated that they would neither renounce the continent to German power nor commit themselves to revive French power. In fact, the revival of the Franco-Russian alliance and reduction of Anglo-German tensions allowed Britain greater independence than it had enjoyed since 1905. If it was not quite so splendid as the isolation of the nineties, Britain's position was at least more satisfactory than the forced involvement of the previous decade.[4]

ALLIANCES UNDER STRESS: THE GREAT POWERS AND THE BALKAN WARS (OCTOBER 1912–OCTOBER 1913)

Alliances fluctuate. During periods of high international tension, alliances tend to tighten as allies drop secondary interests in favor of fundamental concerns. Conversely, during times of low tension, alliances tend to loosen as allies pursue subordinate aspirations. This is logical, since alliances are usually concluded to serve fundamental rather than secondary interests. Allies usually do not accept this logic but try instead to make their alliance serve their own (though not their allies') secondary as well as primary interests. Since allies which have fundamental interests in common frequently have secondary interests at variance, such requests for support in secondary questions are often refused and thereby cause tensions between allies. Conversely, opponents frequently have subordinate interests in common despite their differences over fundamental interests. Consequently, during periods of low international tension when fundamental issues are not at stake, disharmony between allies and harmony between opponents can occur. As long as allies cannot persuade each other to support their secondary interests, the tensions within alliances will remain high and between alliances low. Conversely, when allies support each other's secondary interests as if they were fundamental, tensions within alliance will be low but between alliances high. In short, if fundamental and secondary interests are distinguished, tension tends to decrease between opponents but to increase between allies. Conversely, if interests are not distinguished and all are treated as fundamental, tension tends to decrease between allies but to increase between alliances. During the two years before July 1914, the distinction between fundamental and secondary issues was generally made by both alliances. Allies supported one another in fundamental questions, though seldom to the satisfaction of the ally directly involved. But they did not stand beside each other in secondary questions on which they frequently diverged or even disagreed. Relations among allies accordingly oscillated during this period between harmony and disharmony. Fluidity, rather than rigidity, characterized alliance politics.

The Balkan wars raised both fundamental and secondary issues. The

Balkan nationalism which had provoked the conflict constituted both an opportunity and dilemma for Russia, an ambiguity which would be reflected in the ambivalence of Russian policy during the Balkan conflicts. The opportunity lay in the weapon which Balkan nationalism provided Russia against its two main rivals in southeastern Europe, Austria-Hungary and Turkey. But, if it supported Balkan nationalism, Russia ran the double risk of encouraging uncontrollable forces and causing hostility from the other powers. In the last resort, the Russian government's decision to support the Serb-Bulgarian alliance may have been determined less by the advantages of doing so than by the disadvantages of not doing so. If it did not support the Serbs and Bulgarians, they might win without Russia and thus become less dependent. Alternatively, the Serbs and Bulgarians might come to terms with Turkey and/or Austria-Hungary and thereby become opponents, rather than pawns or allies, of Russia. Or, Bulgaria and Serbia might be defeated and be dominated by Austria-Hungary and/or Turkey. Diplomatic disadvantages were compounded by domestic dangers: the government risked Pan Slav criticism if it refused support. These political impulses were reinforced by the economic imperative of maintaining free passage of the straits for Russian grain exports; a Serb-Bulgarian alliance seemed to provide a buffer against Austro-German penetration toward the straits. Thus, Balkan change generally favored Russia.[5]

The Russians chose not to act alone, however, and sought French support. This request fitted in well with the new French policy of revival. Previously a French government would probably have rejected it and advised Russian abstention or even restraint of the Balkan states. But Poincaré, who dominated French policy at this juncture, was anxious to reassert French independence of German threats, which seemed to necessitate Russian support, which in turn could be insured only if Russia were dependent on France in the Balkans. Although Poincaré recognized the risks involved in backing Russia and the likelihood that the Serb-Bulgarian alliance would precipitate war in the Balkans, he did not seriously object but promised instead to stand by Russia if it became involved as a result in a war with Germany.[6]

Austria-Hungary had perhaps the greatest stake in the Balkans of all the powers, since it was widely assumed that Austria-Hungary would become the sick man of Europe if the Turk died. Austria-Hungary was therefore anxious to preserve Turkey by preserving the Balkan status quo. But such a conservative policy made taking the initiative difficult before the status quo was actually threatened. Nonetheless, Vienna sought—largely alone and unsuccessfully—to encourage Turkish revival and removal of Turkish abuses in the Balkans which provided a stimulant to Balkan nationalism.[7]

German policy was more complex. German patronage of Austria-Hungary and Turkey implied a German commitment to the Balkan status quo. Yet, since this patronage could be perceived as a shift in the Balkan balance of power, Germany had to avoid supporting Turkey and Austria-Hungary too strongly for fear of aligning France and Britain behind Russia. Consequently, it was necessary to present the Balkan status quo as a European, rather than a strictly German, interest.

British policy resembled German in seeking to preserve the status quo and the principle of great power authority in the Balkans. This similarity created the illusion of congruity between British and German interests, whereas in fact they came to the same policy from opposite directions. The Germans wanted to preserve the Balkan status quo because it was worth defending, the British because it was not worth fighting over.

Despite the general disinclination to take any initiative to avoid it, the prospect of war in the Balkans disturbed all the powers and produced the brief but belated phenomenon of great power cooperation on the eve of war. Germany and France urged Russia and Austria-Hungary to warn the Balkan states in the name of all the powers that no change in the status quo would be acceptable. But this last-minute cooperation was too late and perhaps too evidently halfhearted to deter the Balkan states. The outbreak of war at the beginning of October 1912 confronted the great-power alliances with unavoidable issues.[8]

Relations between Vienna and Berlin were initially harmonious. Berchtold, the Austro-Hungarian foreign minister, asked German support with the claims that the Balkan league served both Russian interests and "the English policy of encirclement." Kiderlen-Wächter, the German foreign minister, assured Berchtold that "Austria-Hungary could count unconditionally on the support of Germany as at the time of the annexation" of Bosnia in 1908. But Berchtold's demand for the establishment of Albania to block Serbian access to the Adriatic caused German response to become somewhat less than unconditional. Berlin's ambivalence toward Vienna's policies became evident at the start. Kiderlen regarded Berchtold's condition as a moderate price for Austro-Hungarian acceptance of the new status quo without intervention. But the kaiser was impatient with Vienna and urged an Austro-Serbian reconciliation rather than Austro-Hungarian resistance to Serbia; above all, he opposed risking war in order to achieve Austro-Hungarian demands. Bethmann deviated in the opposite direction when he publically declared German support for Vienna. Berchtold, however, jeopardized this support by his resistance to negotiations with Russia over Serbia. Kiderlen was finally able to persuade Vienna to accept a great power conference on the Balkans. Austro-German cooperation was thereby maintained, though not without disagreements and tensions.[9]

Preservation of the alliance with Austria-Hungary required minimal Austro-Hungarian satisfaction, which in turn depended on Russian acceptance of Austro-Hungarian demands. Kiderlen's task was facilitated by the possibility that the Bulgarians might conquer Constantinople. As the price for Austro-German acceptance of the Russian demand that Constantinople remain Turkish, Russia would have to renounce the Serbian demand for access to the Adriatic and accept Albania. Like the Austro-Hungarians, the Russians wavered between hard and soft lines, their bellicosity perhaps encouraged by French assurances of support and/or the possibility of a political crisis in Serbia. But they finally became less adamant and accepted a conference.[10]

If preservation of the alliance with Vienna had been Kiderlen's only objective, his task would have been simpler and Austro-German relations smoother. He also sought, however, to improve relations with Britain so as at once to win British support in restraining Russia and to loosen British ties with the Franco-Russian alliance. Kiderlen therefore sought to make Russia accept Austro-Hungarian demands rather than risk alienating Britain, which Berchtold's recalcitrance jeopardized, however, by making Austria-Hungary rather than Russia appear to be the threat to peace and by forcing Germany to choose between alienating either Vienna or London. Bethmann's public statement of support for Vienna compounded Kiderlen's difficulties by making Berlin look as obstinate as Vienna. Bethmann's statement provoked a warning from Lichnowsky, the German ambassador in London, that Britain would support France in a war against Germany. Yet it was just such a war from which Kiderlen hoped to exclude Britain by making Russia appear the provocator. He therefore sought to square the circle of looking at once peaceful in London and loyal in Vienna by accepting the British suggestion of a conference but insisting that Austro-Hungarian demands not be discussed. Both Lichnowsky and Grey picked up the contradiction and warned Kiderlen that he risked a war in which Britain would be on the opposite side. This renewed warning caused Kiderlen and the kaiser to reverse roles: Kiderlen accepted it but the kaiser was provoked by it. After overcoming Austro-Hungarian resistance, Kiderlen nonetheless accepted the British conference suggestion in the hope of placating London without alienating Vienna.[11]

Although the danger of a war between the great powers momentarily disappeared, maneuvering continued unabated at the conference table because the powers' objectives were fundamentally different. The success of the conference and great power compromises to maintain the peace most conformed with British objectives. The convocation of the conference in London under the chairmanship of Grey, the British foreign secretary, symbolized Britain's relative disinterest in the continental powers' Balkan rivalries. But Britain was not entirely uninterested and may in fact have been the most desirous of a peaceful solution, since the existing alignment of forces in Europe best served its interests. With a balance of power reestablished by the revival of the Franco-Russian alliance, Britain both became freer for colonial activity and enjoyed greatest influence in Europe. A diplomatic solution of the Balkan problem might even produce special advantages for Britain since it could exploit its mediation to extract concessions elsewhere: from Russia in Persia, from Germany in the naval and colonial questions, and from France in the Mediterranean. British success required restraint of France so that it would restrain Russia and friendliness toward Germany so that it would restrain Austria-Hungary.[12]

A compromise corresponded less with the aspirations of the other powers. Both France and Germany sought to appear peaceful to London, but British admonitions of restraint contradicted German and French reassurances of support to their allies. Russia and Austria-Hungary sought to fulfill their Balkan aspirations without appearing provocative. By these tactics, all the continental powers sought to square their aspirations with their alliances. Although the conference initially appeared successful, in actuality it only formalized what had already been accepted as the basis for the conference. Despite accession to the major demands of Austria-Hungary (Albania) and Russia (Turkish control over Constantinople), Austro-Russian tension soon rose over the question of whether Serbia should get a port on the Adriatic.[13]

The recurrence of Austro-Russian rivalry put new pressures on the Austro-German alliance. Bethmann was anxious to maintain a united front with Austria-Hungary in order to make Britain restrain France and Russia. But he was also impatient with Austro-Hungarian obstinacy and urged a compromise in order to improve relations with Britain as a means of fulfilling German aspirations in Turkey and other colonial areas. It appeared momentarily that Berlin would have to choose between these two objectives when those in favor of a hard line seemed to win the upper hand in Vienna. The dilemma was avoided, however, when Austria-Hungary and Russia opted to compromise. Berlin now sought to make clear to Vienna the advantages of a policy of moderation. Bethmann told Berchtold that Austro-Hungarian provocation would drive the other powers together, whereas Austro-Hungarian restraint might reinforce what Bethmann perceived as a British tendency to separate from its allies and possibly remain neutral in an eventual war. Tension increased again over the Serbian port issue (this time between Montenegro and Austria-Hungary). Anxious to discourage a unilateral Austro-Hungarian initiative which would appear provocative, Jagow,

Kiderlen's successor as foreign secretary, urged Berchtold to seek a European mandate in order to "put Russia and its Balkan clients in the wrong as much as possible." Although a conference of the powers decided in favor of Austria-Hungary, France and Russia would not impose the decision on Montenegro. When Britain seemed prepared to join Austria-Hungary and Germany, it appeared that the German objective of separating Britain from its allies might be achieved. But the British opted to preserve the Entente rather than the great power concert and urged Austro-Hungarian concessions. Although the kaiser again showed little sympathy for Austria-Hungary, Jagow and Bethmann sought to restrain Austria-Hungary while forcing the other powers to support it. Vienna's frustration mounted until Berchtold announced that he would present an ultimatum to Montenegro even without authorization from the other powers. Although the other powers did not authorize it, they did not oppose the Austro-Hungarian ultimatum, and Montenegro acceded. Germany had preserved the alliance with Austria-Hungary but had not loosened British ties with the Franco-Russian alliance.[14]

Conclusion of this crisis might have inaugurated a period of peace in the Balkans. Berlin would have welcomed this eventuality, since it regarded the Balkans as an unhappy diversion from its more important objective of preserving Turkey. In an effort to avoid unnecessary complications and thus crises in the Balkans, Berlin had urged on Vienna a policy of restraint. But Vienna regarded the Balkans as decisive, not divertive, and perceived restraint as tantamount to renunciation. This disagreement would have remained but might have been insignificant if the Balkans had been quiescent. Instead, new violence erupted and imposed increased strains on relations between the two allies during the summer of 1913.

Differences between the former Balkan allies grew during the spring of 1913. Berlin and Vienna agreed that their objective should be "preponderent influence" in the Balkans, but they characteristically disagreed on means. Berchtold argued that fundamental issues were at stake and urged that Entente gains be prevented by establishing a Bulgarian-Rumanian alliance friendly to Vienna and Berlin. Jagow doubted that fundamental issues were involved and commented caustically that "we certainly do not have to join in all of Vienna's stupidities." A reconciliation with Bulgaria would alienate not only Rumania but also Greece, which might then win Entente support against Turkey and threaten its existence. The allies, accordingly, pursued divergent policies: Vienna sought a Bulgarian-Rumanian alliance and supported Bulgaria, whereas Berlin subordinated Balkan politics to the preservation of Turkey by advocating a Rumanian-Turkish-Greek-Serbian alignment and by supporting Greece and Rumania during the crisis. The outbreak of hostilities in the Balkans forced these differences into the open. Berchtold threatened to intervene if Bulgaria were decisively defeated or if Russia intervened to save Serbia from decisive defeat. When the first eventuality occurred, he informed Berlin that he would intervene if Serbia made excessive demands on Bulgaria. The kaiser regarded this threat of intervention as "incredible" and "completely crazy" but worried that war between the powers could result nonetheless. Zimmermann, the undersecretary of the Foreign Ministry, regarded Vienna's "exceptional nervousness" as unjustified because a Serbian threat to Austria-Hungary did not yet exist. With the agreement of Zimmermann, Jagow, and the kaiser, Bethmann therefore warned Berchtold against intervention. Lacking German support, Berchtold renounced intervention despite criticism from hard liners in Vienna and urged a peace conference to save what could be saved for Bulgaria. Hostilities were finally concluded at the end of July. The conflict had placed Russia in an awkward position in relation to the Balkan states and had shattered Russian aspirations for a Balkan league under its aegis. But German hopes that Anglo-Russian complications would develop were also shattered when France restrained Russia. Thus, Austro-German tension and lack of success had resulted from the second Balkan war.[15]

Peacemaking in the Balkans accentuated allied differences because the policies of the powers cut across both alliances. Both Russia and Austria-Hungary were anxious to maintain Rumanian friendship and therefore supported its claims against Bulgaria. But both also wanted to win Bulgarian friendship and therefore supported Bulgaria's claims against Greece. Germany and France competed, however, for Greek favor because of Greece's importance in connection with Turkey and therefore supported Greece against Bulgaria. The peace conference almost foundered over the Greek-Bulgarian disagreement, but Berchtold finally knuckled under and dropped his support for Bulgaria. He and the Russians accepted the peace only subject to revision, however, whereas the other powers regarded it as permanent. Turkish-Bulgarian differences deepened the rift in both alliances when Austria-Hungary and Russia supported Bulgaria and the other powers backed Turkey. It even appeared briefly at the beginning of September that Bulgaria and Turkey might reconcile their differences and combine under Russo-Austrian patronage against Greece, which was supported by the other powers. It seemed that great-power alliances were being remade in the image of Balkan alignments as Austro-Russian conflict was becoming cooperation, whereas cooperation between each and its allies threatened to become conflict.[16]

Appearances were, however, deceptive. The major facts were neither conflict between allies nor cooperation between enemies but competition between Austria-Hungary and Russia for Balkan influence and between Germany and the Anglo-French for influence in Turkey. Nonetheless, genuine rifts had opened up in both alliances. The alliance with Germany was discussed in the Viennese press; Berchtold was pessimistic; Conrad (the Austro-Hungarian chief of staff) threatened not to attend German maneuvers in September; Hungarian Premier Tisza insisted that preservation of the Habsburg Empire required greater German support in the Balkans; and William advocated what amounted to a declaration of independence from Vienna. Vienna and Berlin seemed to be tugged in opposite directions—Vienna toward dependence on Berlin, Berlin toward independence of Vienna. Because it could not negate the Balkans, Vienna feared exclusion; because it feared involvement, Berlin sought to negate the Balkans.[17]

Berlin could not negate the Balkans, however. Austro-Serbian tensions had increased during the late summer of 1913 as Serbia apparently prepared to occupy Albanian territory. When Austria-Hungary asked support of the powers, Russia was ambivalent, but the others agreed halfheartedly. Austro-Hungarian leaders perceived the situation in dire terms and regarded a conflict with Serbia as virtually unavoidable. Berchtold's request for German support of an ultimatum to prevent Serbia from invading Albania confronted Berlin with the usual dilemma. Either it could choose to support Vienna at the risk of alienating Britain and even of war, or it could elect to avoid the risk of alienating Britain and of war at the risk of alienating Vienna. Berlin had chosen to alienate Vienna when confronted with this same choice during the second Balkan war. But, in part because of the previous choice and resulting frictions with Vienna, Berlin now reversed its policy and supported Vienna. Although he regarded Albania as "an untenable situation" and sought to calm Berchtold, Jagow promised German support and warned Serbia. Zimmermann exaggerated but may have been in earnest when he argued that a refusal to support Vienna risked its defection to the Franco-Russian alliance; he therefore not only assured Berchtold of German support even before the kaiser had approved but also warned Serbia. The kaiser was in an uncharacteristically bellicose mood and regarded Berchtold's hope that Serbia would accede to the ultimatum as "regretable! *Now or never!* Order and quiet must be established down there" in the Balkans. But Serbia did give in when Russia withdrew its support.[18]

Once the crisis was over, the operative question became its legacy for subsequent events. Each of the powers sought to exploit it. The French had supported Russia and thereby forced the Russians to assume the responsibility for letting the Serbs down. The Russians sought to make the best of a bad situation by trying to insure that it would not recur. Sazonov, the Russian foreign minister, laid a clever trap for Berlin when he complained to the Germans about Berchtold's "policy of surprises" and "neurotic policy" which confronted Europe with *faits accomplis* and "the unknown." If Berlin admitted its knowledge of the ultimatum, it would appear partially responsible and risk alienating Britain, whereas a claim of German ignorance on the ultimatum implied a disavowal of Vienna and agreement with Sazonov's criticism. Sazonov pushed for the second alternative by suggesting that Berlin had not been informed. Austro-Hungarian policy was also criticized by London, Paris, and Rome. Berlin naturally sought to evade Sazonov's trap by encouraging Vienna while claiming to everyone else that it had been uninformed but could not ask Vienna to revoke the ultimatum without jeopardizing Austro-Hungarian great-power status. The Germans sought thereby to square a diplomatic circle: they supported Vienna confidentially in order to preserve the benefits of Austro-Hungarian dependence, but claimed publicly that Vienna was independent in order to avoid assuming responsibility for its policy and thereby maintain cooperation with Britain. Although Berlin had backed Vienna and reduced the previous summer's antipathies, Vienna was still not satisfied. But Vienna could never be satisfied without alienating the other powers. The circle could not be squared because the two objectives of German policy were contradictory, as the July 1914 crisis would demonstrate.[19]

ALLIANCES UNDER STRESS: THE GREAT POWERS AND TURKEY (OCTOBER 1912–MARCH 1914)

The Balkan and Turkish issues had opposite implications for the great power alliances. In the Balkans, Germany had to choose between alienating Austria-Hungary or the other powers. In Turkey, Russia had to choose between alienating its allies and pursuing its ambitions. The Balkans tended to push Berlin and Vienna apart but the Entente together, whereas Turkey tended to push the Entente apart. It was therefore advantageous to the Entente when the Balkans were at issue, to Germany when Turkey was at issue.

The rapid defeat of Turkey during the first Balkan war raised the issue of total Turkish collapse. Although the surprising resilience of the Ottoman Empire reasserted itself, and only the European portions of the empire were lost, it seemed possible that the empire could dissolve suddenly in the near future. Turkish collapse implied the problem of partitioning its territories among the great powers which involved the danger of disagreement and was regarded with trepidation. The policies of the powers were consequently a conglomerate of efforts to preserve Turkey and at the same time prepare for its partition.

Berlin pursued both these objectives while also seeking to separate Britain from its allies. Bethmann feared that Britain might accede to Franco-Russian pressure for "liquidation" of Turkey-in-Asia and present Germany with a *fait accompli*. Although partition was undesirable and Berlin sought to preserve Turkey, the Germans also prepared for and demanded participation in partition. Berlin sought to fulfill its aspirations in an eventual partition of Turkey through cooperation with Britain which might offer the additional advantage of loosening British ties with its allies. The Turkish and Balkan issues were entangled when the victorious Balkan states demanded financial indemnities from Turkey. Germany, Britain, and France opposed these demands on the ground that they would threaten Turkey with financial collapse and thus great-power intervention. In their efforts to woo Bulgaria, Russia and Austria-Hungary meanwhile supported the Balkan states' demands but Austria-Hungary dropped its support under German pressure and thereby left Russia alone. The issue of internal Turkish reforms constituted another threat of great-power intervention but also an opportunity for Berlin to further cooperation with Britain and strain Entente relations. Anglo-German cooperation in preserving Turkey encouraged negotiation of other colonial questions but produced only limited success. These negotiations pointed up the basic contradiction in German policy toward Britain: Germany sought cooperation with Britain in order to loosen the Entente, but Britain could afford cooperation with Germany only if the Entente were not jeopardized by it. Anglo-German cooperation in preserving the Ottoman Empire would jeopardize the Entente if it implied German success and Russian failure. Ultimately Germany might have to choose between its special interests in Turkey and Anglo-German cooperation. Like Austria-Hungary in its struggle with Serbia, Germany would not always be able to make its own interests look like a mandate from Europe.[20]

The Balkans had obscured Turkey as the primary issue for the great powers during the Balkan wars and their immediate aftermath, but Turkey again became the center of attention at the end of 1913. The crisis grew out of reform measures in Turkey. During the spring of 1913, the Turkish government had asked the French, British, and Germans, but not the Russians, for advisers which the tsar, kaiser, and King George had approved. The German military advisers were not a departure from precedent, since German soldiers had acted in this capacity for twenty years. German preparations were well advanced by the autumn of 1913 and had not complicated great power relations. But the question became an issue among the great powers at the beginning of November when Sazonov complained that a German general (Liman von Sanders) was not only to direct military reforms but also to command a Turkish corps in Constantinople.[21]

The Germans reacted in contradictory fashion, as befitted their dual objectives of preserving Turkey and extending their influence there. In discussions with Russian Minister President Kokovtsev, Bethmann employed arguments designed more to deflate Sazonov's criticism than to explain German behavior. After minimizing the importance of the mission, he insisted that it was necessary to preserve Turkey, revive German military prestige, and prove Sazonov's good faith in Bethmann; in short, the mission was harmless for Russia but essential to Germany. Kokovtsev seems to have been less interested in winning a debate than reaching a compromise and suggested that Sanders either renounce or remove his command from Constantinople. Instead of accepting this escape immediately, Bethmann was dilatory: he would leave the decision up to Sanders. Although he dismissed Turkish "delusions of grandeur" and the possibility of Turkish aggression against Russia, Kokovtsev warned that "things would be different perhaps if Turkey joined other powers." In effect, Russia accepted Turkey as a great power protectorate but not as a German protegé.[22]

Sazonov sought an immediate German concession rather than accepting a postponement. One motive may have been defensive: having swallowed an Austro-Hungarian *fait accompli* the month before, he was in no position to accept one from Germany. But he may also have been motivated by more aggressive considerations. He may have regarded the Sanders mission as an opportunity to disrupt Anglo-German cooperation in Turkey and reestablish an Entente front, objectives possibly encouraged by French Ambassador Delcassé. It is also possible but unlikely that Sazonov was anxious to encourage an outburst of Russian public indignation as preparation for the arms increases which the government would demand during the following spring. Sazonov urged Bethmann to make immediate concessions rather than postpone a decision. Otherwise the issue might become "a prestige question" and Russia "would be forced to revise its relations with Turkey fundamentally."[23]

Rather than escape easily, German leaders chose to do precisely what Sazonov had warned against, i.e., to make the issue a question of prestige. Zimmermann asserted that a concession would destroy German influence in Constantinople, while Bethmann claimed that German and Turkish public opinion precluded a concession. Instead, Berlin argued that a German concession was unnecessary, since the German mission was no different from the French or British missions. But Sazonov avoided this trap by speaking openly: unlike the German mission, neither the French nor the British mission was perceived as a threat by Russia. This was as undeniable as it was inequitable, yet the inconsistency was not in Russian policy but in German aspirations. If Germany wanted to be regarded by Russia in the same way as France and Britain, it had to pursue a policy in Turkey which was acceptable to Russia. Berlin expected St. Petersburg to prove its good faith by entrusting its interests in Turkey to Germany, whereas St. Petersburg expected Berlin to prove its good faith by respecting Russian interests in Turkey.[24]

The Russo-German confrontation now evolved into competition for Anglo-French support. Sazonov won Anglo-French help initially with the threat that the German mission would require compensation for Russia, but the British backed off when confronted with the German argument that their mission was no different from the others. Sazonov tried to reverse this decision by making ominous comments about the Entente's viability, although he did not press the British because he wanted to maintain at least the appearance of Entente unanimity. The British and French did not, however, support either side and thereby left the Russians and Germans to confront each other alone.[25]

The crisis moved toward its climax when Sanders arrived at Constantinople in December and immediately decided to shift his command away from Constantinople, a solution acceptable to the Russians. But the Turks rejected the move in order to extract greater German support. Despite a German warning against "the risk of serious European complications," Sazonov began to prepare an ultimatum to Turkey with French support. Opinion was divergent among Russian ministers, however, and they decided that negotiations would be preferable to a conflict with Germany. The German government had meanwhile been moving toward a diplomatic solution. Concerned that the Entente would make difficulties for Germany in other parts of Turkey, the Germans bypassed Turkish obstinacy by promoting Sanders out of the Constantinople command in January 1915. Jagow simultaneously warned the Turks that "the affair must not become a question of European prestige which in the end required that we support Turkey more than our interests allow." The crisis was over.[26]

As usual, however, its effects remained for relations between opponents and allies. Characteristically, the Russian and German governments sought to dismantle their positions as quickly as possible by blaming other governments and other elements within their own countries. Bethmann sought to improve Russo-German relations and loosen Entente ties by claiming that Germany had acceded to Russian, rather than Entente, demands. These efforts notwithstanding, the crisis left a reservoir of bitterness in Russo-German relations. Even though they claimed that they had made no concessions, the Germans were disappointed that the Russians did not appreciate German willingness to concede. On the contrary, the Russians angered the Germans by making further demands on Turkey. It was appropriate that the crisis should have left a residue of ill will not because of what had been revised (which was little) but because of what had been revealed. It made explicit what had been implied but denied for a decade. German predominance in Turkey made it difficult to present Turkey as a great-power protectorate. Like German support for Austria-Hungary, German influence in the Ottoman Empire was incompatible with Russian aspirations. Hypothetically, German policy makers had to choose between their aspirations and better relations with Russia but, typically, they did not.[27]

Russian impatience with its allies was almost as great as its animosity against Germany. The crisis revealed the ambivalence of Russian perceptions of France. Although he seemed to accept reassurances of support, Sazonov doubted that France would in fact back Russia unless Britain did so. But Britain was even less certain than France. After initially supporting Russia during the crisis, Britain had drawn back, and Sazonov became skeptical about British support in the future. He feared an Anglo-German agreement over Turkey and possibly British abstention from a Russo-German conflict which might then keep France out. Russian aspirations in southeastern Europe depended, however, on Anglo-French support. It was indicative of Sazonov's logic that this proposition also seemed true in reverse: France and Britain would regard Russia as weak and would not support it against Germany unless Russia actively defended its aspirations. Russian aspirations seemed to depend increasingly on its alliance, which appeared more undependable.[28]

Like all crises, the Sanders episode had tended to obscure other issues which reemerged after the crisis had passed in mid-January 1914. The pattern of alignment along alliance lines which had characteristically recurred during the crisis devolved again into the pattern of cutting across alliances which was more typical of relations between crises. A Russian attempt to be included with the other powers in the administration of the Turkish state debt failed because of Franco-German opposition and lack of British support and in spite of Austro-Hungarian willingness to support Russia in exchange for Russian backing in Albania. Nonetheless, a Russo-Turkish agreement was achieved with German assistance on the question of reforms in eastern Anatolia. While Germany caused Austro-Hungarian and Italian bitterness by rejecting their claims to spheres of influence in Anatolia, the French and Germans agreed on economic spheres of influence in Turkey. Anglo-German negotiations on the Bagdad railroad and Mesopotamia made slow but apparently promising progress, while their negotiations over Portuguese colonies bogged down until March. Although the Anglo-German *détente* feared by the French and Russians did not occur, the British and Germans tacitly agreed to avoid the naval question and thereby reduced mutual tension. It seemed as if the Sanders crisis had not lessened the possibility for cooperation among the powers.[29]

Appearances deceived, however. Russo-German antipathy engendered by the Sanders crisis erupted again at the end of February 1914. This recrudescence of recriminations was more ominous because it did not remain strictly diplomatic but involved public opinion and military questions. When mutual criticism occurred in the Russian and German press, each government sought to extract a disavowal from the other. Although Pourtalès, the German ambassador in St. Petersburg, asserted that the Russian government was not aggressive, the kaiser disagreed and unmercifully criticised Pourtalès' naïveté. The kaiser had already concluded that "Russo-Prussian relations are dead once and for all!! We have become enemies!" The French sought to play the incident both ways: they enjoyed Russo-German tension while it lasted but claimed credit for mediation when tension declined in April. The British reaction was more cautious. The revival of Russo-German tension made the British wary of Germany but no more disposed toward Russia. In the last resort, the prospects for an Anglo-Russian alliance depended less on their perceptions of each other than on German policy toward France. When Lichnowsky, the German ambassador in London, warned that German attacks on Russia might nonetheless tighten rather than loosen Anglo-Russian relations, Bethmann and Jagow were indignant. Their indignation was probably due less, however, to a sense of injustice than to the recognition that the British could not be weaned away from their allies and that Britain and Germany were only fair-weather friends. At the end of March Russian policy seemed to veer away from direct confrontation with Germany. Although Sazonov sought to exploit the Sanders incident again in April, Berlin decided to play down differences with Russia, and Pourtalès predicted "calm weather" when Sazonov again became conciliatory. Russo-German suspicions persisted and the causes of their differences still existed, but Berlin gave Russia less attention during the spring, and the two countries had no direct confrontation until the July crisis.[30]

COLLAPSE OR CONSOLIDATION? THE TRIPLE ALLIANCE AT THE CROSSROADS (DECEMBER 1913–JUNE 1914)

Tensions within alliances were as severe as antipathies between alliances during the spring of 1914. Austria-Hungary and Italy seemed on the edge of conflict, while mutual confidence between Berlin and Vienna was low. Not consolidation or even cooperation but collapse seemed to be the direction in which the Triple Alliance was moving.

Austro-Italian relations degenerated with time. Both sought to move into what appeared to be a power vacuum created by the Balkan wars. The Italians had cooperated during the Balkan wars with Austria-Hungary in order to prevent expansion of its influence, particularly in Albania. Theirs was, therefore, a cooperation based on mutual suspicion, which increased during the autumn of 1913 over Trieste and even precluded cooperation over Albania. Rome sought to extract concessions from Vienna by winning German support and even by making ominous threats involving the existence of the Triple Alliance. To reinforce their demands in Vienna and Berlin, the Italians exploited a French feeler for a Mediterranean agreement. While Berlin sought to neutralize this threat by warning the Italians, Vienna interpreted it as further proof of Italian unreliability. Rome tried to play both ends against the middle by responding sympathetically but vaguely to the French, who let the matter drop for the moment. These tensions were swept under the Triple Alliance rug by a naval agreement between Germany, Italy, and Austria-Hungary in November 1913. The Italians reawakened German suspicions in March 1914, when they seemed over-impressed with Russian military power and overskeptical about Austro-Hungarian viability.[31]

Austro-Italian rivalry and suspicion became open hostility during the spring. Frictions intensified over the problem of Italians living under Austro-Hungarian rule. Relations were not improved by Italian sympathy with Rumanian complaints against Hungary or Italian flirtation with France. But the most serious tension resulted from the degenerating Albanian situation. It had been foreseen by the allies and had been one impulse for the kaiser's meetings with Austro-Hungarian and Italian statesmen in March. Although the Italian king minimized Austro-Italian differences in his discussion with the kaiser, frictions over Albania and Trieste almost precluded the meeting between Berchtold and Italian Foreign Minister San Giuliano in April. When the two foreign ministers met, they maintained the myth of agreement by avoiding rather than confronting issues; in fact, they were agreed only in their effort to persuade the Germans and the public in general that they had not disagreed. When it appeared to Vienna that Rome was fostering Albanian dissolution, Berchtold presented San Giuliano with an ultimatum in June, and an Austro-Italian conflict seemed imminent. It is impossible to predict whether or not a conflict would have erupted to destroy the alliance if the July crisis had not intervened, but clearly Austro-Italian cooperation in the Balkans was unlikely.[32]

Berlin was therefore Vienna's only recourse. Yet little harmony had existed in Austro-German relations since the Austro-Serbian crisis in October 1913. Even then, Vienna had not been entirely satisfied with Berlin's support, and German refusal to accede to Austro-Hungarian (and Italian) requests for spheres of influence in the Ottoman Empire further alienated the allies. Above all, Berlin and Vienna differed in their perceptions of Balkan prospects: Berlin preferred Austro-Hungarian restraint, maintenance of Rumanian and Greek friendship, and a *détente* with Serbia, whereas Vienna advocated friendship with Bulgaria, forcing Rumania to choose sides, and preparation for conflict with Serbia. Berlin and Vienna likewise disagreed on whether the Balkan league was likely to be revived — Austro-Hungarian leaders' fears that the Franco-Russian alliance was seeking to reestablish the league were dismissed as premature by Jagow, and rumors of a Serb-Montenegrin union concerned Vienna but were discounted by Berlin. Berlin and Vienna saw the international situation during the spring of 1914 in quite different terms.[33]

Their perception of a worsening international situation during the spring of 1914 made Austro-Hungarian leaders increasingly anxious to win German support. Chief of Staff Conrad urged Berchtold to win from the Germans a firm commitment to a strong line against Russia and France, which he asserted were preparing to attack Austria-Hungary and Germany. Hungarian Premier Tisza, meanwhile, claimed that it was essential to persuade Berlin that its interests in the Balkans were identical with Vienna's. Berchtold complained that he had sought to do just that for a year, but that the prevailing German policy amounted to "a revival of the Bismarckian theory of the bones of the Pomeranian grenadier." Although Francis Ferdinand, the heir to the throne, also advocated Austro-German cooperation, he urged an accommodation of Austro-Hungarian to German policy rather than the reverse, as demanded by his countrymen. The Austro-Hungarian ambassador to Turkey, Pallavicini, thought Turkey and the Balkans could be rescued "from Russian claws" only by firm support of a Bulgarian-Turkish alliance, which Berlin opposed. He blamed the apparent drift of Turkey toward Russia in large measure on Germany and concluded that "the Triple Alliance powers must finally shed their passivity." If they did not, the Balkans would fall under Russian influence, at which point Austria-Hungary would have to reconsider its alliance policy, since the Triple Alliance would no longer give it "protection against Russia." If a pro-Russian Balkan constellation occurred, "this problem of immeasurable importance would imply the further question of whether an understanding between us and Russia would not have to be sought." Pallavicini therefore urged that Vienna persuade Berlin to pursue an "identical

Balkan policy," in the formulation of which Austria-Hungary must have "unrestricted leadership since [the Balkans] affect [Austria-Hungary's] most vital interests." Pallavicini in effect wanted a German blank check in the Balkans. Similar criticism came from Szapary, the Austro-Hungarian ambassador in St. Petersburg, who asserted that Russo-German relations had been improved only because Germany had given in all along the line. Baron Ludwig von Flotow, the new section chief at the Austro-Hungarian Foreign Ministry, argued that the Triple Alliance had to cooperate if it were to salvage anything from the degenerating Balkan situation. Czernin, the Austro-Hungarian ambassador in Bucharest, made the most specific proposal: after painting the Balkan picture in desperate terms, he urged Berchtold to send a special delegation to make the kaiser comprehend the seriousness of the Balkan situation. The need for salvation seemed great, and it could be found only in Berlin.[34]

Berlin was, however, both ambivalent and ambiguous. Austro-Italian differences were difficult and perhaps impossible to resolve, as the Austro-Hungarians and Italians were well aware. The Germans were deeply concerned about the rivalry of their allies in Albania, which they regarded as the weak point of the Triple Alliance, and an opportunity which the French and Russians were seeking to exploit. They therefore urged their allies to resolve their differences but themselves worked less to compose than to conceal these disagreements. When he met Austro-Hungarian leaders in March, the kaiser spirited away their concerns and reinforced their prejudices rather than faced their problems. He characteristically accepted the Italian king's reassurance that Austro-Italian relations were "competely normal and satisfactory" rather than raise issues he knew existed. Berlin's efforts to arrange more contact between Rome and Vienna were designed primarily for their effect on public opinion. German leaders tended to be impatient with Vienna because of what they regarded as its oversensitivity. The kaiser criticized Vienna when an insignificant issue almost prevented the meeting between San Giuliano and Berchtold. Hans von Flotow, the German anbassador in Rome, argued that Vienna should be more conciliatory toward its Italian subjects if it really wanted a "consolidation of the alliance with Italy." The kaiser agreed when he condemned Berchtold's policies as "shameful" after Rome complained about new frictions over Trieste.[35]

Berlin was hardly more sympathetic toward Vienna's problems elsewhere in the Balkans. German leaders were unmoved by Vienna's concerns over a possible Serb-Montenegrin union and merely repeated their remonstrances to seek a reconciliation with Serbia. The kaiser was outraged when he learned that Vienna had sought to keep Rumania out of the second Balkan war; as in the case of Austro-Italian differences, Berlin assumed the role of mediator in Austro-Rumanian frictions rather than that of unqualified supporter, as Austro-Hungarian statesmen desired. In fact, Berlin's perception of future Balkan alignments conformed much more closely with the Rumanian rather than the Austro-Hungarian view, and the prospects were unfavorable for German response to Austro-Hungarian requests for support.[36]

Berlin was thus exposed to increasing pressure from Vienna, Rome, and Bucharest for a more active policy in the Balkans. German leaders were aware of the drift of events. Moltke, who had urged restraint on Conrad in the Serbian question during March, encouraged Austro-Hungarian activism in May and warned Bethmann that Rumania might divert Austria-Hungary from an offensive against Russia. Jagow commented to Goschen, the British ambassador in Berlin, that Germany might have to face Russia and France "practically alone" if war broke out. Although Austria-Hungary would be necessary for Germany as a diversion for Russia in a two-front war, the alliance was neither easy to consolidate nor an unmixed blessing for Germany. Tschirschky, the German ambassador in Vienna, told Jagow in May that he had long been concerned "whether it is really worth while to commit ourselves so firmly to this construction [i.e., Austria-Hungary] which is creaking at every joint and to continue the laborious task of dragging it along." The difficulty was that there was no other existing "political constellation" which could be substituted for the alliance. The alternative was "to aim at the dissolution of the monarchy," which would involve the reconstruction of central Europe and thus implicate the other powers. "Whether we would receive *carte blanche* from England to do so—even if [England] had been brought into a really firm arrangement with us—is doubtful." Tschirschky was not even certain that an *anschluss* with the German provinces of the monarchy would prove advantageous for Germany. He therefore reverted to the existing policy of preserving the Habsburg Empire. Yet success in doing so depended on the difficult task of consolidating the empire. If consolidation proved impossible, "then the decomposition will certainly proceed very rapidly and we would have to adjust our policy accordingly." Thus, at least one important German diplomat and one important Austro-Hungarian diplomat—Pallavicini—discussed the possible demise of the Triple Alliance during the spring of 1914. Both preferred preservation to dissolution of the alliance as the lesser of evils, more because it was familiar than because the prospects were favorable.[37]

This negative approach characterized relations between the allies during the spring of 1914. Since their perceptions of the Balkans were irreconcilable, Berlin and Vienna sublimated rather than settled their differences. There could be no coordination of policies until events forced one or both to give way. Ultimately, the alliance would be consolidated not by resolution of differences in the Balkans, but only by their subordination to more important issues.

ALLIANCE OR NOT? TESTING AND TIGHTENING THE ENTENTE (SPRING 1914)

Both alliances were confronted by problems in the spring of 1914. But these problems were different. The main questions for the Triple Alliance were whether the existing alliance could survive tensions between two of its members (Austria-Hungary and Italy) and whether the third member (Germany) would feel compelled to support the Balkan interests of its main ally (Austria-Hungary) in order to preserve their alliance. The issues for the Triple Entente were whether it would be transformed into an alliance and whether that alliance would apply to the Balkans as well as the European balance of power.

Negotiations over subordinate issues between members of opposing alliances might have deemphasized alliance politics. Anglo-German negotiations over Portuguese colonies continued but were dropped without agreement in April. They revealed a contradiction in German policy: although anxious to achieve a *détente* with Britain in order to draw it away from its allies, the Germans were unwilling to pay with colonial concessions. Anglo-German negotiations over the Bagdad railroad reached a highpoint in March but continued into the July crisis. French and British negotiations with Turkey were successful, but lack of progress in German-Turkish talks retarded a general agreement on Turkey. The Turks also complicated an Anglo-German agreement on Persia by making their acceptance conditional on Anglo-German protection against Russian demands for compensation in Armenia. Despite their limited progress, these Anglo-German negotiations caused Britain's allies concern.[38]

This concern made them press Britain for a consolidation of the Entente. The initiative came from the Russians but was actively supported by the French. The Russians were disappointed with British lack of support during the Sanders crisis and concerned by the simultaneous rise in Russo-German tension. Russian policy moved on several fronts at once. One response had been increased arms expenditures and reduction of tension with Germany in order to allow military preparations to be completed. Another involved renewed efforts to revive the Balkan league. A third was pressure to tighten the Entente. Sazonov and the tsar urged Benckendorff, the Russian ambassador in London, and Paléologue, the new French ambassador in St. Petersburg, to work for conversion of the loose Triple Entente into a firm defensive alliance in order to deter Germany. Although Benckendorff asserted that Grey would do so if he could, Grey actually felt that it was impossible to improve the problematical Anglo-Russian relations. Nonetheless Buchanan, the British ambassador in St. Petersburg, worried that a British refusal risked dissolution of the Entente. Consequently, although British leaders regarded a formal alliance as impractical and Grey's maxim was postponement as long as possible, British leaders decided to consider a colonial and even naval agreement to appease the Russians.[39]

The issue was raised during the visit of King George and Grey to Paris in April. This event turned out to be all things to all men and thereby accurately reflected the ambivalence of the Anglo-French Entente, the tenth anniversary of which was the formal occasion for the visit. The French were anxious to make more, the British less, of the event; indeed everyone attributed importance to it except the British, who were the only ones who could have made it significant. Such confusion was understandable, since the British appeared to tighten relations with the French and Russians even as they insisted that closer association was impossible. It was indicative of Grey's reserve toward the Entente that he suspected the French of having invented the claim that it was necessary to do "something to make relations with Russia more secure." According to Grey, he spent his time avoiding commitments. He trumped French arguments with the suggestion that they discourage Russian demands by informing St. Petersburg how loose the Anglo-French Entente actually was. He asserted that military cooperation with Russia was impractical in any case, since all British land forces would aid France. These objections notwithstanding, Grey finally agreed to initiate discussions which "could not amount to very much but would be something" to pacify the Russians, French, and some of his own advisers (including Nicolson and Buchanan). The French, naturally, presented Grey's reluctant acquiescence as enthusiasm to the Russians. Although he cautioned the Russians by making clear the informality of the Anglo-French Entente, Grey agreed to the initiation of discussions at the end of May between naval representatives for "eventual cooperation of the Russian and English navies." The Russians drew precisely the conclusion Grey had sought to discourage: the talks would be "an important step toward joining England to the Franco-Russian alliance." Franco-Russian enthusiasm is probably not explained in military terms, since they probably realized as well as Grey that an Anglo-Russian naval agreement could have little practical value. Their main concern was diplomatic, i.e., for the effect on Germany. In this consideration they were not mistaken.[40]

Berlin was optimistic in regard to Britain during the early spring. When Lichnowsky, the German ambassador in London, repeated his warning in February that Britain would stand by France in a war with Germany, Jagow and Stumm, director of the political section of the Foreign Ministry, expressed doubts and continued to hope for a loosening of British ties with the Franco-Russian alliance. Austro-Hungarian and German leaders were aware of Franco-Russian efforts to tie Britain more closely, but many (including Lichnowsky, the kaiser, Jagow, Schoen, the German ambassador in Paris, and several Austro-Hungarian diplomats) accepted the British assurance that nothing had changed. Since Anglo-French relations seemed unchanged, Anglo-German cooperation seemed unthreatened and indeed reinforced by colonial negotiations and the possibility of a naval *détente* in May and June. Although Lichnowsky repeated his warning against doing so, the kaiser, the crown prince, Tirpitz, Bethmann, Jagow, and Tschirschky, but not Moltke, interpreted Anglo-German cooperation and nonconsolidation of the Entente as uncertainty about British support of France in war.[41]

Berlin's perception of Britain altered radically, however, during the second half of May. When the Anglo-Russian naval talks became known in Berlin, Jagow arranged a leak in the German press and warned London. Although the British press reaction was angry, the British and Russian governments both denied the reports. But the rumors persisted through June, and the Germans became alarmed because their policy of separating Britain from its allies was at issue. It was not surprising that the kaiser ordered Bethmann to "create clarity" in relations with Britain, since the Kaiser felt that the "third Balkan war" was imminent and being prepared for by the Franco-Russian alliance. Consequently, Bethmann and Jagow made their most concerted effort to divide Britain from its allies when they warned that an Austro-Russian conflict in the Balkans could be avoided only by Anglo-German cooperation. This cooperation required that the British not encourage Russian chauvinism in ways such as the reported naval talks. The Germans doubted Grey's renewed denials because they were informed about not only the Anglo-Russian naval talks but also the earlier Anglo-French military conversations. Lichnowsky tried to smoke Grey out in a conversation on 6 July, but the Germans were already committing themselves on that same day to the support of Austria-Hungary against Serbia, which would put Anglo-German cooperation to its ultimate test.[42]

Contrary to German anxieties, the apparent Anglo-Russian amity of May became enmity in June. The British government postponed the Anglo-Russian naval talks until August because of German complaints and British press criticism. An additional consideration was probably

Anglo-Russian negotiations over Persia in which the naval talks provided the British with a convenient bargaining point to extract concessions from the Russians. Sazonov may have perceived the same relationship in reverse: just as serious negotiating on the naval question began, he protested about British press criticism of Russian policy in Persia. Grey responded ominously that Anglo-Russian differences in Persia "must react upon the general political relations of Russia and the European situation." In fact, Buchanan, Grey, Asquith, and Nicolson were all concerned about the possibility of an Anglo-Russian conflict over Persia, Tibet, and India. When the Russians made further difficulties about Persia, Grey sought officially to dispel Russian concerns and reduce Anglo-Russian friction but was actually impatient with the Russians and refused to continue discussions. Sazonov openly linked the Persian and naval questions when he offered concessions in Persia in exchange for immediate resumption of the naval talks. Although the atmosphere was improved both by Grey's inclination to accept and by a British naval visit to Russia, Anglo-Russian relations remained ambivalent.[43]

Russo-German relations presented a similarly contradictory and changing picture. Enmity in March was followed by amity in April and May but enmity in June. Evaluation of these vicissitudes is complicated by the fact that both Germany and Russia were anxious to persuade the British that the other power was aggressive. After their press feud in March, Russia attracted less German attention. Bethmann made no public statement on Russia during the spring, and Jagow claimed in the Reichstag that "no real hindrance to peaceful coexistence between Russia and Germany" existed. Although Sazonov gave what he claimed was a friendly response, he revived the Sanders question, and Russian military preparations continued. Despite Russian efforts, the British remained unconvinced of German aggressiveness and the imminence of a Russo-German conflict. The outward calm of April and May gave way in June to new Russo-German tensions as a result of Russian military preparations and press bellicosity. An article in the Russian press boasted of Russian military preparations and urged a similar policy on the French. Pourtalès' argument that the article was designed more to encourage the French than to frighten the Germans was lost on the German public and government. The article was widely republished in Germany, was generally interpreted as a threat, and confirmed the kaiser's fears about Franco-Russian preparations. But it also served to buttress the German case that Russian bellicosity required Anglo-German cooperation. Grey remained unconvinced, however, that Russia was genuinely aggressive.[44]

German relations with France were perhaps more difficult to fathom. Since the Germans paid relatively limited attention to France during the spring of 1914, there is little evidence of either enmity or amity. Although concerned by French efforts to convert the Anglo-French Entente into a formal alliance, the Germans properly assumed that such a development was more dependent on British than French policy. Franco-German relations in the Near East were mixed: amiable in Turkey, acrimonious in the Balkans. The primary German concern in regard to France was, in fact, less with their direct relations than with the French domestic crisis over military expansion and its implications for the Franco-Russian alliance. Statements in the Russian press were probably reinforced with confidential warnings that the Franco-Russian alliance depended on French expansion. The French government sought to paper over the crisis with vague statements on expansion and reassurances to its allies. The kaiser expressed concern about French preparations but predicted that France would sink into "the red flood" of revolution and would not be able to expand militarily. He reflected the contradictory but prevalent German view that France was both dangerous and decadent.[45]

FLUID NOT RIGID: THE NATURE OF ALLIANCES

Alliances have frequently been regarded as a major cause of war in 1914.[46] Relations between and within the alliances undoubtedly constituted an important consideration during the spring of 1914. The operative question is: in what way did alliances affect the course of events? The contention that alliances caused war usually implies and sometimes states that the rigidity of the alliances was the critical factor.[47] The evidence can be interpreted, however, in precisely the opposite way. Both alliances were in a state of flux and redefinition during the spring of 1914. It was uncertain precisely how allies would behave toward one another in any particular issue or whether alliances would be tightened or loosened. This uncertainty had caused tension and mutual recriminations. It was due in the last resort to differing perceptions of what constituted secondary (i.e., individual) and primary (i.e., alliance) interests. As long as the distinction was made, the danger of war was limited. But, if all questions became alliance questions and secondary interests became identical with existence, the danger of war would increase. The reactions of the various powers to these questions seemed unpredictable. Indeed, this was precisely the danger. If the alliances had been rigid in the sense of being secure and defined, the responses of allies, and therefore the course of events, would have been more predictable. Instead, the fluidity of alliances made responses uncertain and reinforced anxieties. Thus, the fluidity rather than rigidity of alliances increased the likelihood of war.

NOTES

1   Joseph J. C. Joffre, *Memoirs* (New York, 1932), 1:11, 23, 37, 56; *Der Weltkrieg 1914–1918* (Berlin, 1925), 1:85; Barbara W. Tuchman, *The Guns of August* (New York, 1962), pp. 34–37, 42–43, 57–58; Gerhard Ritter, *Staatskunst und Kriegshandwerk* (Munich, 1960), 2:107; Taylor, *Struggle*, pp. 472, 486–89.

2   For an example of an apology for tightening the Franco-Russian alliance, see: Taylor, *Struggle*, pp. 483–84, 486–88. For an example of criticism, see Sidney B. Fay, *The Origins of the World War* (New York, 1966), 1:312–42.

3   Taylor, *Struggle*, pp. 472, 478; *Der Weltkrieg 1914–1918: Kriegsrüstung und Kriegshandwerk* (Berlin, 1930), 1:145–46, 150–51. See chapter 5 of this book for details of domestic politics and chapter 6 for details of arms increases.

4   Taylor, *Struggle*, pp. 476–81.

5   Ibid., p. 484.

6   Ibid., pp. 487–88; Fay, *Origins*, 1:434.

7   Taylor, *Struggle*, p. 490; Fay, *Origins*, 1:436–37.

8   Taylor, *Struggle*, p. 492; *Die Grosse Politik der Europäischen Kabinette, 1871–1914*, ed. J. Lepsius, A. Mendelssohn-Bartholdy, F. Thimme (Berlin, 1922–27), 33:458–59.

9   *GP*, 33:185–86, 258–59, 273–76, 295–96, 302–4, 424–26, 428–30, 451–53, 458–62, 472–76; *GP*, 34:16; Fay, *Origins*, 1:442; Schulthess, *Europäischer Geschichtskalender, 1912* (Munich, 1915), p. 243; Karl Helfferich, *Der Weltkrieg* (Berlin, 1919), 1:105.

10   *GP*, 33:279–81, 306–7, 341–42, 347–48, 359, 393–94; *GP* 34:5–6; Taylor, *Struggle*, pp. 492–93; Helfferich, *Weltkrieg*, 1:103–4.

11   *GP*, 30:574–75; *GP*, 31:552–56; *GP*, 33:189–93, 228–37, 244–47, 296, 348, 355–56, 360–61, 372–73, 424–26, 428–30, 451–54, 458–67, 472–76; *GP*, 34:16, 24–25; *GP*, 39:119–23; Schulthess, *Geschichtskalender*, p. 243; Helfferich, *Weltkrieg*, 1:105; Fay, *Origins*, 1:442.

12   Taylor, *Struggle*, p. 493; *British Documents on the Origins of the War, 1898–1914*, ed. G. P. Gooch and H. Temperley (London, 1938), 11:193–94.

13   *GP*, 33:222–23, 261–62; *GP*, 34:44–46, 63–64, 70–73, 90, 102–3, 346–48; *GP*, 39:9–11; Taylor, *Struggle*, p. 494.

14   *GP*, 34:227–28, 281–83, 309–11, 316–18, 346–48, 367, 409, 414–15, 430, 495–99, 503–4, 528–29, 531–32, 537–38, 546–47, 551, 554–55, 557–58, 562, 564–65, 595–96, 600, 603–5, 625–26, 631, 636–37, 640–42, 702–3, 717–20, 725, 727–28, 734–39, 741–42, 746–48, 753–58, 760–62, 770–73, 779–82, 784, 786–87, 796, 801–2, 808–10; Schulthess, *Geschichtskalender*, p. 614.

15   *GP*, 34:356–57, 409–11, 444–46, 459–61, 742–43, 820–27, 827–30, 864–65, 873–74, 876–77, 884; *GP*, 35:13–14, 19, 33–35, 46–48, 61–62, 66–70, 78, 89–100, 115–16, 122–24, 128–30, 140, 142, 146–48, 181–82, 207–8, 216–19, 237–39; Franz Conrad von Hötzendorf, *Aus meiner Dienstzeit* (Vienna, Leipzig, Munich, 1925), 3:402–4.

16   *GP*, 35:323–32, 334–36, 342, 346–53, 356–57, 365–67, 370–71, 378–79; *GP*, 36:24–25, 40, 58–60, 73, 76–77, 84–85; *GP*, 39:383–84; *Österreich-Ungarns Aussenpolitik von der*

bosnischen Krise 1908 bis zum Kriegsausbruch 1914, ed. L. Bittner, A. F. Pribram, H. Srbik, H. Uebersberger (1930), 7:116–18, 123, 145, 152–54, 173–74, 178–81, 190.

17   *GP*, 35:372–76; *GP*, 36:27–31; *GP*, 39:441–42; *OU*, 7:114–16, 198–201, 205, 216–17, 219–21.

18   *GP*, 39:441–42; *GP*, 36:388–89, 397, 399–401; *OU*, 7:188–89, 192–95, 248, 256, 258, 261–62, 265–67, 290, 315–16, 346, 353–58, 374, 376, 384–88, 397–403, 427–28, 430–33, 435–36, 445–46, 451–52, 454–55, 459–61, 470, 473, 475; Fay, *Origins*, 1:470.

19   *GP*, 36:402, 407, 413, 420–21; *GP*, 39:460–62; *OU*, 7:470–71, 478–81, 483, 487–88, 491–92, 506–8, 512–15, 525–29.

20   *GP*, 34:240–42, 247, 255–56, 262–63, 266–67, 281–83; *GP*, 35:16–18; *GP*, 37:60–66, 154–55, 181–84, 196–200, 207–8, 474–76, 643–50, 655–57, 660–61, 822–25, 829–30; *GP*, 38:30–31, 41–48, 50–52, 54–56, 81–82, 86–87, 98–99, 100, 114–17, 124–27, 195; Taylor, *Struggle*, pp. 504–5.

21   Fay, *Origins*, 1:506–10, 599–600; Taylor, *Struggle*, p. 508.

22   *GP*, 38:212–17; Fay, *Origins*, 1:510–12.

23   *GP*, 38:225–27; Fay, *Origins*, 1:500–1, 516–17.

24   *GP*, 38:225–27, 244–45.

25   *GP*, 38:225–28; Fay, *Origins*, 1:514–21; Taylor, *Struggle*, p. 501; Schulthess, *Geschichtskalender*, p. 404; Fritz Fischer, *Griff nach der Weltmacht: Die Kriegszielpolitik des kaiserlichen Deutschland 1914/18* (Düsseldorf, 1964), pp. 46–47.

26   *GP*, 38:283–86, 293–97; Fay, *Origins*, 1:513, 522, 529–35.

27   *GP*, 38:293–97, 303–4, 306–12; Fay, *Origins*, 1:536.

28   Fay, *Origins*, 1:481, 520–21, 528, 530–40; Taylor, *Struggle*, pp. 501, 511, 531; Raymond Poincaré, *Au Service de la France: Neuf années de souvenirs* (Paris, 1928), 1:228.

29   *GP*, 37:240–552, 566–83, 589, 596, 606–9, 669–70, 680–82, 686–88, 690–93, 695–97, 700, 704–5, 711–34, 739–45, 822–25, 891; *GP*, 38:79–84; *GP*, 39:69–99; Taylor, *Struggle*, pp. 486, 508; Fischer, *Griff*, pp. 46–47.

30   *GP*, 38:313–17; *GP*, 39:544, 547–61, 570–73, 578–84.

31   *GP*, 39:383–84, 390–92, 414–20, 423, 539–40.

32   *GP*, 39:328–31, 338–41, 343–58, 400–6, 427–29, 716–17; *OU*, 8:177, 184–85, 203–4, 207.

33   *GP*, 37:60–66, 154–55, 181–84, 196–200, 207–8, 474–76, 643–50, 655–57, 660–61; *GP*, 38:30–31, 41–48, 50–52, 54–56, 81–82, 86–87, 98–100, 114–17, 124–27, 195, 325–27; *GP*, 39:458–62, 466, 469–71, 545–47; Taylor, *Struggle*, pp. 504–5, 515; *OU*, 7:525–29, 626–29; Fay, *Origins*, 1:479, 481–86, 490, 497.

34   *OU*, 7:974–79, 1028–31; *OU*, 8:1–3, 25–27, 32–34, 173–76, 180–82; Conrad, *Dienstzeit*, 3:597–98, 615–16, 627–28.

35   *OU*, 8:99–100, 197, 236; *GP*, 36:402–4, 540–46, 560, 562–63, 571, 585–86, 602–4, 613–15, 645–46, 649–61, 665–66, 671–74, 687–90, 694–710, 716–20; *GP*, 38:348–52; *GP*, 39:332–51, 402–4.

36   *GP*, 38:331–35, 516–22; *GP*, 39:487–97; *OU*, 8:168–69, 172.

37   *GP*, 39:361–64; Conrad, *Dienstzeit*, 3:670; Ritter, *Staatskunst*, 2:311; *BD*, 10:802–3, part 2.

38   *GP*, 31:367, 375–76, 379; *GP*, 38:102–7, 111–18.

39   *GP*, 37:593; *BD*, 10:775–85, part 2; Taylor, *Struggle*, p. 511.

40 GP, 37:107, 612–14, 624–25, 631; BD, 10:787–90, 979, part 2; Edward Grey, Twenty-Five Years, 1892–1916 (New York, 1925), 1:284.

41 GP, 31:426, 433–40; GP, 37:99–105, 108–11, 120–32, 435–44, 447–48; GP, 39:361–64, 593–608; OU, 7:1062–63, 1080, 1085–87; OU, 8:21–22; BD, 10:392, 396–97, 609–11, 741–53, part 2; Conrad, Dienstzeit, 3:668–73; Edward House, The Intimate Papers of Colonel House, ed. C. Seymour (London, 1926), 1:278; Alfred Tirpitz, Erinnerungen (Leipzig, 1919), p. 195.

42 GP, 39:617–33; BD, 10:791–97, 802–4, part 2; Fischer, Griff, pp. 57–58.

43 GP, 39:624–27, 632–36; BD, 10:745–46, 776–77, 797–813, part 2.

44 GP, 39:580, 586–87, 628–36; BD, 10:743–46, 802–4, part 2; House, Papers, 1:278; Fischer, Griff, pp. 57–58; A. Hoyos, Der deutsch-englische Gegensatz und sein Einfluss auf die Balkanpolitik Österreich-Ungarns (Berlin, Leipzig, 1922), p. 82; Theobald Bethmann Hollweg, Betrachtungen zum Weltkriege (Berlin, 1919), 1:93, 99.

45 GP, 39: 260–74, 582, 587; Fischer, Griff, pp. 57–58.

46 For example, see Fay, Origins, 1:34.

47 For example, see Felix Gilbert, The End of the European Era, 1890 to the Present (New York, 1970), p. 91.

IV / THREAT OF CHANGE:

The Balkan Wars and the Survival of the Habsburg and Ottoman Empires (October 1912 – June 1914)

THE ISSUES INVOLVED: AUTHORITY, CHANGE, SURVIVAL, VIOLENCE

Balkan events during the years 1912–14 are important both as an influence on and an indicator of great-power policies. But these events are significant for several other related reasons. They revealed the nature of great-power authority and cooperation; confronted Europe with the problem of territorial change; threatened the existence of the two contiguous empires, Turkey and Austria-Hungary; and involved violence. The cumulative effect of these impulses would alter the international situation by June 1914.

Although these issues were interrelated, they arose at different stages. Great-power authority and cooperation were involved most specifically during the Balkan wars but also during the spring of 1914. Change occurred most clearly during the wars but was frequently implied thereafter. Ottoman survival seemed most jeopardized during the first Balkan war, but the problem lingered thereafter and was revived during the Sanders crisis at the end of 1914. Habsburg survival was raised indirectly by the Balkan wars and became an increasingly real issue until the spring of 1914, when it seemed threatened to many statesmen, especially in Vienna. Violence was most evident during the two Balkan wars, but the threat increased thereafter and actually recurred in the Balkans during the spring of 1914.

THE CONCERT COLLAPSES: THE FAILURE OF GREAT-POWER COOPERATION IN THE BALKANS AND TURKEY

Balkan events were complicated by their involvement in the eastern question in which a subtle but significant shift had occurred since the 1890s. Whereas Bismarck had generally resisted German involvement in the eastern question, William and his advisers had encouraged it. Consequently, Germany gradually became engaged, like France and Britain, in economic penetration into the Ottoman Empire. This development had not been particularly notable as long as the Near East had remained relatively somnolent and the great powers had been busy elsewhere. The question, however, became more immediate at the end of the first decade of the twentieth century. The French, British, and Russians had avoided conflicts elsewhere and again turned their attention increasingly to Europe. Austro-Russian tension in the Balkans revived during the Bosnian crisis. Germany's involvement in the crisis and humiliation of Russia publicized its new interest in the Balkans and Near East in general.

The eastern question was revived not only by great-power but also Turkish actions. Turkish authority in the southern Balkans, and indeed to a certain extent elsewhere, rested as much on what amounted to a great-power mandate as on Turkish power. This mandate would continue only as long as Turkish rule remained acceptable to the powers, which in turn depended on Turkey's being sufficiently strong to police its subjects but sufficiently weak to respond to great-power pressures. These preconditions were jeopardized by a Turkish reform movement which might strengthen Turkey enough to allow it to resist or choose among the powers. Like many peoples under European colonial domination, the Young Turks advocated reviving Turkish strength through modernization in order to rule by virtue of their own power rather than as agents of the European powers. These aspirations were made even more ominous for the European system by the tendency of the Young Turks to turn to Germany for assistance.

Characteristically, the Balkan crisis was precipitated by the Balkan peoples themselves. Balkan nationalism and self-consciousness had intensified at the beginning of the twentieth century. The central question, however, was not, and had never been, the strength of Balkan nationalism, but rather the policies of the great powers. When the powers cooperated and maintained their authority, Balkan aspirations were subordinated to great-power interests; when the powers did not cooperate, the Balkan states could exploit great-power rivalries. At the beginning of 1912, two of the Balkan states—Serbia and Bulgaria—questioned great-power authority in the Balkans by plotting violent alteration of the Balkan status quo. The immediate impulse was the. Italo-Turkish war, which could be interpreted as an indication that Turkey was still weak despite reforms, and that the powers might not intervene to protect it. Serbia and Bulgaria committed themselves not only to expel the Turks and exclude the Austro-Hungarians from the Balkans but also to destroy great-power authority in the Balkans.[1]

The eastern question was therefore revived under particularly unpropitious circumstances. The previous decade had marked an increase in great-power tensions, culminating in an arms race on the continent after 1912. Meanwhile, Germany had become involved in the question, and Turkish and Balkan nationalism were both on the rise. All factors conspired to jeopardize great-power authority and thus peace in the Balkans. The myth of great-power authority in the Balkans and Near East persisted up to the July crisis. Ultimately, it depended on great-power cooperation and determination to control events. The powers went through the motions of anticipating war in the Balkans and warned the Balkan states that no change in the status quo would be accepted. But Russia, with French approval, had condoned the Serb-Bulgarian alliance's intention to alter the status quo. The great-power warning proved unsuccessful when the Balkan states attacked Turkey at the beginning of October 1912. Great-power authority had thus been unable to deter war. It remained to be seen whether it could preserve the status quo.[2] Three hypothetical options confronted the great powers. They could cooperate, conflict, or condone. Cooperation had already proven unsuccessful. A great-power conflict seemed possible as the result of Austro-Hungarian intervention against Serbia or Russian intervention against Bulgaria. But Anglo-German restraint eventually deterred both, and the powers reverted to passive observation of events. Under British, German, and French prodding, Austria-Hungary and Russia finally accepted the principle of negotiating a new Balkan status quo.[3]

War forced the powers to face the Balkan problem. With the expulsion of Turkey and absence of anyone prepared to reestablish it, the possibility of a great-power mandate to Turkey disappeared. Another alternative was war over the Balkans between the powers and/or the Balkan states, but for the moment this danger had been avoided when Austria-Hungary and Russia demurred. There remained the options of Balkan autonomy and great-power authority, which were logically incompatible and might have precipitated a conflict. In attacking Turkey, the Balkan states had attacked the great powers' policeman in the Balkans and thus their authority. At the beginning of the war, the powers had specifically warned the belligerents that no change in the Balkan status quo would be acceptable. In their preparations for an ambassadorial conference on the Balkans, the powers specifically recognized that the central question would be to what extent they would permit changes in the status quo. Conversely, Balkan strength rested not on recognized authority but on the accomplished fact of their victory and the assertion of national aspirations. The Balkan states had accepted great-power—i.e., Russian—support but not great-power authority. A consistent solution necessitated a choice.[4]

As it turned out, not a choice but a compromise was made as Balkan autonomy was tacitly recognized in some cases, great-power authority reimposed in others. This compromise was illustrated by the simultaneous convening in London of both the great-power ambassadorial conference and the peace conference between the Balkan states and Turkey. This outcome was due, however, less to rational decision or agreement than to disagreements among the powers on the one hand and among the Balkan states on the other. By avoiding the central issue of great-power authority versus Balkan autonomy, conflict was made less likely immediately but more likely eventually. The differences among the powers and the Balkan states deterred a conflict between the two groups at this time but would erupt into subsequent conflicts—among the Balkan states in 1913 and among the great powers in 1914.

The great-power ambassadorial conference in London gave the impression of immediate success. In actuality, like most successful diplomatic conferences, it only succeeded in formalizing what had already been accepted as the basis of the conference. It granted the Austro-Italian demand for an autonomous and neutralized Albanian state under great-power protection and accepted the Franco-Russian insistence that Constantinople and a zone on the European shore remain Turkish. The initial success was, however, deceptive since the great-power agreements on Albania and Constantinople did not reverse events in the Balkans so much as they drew limits to further change. They depended on great-power cooperation to agree on the details and defend their decisions.

The powers found it difficult to agree on the details. Since Turkish authority had existed in Constantinople, it presented no immediate problem, but Albania was a new creation and therefore by no means clear. Austro-Russian disagreement soon emerged over Albania's borders. Anxious to block Serbian access to the Adriatic, Austria-Hungary demanded that the port of Scutari be awarded Albania, whereas the Russians insisted Scutari be given Serbia. Despite the tensions which the issue had created among the great powers, an Austro-Russian agreement was finally reached when Russia acceded. Reluctant accession was not, however, cooperation, and a great-power agreement had to be instituted. Great-power willingness to defend their decisions was tested when Montenegro demanded Scutari. Berchtold argued for the threat of force, but Jagow prevailed upon him to seek a great-power mandate. Although the great powers confirmed Albanian possession of Scutari, they were reluctant to enforce their decision when Montenegro took Scutari in April 1913. They did not resist, however, when Berchtold presented Montenegro with an ultimatum and forced it to back down. The Scutari crisis revealed the sham of great-power authority in the Balkans and the contradiction on which great-power cooperation was based. While the concert could succeed in the Balkans or elsewhere only if the powers' interests were not directly involved, all the powers except possibly Britain sought to exploit the Balkan situation for their own purposes. The concert was, therefore, unlikely to function effectively.[5]

The destruction of great-power authority in the Balkans was accelerated by the second Balkan war in June 1913, since events were again determined by the Balkan states rather than by the great powers. But the second Balkan war also precluded Balkan autonomy as a solution for the problem of power in the Balkans. As great-power authority depended on great-power cooperation, Balkan autonomy could be defended against great-power interference only if the Balkan states cooperated. Persistence of the Balkan league was hypothetically possible but assumed the subordination of its members' mutual antipathies to an outside threat or opportunity such as Turkey or Austria-Hungary. When Turkey was effectively expelled from the Balkans, it ceased to act as a unifying force. A Balkan league based on antipathy toward Austria-Hungary was unlikely, since Bulgaria and Greece had little to gain from it, but Rumania and Serbia had much. On the contrary, Austro-Hungarian resistance to a Serbian port on the Adriatic had a disunifying effect on the Balkan states. Frustrated in its desire for a port, Serbia refused to fulfill its promises to Bulgaria. Having done most of the fighting against Turkey, Bulgaria assumed it could substitute domination for cooperation with its former allies. The issue had now become not Balkan cooperation and autonomy but Balkan conflict and either a Balkan balance or Bulgarian domination. Although the Scutari crisis had indicated that the powers were unlikely to assert their authority, the individual powers were not disinterested in Balkan events. Russian hopes for a Balkan league under its auspices were shattered by the conflict, whereas Austria-Hungary was anxious to preclude a league and thus encouraged the conflict but opposed a Serbian victory. Renewed Balkan violence accordingly revived the possibility of great-power intervention, which threatened to precipitate a great-power conflict but was avoided when the allies of Austria-Hungary and Russia restrained them. A Balkan balance rather than Bulgarian domination occurred when Bulgaria was resoundingly defeated. Consequently, the Balkan states had again asserted their independence of great-power authority.[6]

The peace of Bucharest both marked the end of great-power authority in the Balkans and formalized the Balkan balance. Not only did the powers fail to reassert their authority, but they specifically renounced it. Berlin opposed great-power participation in the peace conference, and Sazonov urged the belligerents to negotiate directly with one another. The powers thus completely reversed themselves since the first Balkan war. Whereas they had then rejected any change in the status quo, they now insisted that the Balkan states establish a new status quo themselves. This turned out to be a maneuver, however. Although the powers refused to take responsibility for the Balkan status quo, each sought to exploit it for his own profit and great-power rivalry replaced cooperation and authority in the Balkans.[7]

These tendencies were confirmed during the autumn of 1913 and spring of 1914. When Serbia threatened Albania in the autumn of 1913, the powers failed to act and Serbia remained obstinate. Berchtold again resorted to an ultimatum, as he had done during the Scutari crisis. Although they did not endorse the ultimatum, the other powers did not oppose it, and Serbia backed down. Berchtold rejected Entente criticism with the inconsistent, but not altogether incorrect, assertion that the myth of great-power unanimity could be preserved only if one power took the initiative. But, if great-power unanimity were a myth, one power would hardly be allowed to take the initiative repeatedly. It would only be allowed to do so if great-power agreement existed, in which case it would be unnecessary, since no small state would resist a genuine great-power mandate. The same problem recurred during the spring of 1914 when Vienna again sought great-power support to preserve the existence of Albania, which was threatened by Greek agitation and internal dissension. Although the powers managed to arrange a solution with Greece, the internal disruption continued; eventually, Austria-Hungary intervened with force and threatened Italy with an ultimatum. The transition was complete from great-power authority to great-power rivalry, and Balkan issues had become so clearly partisan that cooperation was virtually precluded.[8]

Great-power cooperation in the Ottoman Empire, meanwhile, persisted but declined. After it had become clear at the end of 1912 that Turkey would survive defeat, Britain, France, and Germany acted together to preserve the empire. They agreed to supply advisers to help the Turks modernize their army, navy, administration, and finances and resisted Russian moves which seemed to jeopardize the survival of Turkey. But this pattern was altered during the Sanders incident. At first Russia was able to win Anglo-French support against the German military mission. The Germans finally managed to persuade the British to drop their support of Russia with the argument that the German mission was the same as those of the British and French. But the British and French did not support the German mission and thus the principle of cooperation. Instead, they left the Germans and Russians to confront each other. Thus, the role of protecting Turkey seemed to have been assumed by Germany and the principle of cooperation to have been jettisoned. As it turned out, cooperation between Germany, Britain, and France against Russian pressures recurred in the spring of 1914 but became less significant because Russia pursued a more benevolent policy toward Turkey and Turkey was more active in the Balkans.[9]

POWER IN JEOPARDY: THE ISSUE OF HABSBURG SURVIVAL

The issues of great-power authority in the Balkans and Habsburg survival were interrelated. The persistence of the status quo and great-

power authority in the Balkans would serve Austro-Hungarian purposes, since it was widely assumed that Austria-Hungary would become
the sick man of Europe if the Turk died. The Balkan wars, therefore,
implicated both great-power authority and Habsburg survival. But,
whereas great-power authority and Habsburg survival reinforced each
other as long as the Balkan status quo was not threatened, they conflict-
ed when the status quo was altered. Great-power authority depended on
cooperation, which assumed that the existence of no power was directly
involved. Habsburg survival was, however, implicated by the expulsion
of the Turks and intensification of Balkan nationalism. The more threatened Austria-Hungary seemed, the more it intervened in the Balkans.
The more it intervened, the more events were interpreted in terms of
Habsburg survival, and the less the powers could cooperate to control
events. Consequently, European authority and Habsburg survival became increasingly incompatible.

The danger to Habsburg survival posed by expulsion of the Turks
from the Balkans was perceived from the start by the statesmen in Vienna. They sought unsuccessfully to deter war by urging reforms on the
Turks and warning the Balkan states against changing the status quo.
The outbreak of hostilities was immediately seen as a threat. Berchtold
felt the Balkan league could become a Russian tool, and the possibility
of a united Balkan front against Austria-Hungary would remain the
central concern of Vienna's policy up to the war. With the victory of the
Balkan league over Turkey, Vienna's fears intensified as Berchtold saw
drastic alternatives. He felt that victorious Serbia would now have to
choose between conciliation and conflict with Austria-Hungary. As a
means of conciliating Russia, he revived the plan for partition of the
Balkans which had been mooted on the eve of the Bosnian crisis in 1908.
He hoped that Russia would renounce Serbia in exchange for Austro-
Hungarian recognition of Russian preponderence in Bulgaria. To make
Serbia dependent on Austria-Hungary and thus force it into friendship,
Berchtold rejected the Serbian demand for an Adriatic port and insisted
instead on the establishment of Albania, which would block Serbian
access to the Adriatic. At first, it seemed possible that Austria-Hungary
might intervene against Serbia or refuse to negotiate with Russia over
Serbia. But the combination of German reassurances of support and restraint against action eventually persuaded Vienna to accept a conference on condition that Albania be established. When frictions with Russia over Albania recurred in the winter of 1913, the advocates of war
momentarily won the upper hand in Vienna, but Germany again restrained its ally and an Austro-Russian compromise was worked out.[10]

The Scutari crisis of the spring of 1913 reinforced the Austro-

Hungarian belief that Austro-Serbian coexistence was impossible. The powers' unwillingness to impose their decision on Montenegro confirmed the Austro-Hungarians in their belief that they could not rely on great-power authority to preserve Albania. Both the success of their ultimatum to Montenegro and the powers' acceptance of it encouraged Viennese threats of violence to defend its interests. Nonetheless, Vienna was confronted with a dilemma. The Germans urged their ally to preserve its great-power status by relying on the concert. The concert was not only cumbersome and frustrating—as the Scutari crisis indicated— but also contradictory. A great power could not preserve itself with the concert's approval but only by the assertion of its own interests. If its preservation depended on European approval, it lost its power status and became a European mandate like Turkey. Thus, if Austro-Hungarian statesmen pursued the policy advocated by Berlin, they risked losing their great-power status. Yet, if they asserted their own interests despite the concert, they risked losing German support and provoking war.[11]

This dilemma became clearest during the second Balkan war. The possibility of a united Balkan front against Austria-Hungary was destroyed for the moment by the conflict among the former Balkan allies. But a new danger immediately emerged in the form of a crushing Bulgarian defeat and Serbian victory. Berchtold informed Berlin that Vienna would intervene either if Bulgaria were decisively defeated or if Russia intervened to save Serbia from decisive defeat. He argued that Germany and Austria-Hungary should exploit the war to insure against Entente success. He regarded Bulgaria as critical to future developments in the Balkans. If Bulgaria chose to remain under Russian influence and perpetuate the Balkan league, Rumania and Austria-Hungary would be diverted from a war against Russia, and Germany would have to send more troops east. But, if Bulgaria were induced to join the Austro-German side, Rumania and Austria-Hungary would be freed to join in the war against Russia, and Bulgaria would check Serbia. Berchtold therefore urged retaining Rumanian friendship and encouraging a Rumanian-Bulgarian reconciliation by winning concessions for Rumania from Bulgaria, which would be compensated with concessions extracted from Serbia and Greece. When a Rumanian-Bulgarian arrangement proved impossible and Bulgarian defeat was imminent, Berchtold became anxious. He warned Berlin that Austria-Hungary's South Slavs would become uncontrollable if Serbia became "overly powerful" and threatened intervention if Serbia made excessive demands. But, when the Germans refused support for intervention, Vienna's only recourse was to save Bulgaria by urging an end to hostilities and defending Bulgarian interests at the peace conference. As a result, the mood among Austro-Hungarian statesmen was dark in the late summer of 1913, and Hungarian Premier Tisza even spoke hypothetically of the empire's dissolution.[12]

Austro-Hungarian frustrations and anxieties intensified during the autumn of 1913. Austro-Serbian tensions had risen during the late summer and increased when Serbia threatened Albania. Vienna was again frustrated by the other powers' unwillingness to force Serbian compliance. The renewal of Austro-Serbian tensions caused a wide-ranging and revealing discussion of policy in Vienna. Berchtold argued that the Balkan wars had created a new situation. After the expulsion of Turkey, Austria-Hungary was confronted with powerful Balkan states, of which Serbia and Rumania had aspirations incompatible with the empire's existence. Serbia could always reestablish the Balkan league by buying off Bulgaria with Macedonia. Conrad advocated annexation of Serbia and Montenegro since they were presumably only awaiting an opportunity to attack Austria-Hungary. But Berchtold, Tisza, Austro-Hungarian Finance Minister Bilinski, and Austrian Minister President Stürgkh opposed an attack of Serbia because it would be resisted by the other powers. They nonetheless regarded an Austro-Serbian conflict as both inevitable and essential: "A conflict resulting in the humiliation of Serbia is the necessary precondition for the existence of the monarchy." This assertion implied that the reverse was also true: the monarchy could not survive unless such a conflict occurred. Although all his colleagues rejected immediate violence, Conrad was pleased by their acceptance in principle of his argument that an eventual solution would require violence. Austro-Hungarian leaders therefore supported Berchtold's ultimatum to Serbia. As Tisza commented, the Balkan wars had demonstrated that only powers which threatened were respected, a conclusion apparently justified when Serbia gave way before the Austro-Hungarian threat. The Balkan wars had evoked a new Viennese attitude which rendered ominous warnings normal and violence thinkable or perhaps even necessary.[13]

Developments in the Balkans during the winter and spring of 1914 were unpropitious to Austria-Hungary. Austro-Serbian tensions rose again during the winter because of rumors of a Serb-Montenegrin union. Councils in Vienna were divided: Conrad characteristically urged opposition; Tisza typically advocated flexibility and preparing for the union; while Berchtold was ambivalent as usual in regarding the union as virtually unavoidable but unacceptable. Action was made less palatable by the lack of sympathy of Vienna's allies. The problem disappeared, however, when the rumors desisted. During the spring of

1914, no direct conflicts occurred in Austro-Serbian relations and Vienna paid remarkably little attention to Serbia. This apparent paradox can be explained in part by the fact that the conflict with Serbia was so basic that it need not be repeatedly articulated; active or somnolent, it remained the starting point and rationale for Austro-Hungarian policy. Nonetheless, the decline in Viennese concern for Serbia during this period is striking, particularly in consideration of the July crisis, and is explained in large measure by Austro-Hungarian distraction with other Balkan problems.[14]

Bulgaria remained critical for Austria-Hungary because its antipathy toward Serbia was the primary stumbling block for a Balkan league against Austria-Hungary. Increased Austro-Rumanian tensions during the spring of 1914 were accompanied by greater Austro-Hungarian attention toward Bulgaria. Vienna sought German financial assistance in competing with France for influence in Bulgaria. But Berlin refused and evidenced relatively little interest in Bulgaria during the spring. After its defeat in the second Balkan war, Bulgaria was the main Balkan revisionist, but it could revise the new status quo only if it divided its former opponents. Bulgaria sought an alliance with Rumania which foundered on Bulgarian-Rumanian disagreements, while a Bulgarian-Turkish alliance failed when Austria-Hungary and Germany refused to meet the Bulgarian demand for a guarantee against Rumania and Serbia. The Bulgarians accordingly elected restraint instead of revision until developments were more favorable. Vienna could therefore expect little help for the moment from this quarter.[15]

Meanwhile, Austro-Hungarian relations with Rumania degenerated further. In an effort to salvage the situation, Berchtold sent to Bucharest a conciliatory envoy (Czernin) in October 1913. When it became clear that relations had reached a critical stage, Vienna favored forcing Bucharest to choose between the great-power alliances but was restrained by Berlin. Yet Vienna's anxieties were generally justified by Rumanian aspirations, and Austro-Rumanian tension rose so rapidly during the spring of 1914 that Rumania attracted more attention than any other problem except Albania.[16]

Rumania pursued a dual policy because, like all the Balkan states, it had interests both inside and outside the peninsula. In the Balkans, it had the conservative objective of preserving the anti-Bulgarian coalition to prevent Bulgarian revision of the favorable status quo established by the second Balkan war. It therefore refused the Turkish suggestion of a Turkish-Bulgarian-Rumanian alliance (since it would have alienated Greece and Serbia) and sought instead to reconcile Greece and Turkey. Rumania also tried to avoid Serbian and/or Greek involvement in Albania, which might have diverted them from opposition to Bulgaria. But Rumanian policy outside the Balkans became increasingly revisionist toward Austria-Hungary. Although superficially contradictory, these two aspects of Rumanian policy were complementary and correlated. Only when Rumania had insured that the anti-Bulgarian alliance would persist could it afford the luxury of pursuing irredentism against Austria-Hungary. It was, consequently, fortunate for Rumania that Bulgaria pursued a less active role in the spring, since Bucharest could press Vienna for concessions to Rumanians living under Habsburg rule in Transylvania.[17]

Meanwhile, Austro-Hungarian relations with Italy over Albania reached the breaking point. The Albanian problem attracted more attention in Vienna and Berlin during the spring of 1914 than any other question. Despite their formal cooperation in establishing a monarchy in Albania, Austro-Hungarian and Italian agents immediately began to compete for influence in the country. Briefly forced into cooperation by a Greek threat to Albania in the early spring of 1914, Rome and Vienna were driven apart again by internal revolts in Albania during May and June. The Italians sympathized with the rebels when the Austro-Hungarians seemed to dominate the new monarch. His apparently imminent demise in June caused the Austro-Hungarians to demand an international force but to reject internationalization of Albania, with the implication that it was an Austro-Hungarian sphere of influence. Despite a warning from his ambassador in Rome, Berchtold presented Rome with what was designed to appear as an ultimatum but was probably a bluff. San Giuliano's refusal to be browbeaten and his counter-threats made an Austro-Italian conflict seem possible.[18]

These problems were compounded by Russian efforts to exploit them. During the spring of 1914, the Russians were more active and apparently more successful in the Balkans. They bettered relations with the Ottoman Empire. More ominous for Vienna, Russo-Rumanian relations improved as Austro-Rumanian relations degenerated. The Russians encouraged the Rumanian-Serbian-Greek grouping of the second Balkan war during visits of Serbian President Pashich and Greek President Venizelos to St. Petersburg in February 1914. Russian efforts seemed to bear fruit in the Rumanian crown prince's trip to Russia in March and the return visit of the tsar and Sazonov in June, but no concrete agreement was reached.[19]

Balkan developments caused a serious reappraisal of policy as well as pressure for action in Vienna. Austro-Hungarian leaders had already been pessimistic during the autumn, when at least some had perceived only two alternatives. Vienna could elect a "policy of calm," which offered the advantage of pursuing the established objectives of maintaining friendship with Rumania, seeking cooperation with Greece, working for an "acceptable relationship" with Serbia, and thus remaining "in complete harmony with Germany"; this option had the distinct disadvantage of leading to "certain suicide for Austria over the long run." The alternative was a policy of action which might rescue the monarchy but required the radical departures of preparing for a conflict with Serbia, seeking Bulgarian friendship, regarding Rumania as "uncertain," and thus risking disharmony with Berlin. Bitterness toward Berlin because of its behavior during the Balkan wars generally disposed Vienna toward the second alternative. Pressure for greater activism increased during the spring of 1914. Conrad concluded that Russia "undoubtedly wants a new Balkan league and is working in that direction at high pressure." Tisza agreed and asserted that Russia's purpose was to divert Austria-Hungary in order to allow Franco-Russian concentration against Germany. Since the league could not be recreated without Bulgaria, Vienna should seek to win over Bulgaria, draw Rumania and Greece away from Serbia and reconcile them with Bulgaria. Agreeing with Tisza that "there is no time to be lost," Berchtold authorized Flotow, the Foreign Ministry expert on the Balkans, to develop Tisza's ideas into a program which emphasized the dangers of the situation. Flotow concluded that Rumania was threatening and should be forced back to the side of the Triple Alliance by arranging an alliance with Bulgaria, but, if Rumania proved recalcitrant, a Bulgarian-Turkish alliance should be sought.[20]

The concerns of Austro-Hungarian leaders in Vienna were reinforced by warnings of disaster which poured in from Austro-Hungarian representatives in the Balkans. Pallavicini, the ambassador in Constantinople, argued that it was pointless to seek an association between Bulgaria and Rumania, as Vienna had previously sought to do. The apparent Russian success in Turkey and Rumania was "unfavorable and full of possible dangers for us," and his deputy in Constantinople feared that a Balkan league under Russian patronage was imminent. Pallavicini therefore urged Berchtold to "save what was still to be saved." The most persistent pressure was exerted on Vienna by Czernin, the recently appointed ambassador in Bucharest. He told Berchtold in March that only decisiveness could "avert unfathomable disaster" in the Balkans. Vienna would have to make certain of its alliance with Rumania or seek the alternative of an arrangement with Bulgaria against Rumania. Czernin regarded the tsar's visit to Rumania as a "milestone" in Rumanian and possibly Austro-Hungarian history, i.e., the point at which Rumania passed over to the Entente side. In more desperate terms than ever, he urged Berchtold to take the initiative before the empire's fate had been decided by its enemies. The increased anxieties were evident in the growing tendency to use the vocabulary of panic.[21]

Berchtold seems to have been more acted upon than actor during the spring of 1914. He agreed with some dire predictions: as he told Tschirschky, all Austro-Hungarian statesmen suffered from the nightmare of a revived Balkan league. But he seemed unable or unwilling to decide between alternative courses of action. Confronted with Czernin's mounting pressure for a departure toward Rumania, Berchtold procrastinated and sought to pacify him with justifications for inaction. Berchtold was finally prevailed upon at the end of June to work over the Tisza-Flotow outline of policy and seek German support. His version of the program accumulated all the pessimism prevailing in Vienna. Turkey, which had a community of interests with the Triple Alliance and constituted a counterbalance to Russia in the Balkans, had been driven out during the first Balkan war. Serbia, which was hostile to Austria-Hungary, had come under Russian influence, gained greatly during the Balkan wars, and might gain more by a union with Montenegro. Relations with Rumania had become progressively worse. The Franco-Russian alliance sought to revive the Balkan league as a diversion for the Triple Alliance. Franco-Russian success depended on drawing in Turkey by arranging a Turkish-Greek agreement and winning Bulgaria by reconciling it with Serbia and Rumania. It was therefore necessary for the Triple Alliance to bring over Bulgaria and possibly Turkey in order to control Rumania and preclude a Balkan league. Having himself delayed, Berchtold now argued that an initiative must be taken "at once, while the road to Sofia and also to Constantinople is still open." Unless a "timely and energetic counter-action" were initiated against Russia's "encirclement policy," it could perhaps not be undone at a later date. Thus calm and inaction seemed tantamount to surrender and action the only recourse. But action required German support, which necessitated persuading Berlin that Austro-Hungarian existence was jeopardized. The seeds of desperation were sown in Vienna by June and would be reaped in Berlin during July.[22]

PROTECTORATE, PARTITION, PROTEGÉ, OR PARTICIPANT? THE ISSUE OF OTTOMAN SURVIVAL

The revision of authority in the Balkans raised the issue of Ottoman as well as Habsburg survival. Four eventualities seemed possible: protectorate, partition, protegé, and participant. The Ottoman Empire could probably survive if it elected to remain the great powers' protectorate, an option which had the virtue of being traditional and avoiding funda-

mental change, but which depended for success on great-power cooperation and did not satisfy Turkish aspirations for independence. Turkey
could be partitioned, an alternative which had the appeal of removing
the problem but which would be resisted by the Turks and thus risked a
great-power conflict. Turkey could become a protegé of one of the great
powers, which had the attraction to the Turks of renouncing the status
of great-power mandate and to one great power of dominating Turkey,
but it risked the opposition of the other powers. Finally, Turkey might
become another participant in Balkan politics, an option which had the
virtues of avoiding a great-power confrontation over Turkey and satisfying Turkish desires for independence, but implied renunciation of the
status of great-power protectorate and thus risked Turkish survival.
These possibilities appeared in successive stages.

The defeat of Turkey during the first Balkan war made its collapse a
distinct possibility and caused the traditional response from the powers
of cooperating to maintain their protectorate. Perceiving Turkey as a
useful policeman in the Balkans, and thus anxious to preserve its authority as long as possible, Vienna had encouraged internal reform and
discouraged attacks by the Balkan states. The Russians and French
pursued the contradictory policies of condoning the Serb-Bulgarian attack of Turkey, but, when it seemed possible that Bulgaria would take
Constantinople, insisting that the straits remain under Turkey, which
seemed more amenable to pressure than Bulgaria. In effect, the French
and Russians favored ejection of Turkey from the Balkans but not from
the straits, the latter of which was in fact reaffirmed at the London conference in December 1912. When Turkey managed to survive defeat, the
powers reaffirmed their policy of protection by providing advisers for
financial, naval, and military reforms and by rejecting demands of the
Balkan states and Russian maneuvers which might retard or jeopardize
Turkish revival. Russian resistance to the appointment of Sanders can
be interpreted as a protest against this protection of Turkey, although it
was probably motivated more by a desire to split Germany from the
other powers and resist its predominance in Turkey. The British,
French, and German efforts to preserve Turkey persisted into the spring
of 1914.[23]

The powers nonetheless prepared for the eventuality of partition. The
negotiations among the powers over spheres of influence in Turkey anticipated this possibility and the advisers sent to expedite Turkish reforms implied extension of control in Turkey, as the Sanders episode
indicated. Russian plans for naval expansion during the winter of 1914
were based in large measure on the determination to take over Constantinople if a war broke out among the great powers. Turkish recovery and

great power support, however, made partition less likely in the spring of 1914, as indicated by the change in Russian policy toward Turkey from threat to benevolence.[24]

More ominous was the possibility that Turkey might become a protegé of one of the great powers, which, under the circumstances, probably could be only Germany. This eventuality was one of the issues in the Sanders incident. Although anxious to disrupt the cooperation of the other powers in preserving Turkey, the Russians may actually have perceived the danger of German predominance in Turkey as a result of military command at the straits. This was probably not the immediate and conscious goal of German policy makers in sending Sanders, but it was a possible result of the mission since advisers implied influence. British refusal to support the Russian protest indicated both that they did not perceive the Sanders mission as a threat and that they did not place relations with Russia above cooperation with Germany to preserve the Ottoman Empire. But British failure to support Germany against Russia also showed the limits of great-power cooperation in Turkey. The German compromise on the Sanders mission was a demonstration that they were not prepared to risk war in order to establish their predominance in Turkey. But their unwillingness to resist Russia alienated the Turks, and German relations with Turkey during the spring of 1914 became problematical. Thus, Germany was the most likely power to dominate Turkey but was still far from doing so.[25]

Increasingly, it seemed that Turkey would become a participant in Balkan politics. This role became possible when Turkey entered the second Balkan war and became more likely in the maneuvering which followed the war. By the spring of 1914, Turkey was regarded by all the powers as a factor in the Balkan equation. To encourage a Greek-Turkish *détente* as the prerequisite for a new Balkan league (including Turkey, Greece, Rumania, and Serbia), Russia during the spring of 1914 pursued a more friendly policy toward Turkey which culminated in a meeting between Sazonov and a Turkish statesman in May. The Turks themselves sought an understanding with Rumania and Bulgaria as a tool in their dispute with the Greeks over the Aegean Islands. But the Rumanians were anxious to mediate the Turkish-Greek dispute in order to prepare the way for a "Quadruple Alliance" of Greece, Turkey, Rumania, and Serbia against Bulgaria. The Turks then sought unsuccessfully to arrange an alliance with Bulgaria. Anxious to maintain their influence in both Greece and Turkey, the Germans encouraged resolution of the Greek-Turkish dispute and a Greek-Turkish *détente* which would be the first step toward a Turk-Greek-Rumanian alignment against Bulgaria. But Vienna reversed the proposition by opposing a

Turk-Greek *détente* which might facilitate a new Balkan league and by seeking instead a Turk-Bulgarian alignment. Although all these maneuvers had come to little by the spring of 1914, they indicated that Turkey had become an active participant in a fluid political situation.[26]

IMPLICIT BECOMES EXPLICIT

The disturbing after effects of political crises have been compared to the "sequelae" which pathologists observe after serious diseases.[27] The Balkan wars and the crises which followed them had repercussions susceptible to this interpretation. One was the shock of rapid change. The Balkan wars caused the first significant territorial change in Europe since the Congress of Berlin (1878), i.e., in the memory of most Europeans living in 1912. Europe had become accustomed to rapid change in the colonial world but to stability in Europe. The Balkan wars shook this assumption. They presented the curious spectacle of having been predicted but unexpected. The demise of the Ottoman Empire had long been described as inevitable and even imminent. Once the Turks had been expelled from the Balkans, no one seriously considered putting them back. Nonetheless, the collapse of Turkish power in the Balkans came as a shock. What appeared stable might prove illusory. It suggested that all those "inevitable" events which had been predicted but had not occurred should be taken more seriously: the dissolution of the Ottoman Empire in Asia, the decline of the Habsburg Empire, revolution in Russia, and war in Europe. In short, war in the Balkans may have helped transform some platitudes into self-fulfilling prophecies.

The Balkan wars affected European attitudes toward violence. No violence had occurred between European states since 1871 or 1877, if Turkey is defined as a European state. Although they had raised tension, the crises of the decade before the Balkan wars had remained diplomatic. But violence was implied during these crises as it is in all crises. The Balkan wars made violence explicit. Violence had, furthermore, proven successful. Consequently, the relationship between war and diplomacy had been altered. For a generation before the Balkan wars, diplomacy had prevailed over war, and peace had been regarded as normal. Suddenly, success became associated with violence. Diplomacy during the Balkan wars had been least successful in preventing or punishing violence and most successful in preparing it, i.e., in organizing the Balkan league. The great-power alliances were criticized by their members in the same spirit—not because they had not prevented war, but because they had not exploited it.

The possibility of change and premium on violence affected the great-power alliances. Change was perceived variously as an opportunity and a threat. All the powers sought to exploit the situation for their own purposes. The interests of allies were seldom identical and frequently competitive. Paradoxically, these cross purposes between allies tended to neutralize the alliances and thus act as a factor for peace. As long as allies competed and opponents cooperated, the alliances were less likely to confront one another. But the ultimate objective of great-power alliances was power, not peace. Consequently the revelation of this lack of unanimity caused tensions within alliances. Their ominous result was a determination to tighten alliances and coordinate policy in anticipation of the next crisis.

The possibility of change likewise affected great-power authority. Great-power authority was dependent in part on great-power cooperation. Cooperation required stability, i.e., an absence of fundamental problems which implicated the important interests of any of the powers. The possibility of further change, however, involved the interests, if not indeed the existence, of two important states, Austria-Hungary and Turkey. At the same time, it implied opportunities. Consequently, change encouraged rivalries over possible gains and defensivism over possible losses. Some cooperation occurred in pursuit of these objectives: Germany, Britain, and France negotiated over spheres of influence in Turkey, and Austria-Hungary and Russia acted together in supporting Bulgarian interests. Yet these instances were more the result of parallel purposes rather than a basic desire to cooperate as a means of controlling events. As the rivalries intensified, the issues became more partisan. Competition therefore discouraged cooperation, which was essential to great-power authority and control over events. The possibility of fundamental change created a vicious cycle: change encouraged competition which both precluded cooperation to control change and indeed encouraged change. The possibility of change and war which was always implicit in the European system now became explicit.

NOTES

1   Taylor, *Struggle*, p. 485; Ernst C. Helmreich, *The Diplomacy of the Balkan Wars, 1912–1913* (Cambridge, 1938), pp. 36–59.

2   Taylor, *Struggle*, pp. 484, 487–88, 492; Fay, *Origins*, 1:434; *GP*, 33:458–59.

3   See pp. 75–78 above.

4   *GP*, 34:9–10, 24–25.

5 *GP*, 34:63–64, 80–81, 90, 102–3, 129–31, 165–67, 191–93, 220–22, 227–28, 268, 281–83, 309–11, 316–18, 346–48, 367, 409, 414–15, 430, 495–99, 503–4, 528–29, 531–32, 546–47, 551, 554–55, 557–58, 562, 564–65, 595–96, 600, 603–5, 636, 702–3, 718–20, 725, 734–36; Conrad, *Dienstzeit*, 3:144–47; Schulthess, *Geschichtskalender*, p. 614.

6 *GP*, 34:444–48, 742–43, 820–30, 864–65, 873–74, 876–77, 884; *GP*, 35:7–8, 13–14, 19, 33–35, 46–48, 61–62, 66–70, 78, 89–100, 115–18, 120, 122–24, 128–31, 140, 142, 146–48, 207–8, 216–17, 237–39; Conrad, *Dienstzeit*, 3:144–47, 375–76, 402–4.

7 *GP*, 35:142–43, 323–36, 346–53, 356–57, 365–67, 370–71, 378–79; *GP*, 36:24–25, 40, 58–60, 73, 76–77, 84–85; *GP*, 39:383–84; *OU*, 7:116–18, 123, 145, 152–54, 173–74, 178–81, 190.

8 *OU*, 7:188–89, 192–95, 248, 256, 258, 261–62, 265–67, 290, 304, 315–16, 328, 332, 341–46, 350–58, 374–77, 384–91, 396, 405, 414, 427–36, 442–46, 449–67, 470–72, 478–81, 487–88; *OU*, 8:9, 17–18; *GP*, 36:386–91, 397–402, 407, 413, 420–21, 425–66, 486–522, 527–28, 548–50, 559–75, 580–84, 587–88, 598–609, 613–17, 624–33; Fay, *Origins*, 1:470, 473–75; Conrad, *Dienstzeit*, 3:69, 585, 676.

9 *GP*, 33:222–23, 261–62; *GP*, 35:16–18; *GP*, 37:643–49, 822–25, 829–30, 891; *GP*, 38:30–31, 50–52, 54–56, 81–82, 86–87, 98–100, 195; Taylor, *Struggle*, pp. 484–92, 504–5, 508; Fay, *Origins*, 1:434–37, 506–10, 599–600.

10 *GP*, 33:185–86, 258–59, 273–76, 296; *GP*, 34:16, 309–11, 316–18, 367, 409, 414–15, 430; Taylor, *Struggle*, p. 490; Fay, *Origins*, 1:436–37; Conrad, *Dienstzeit*, 3:144–47.

11 *GP*, 34:495–99, 770–71, 779–87, 796, 801–2, 808–10.

12 *GP*, 34:820–27, 873–77; *GP*, 35:7–8, 46–48, 61–62, 66–70, 78, 89–90, 98–99, 115–16, 120–24, 128–31, 142, 146–48, 323–36, 342, 346–53, 356–57, 365–67, 370–79; *GP*, 36:24–25, 40, 58–60, 73, 76–77, 84–85; *GP*, 39:383–84; *OU*, 7:114–18, 123, 145, 152–54, 173–74, 178–81, 190, 198–201, 219–21; Conrad, *Dienstzeit*, 3:375–76.

13 *OU*, 7:188–89, 192–95, 248, 256–58, 261–62, 265–67, 290, 304, 315–16, 328, 332, 341–46, 388–89, 387–403, 442–46, 449–57, 461–67, 470–75; *GP*, 36:386–91, 397–402; Fay, *Origins*, 1:470; Conrad, *Dienstzeit*, 3:69.

14 *GP*, 38:325–27, 331–52; *OU*, 7:916–17, 936, 939–41, 980–84, 1063–69; Conrad, *Dienstzeit*, 3:580–81, 616, 661.

15 *GP*, 39:462–63; *OU*, 7:918–20, 926–29, 936–38, 943–44, 950, 1005, 1009–10, 1026–27; *OU*, 8:12–13, 18, 35–38, 40–41, 61–62, 80–81, 124–26, 146–47, 156–57.

16 *GP*, 39:458–62, 466, 469–71; *OU*, 7:626–29; Fay, *Origins*, 1:490, 497; Taylor, *Struggle*, p. 515.

17 *OU*, 8:931–32.

18 *GP*, 36:425–66, 486–522, 527–28, 548–50, 559–75, 580–84, 587–88, 598–609, 613–17, 624–33, 716–17; *OU*, 8:17–18, 162–65, 169–71, 177, 184–85, 203–4, 207; Conrad, *Dienstzeit*, 3:585, 676.

19 *GP*, 39:483, 494, 497, 516–17, 525–28; *OU*, 7:1018, 1037–38, 1095; *OU*, 8:376–77; Fay, *Origins*, 1:482–87.

20 *OU*, 7:931–35, 961–63, 1053–56; *OU*, 8:1–3; *GP*, 39:460–62; Conrad, *Dienstzeit*, 3:55.

21 *GP*, 36:790–91, 795–97, 931–35, 974–79, 1055–56; *OU*, 7:931–35; *OU*, 7:1–3, 32–35, 45, 49–50, 65–66, 76–77, 80, 83–93, 103–4, 121, 126, 201–2; Fay, *Origins*, 1:491–92.

22 *OU*, 7:974–79, 1006–11, 1022–26, 1041–44, 1073–79, 1085, 1092–93; *OU*, 7:5–6, 13–15, 36–37; *GP*, 36:776–79.

23 *GP*, 31:367, 375–76; *GP*, 33:222–23, 261–62; *GP*, 35:16–18; *GP*, 37:643–49, 822–25, 829–30; *GP*, 38:30–31, 50–56, 81–82, 86–87, 98–100, 195.

24 *GP*, 31:367, 375–76; *GP*, 32:896–900; *GP*, 34:262–63, 281–83; *GP*, 36:795–97; *GP*, 37:120–32, 154–55, 181–84, 196–200, 207–8, 435–44, 447–48, 474–76, 566–83, 589, 596,

606–9, 643–50, 655–57, 660–61, 669–70, 680–82, 686–97, 700, 704–5, 711–34, 739–45; *GP*, 38:41–48, 317–18; *OU*, 7:974–79, 994–96, 1004, 1006, 1020–21, 1028–31, 1051–53, 1056, 1059; *OU*, 8:9–16, 20, 22–24, 31, 35, 45, 49–50, 65–66, 90–91; *BD*, 10:392, 396–97, 780–82, part 2; Taylor, *Struggle*, pp. 486, 508; Fischer, *Griff*, pp. 46–47.

25   *GP*, 31:367, 375–76; *GP*, 38:284–86; Fay, *Origins*, 1:513.

26   *OU*, 7:909–12, 931, 939, 961–63, 974–79, 994–96, 1004, 1006, 1019–21, 1028–32, 1035, 1038–39, 1046–53, 1056, 1059, 1078–79, 1085, 1087–90, 1096–97; *OU*, 8:9–16, 19–31, 35, 45, 49–52, 65–66, 81, 86–91, 99, 103–4, 114, 126; *GP*, 36:365–69, 569, 755–60, 793–97, 800–1, 815–25; *GP*, 39:481–87, 506; Conrad, *Dienstzeit*, 3:644; Fay, *Origins*, 1:541.

27   Penfield Roberts, *The Quest for Security, 1715–1740* (New York, 1947), p. 240.

V / DETERMINANT, DISTRACTION, OR DEVICE?

The Influence of Domestic Politics on Foreign Policy (1912–June 1914)

THE POSSIBLE INTERPRETATIONS

An understanding of the international behavior of Germany and the other powers on the eve of war necessitates an analysis of the relationship between foreign policy and domestic politics. Several general interpretations suggest themselves. Politics can be perceived as the primary determinant of foreign policy. Alternatively, politics can be regarded either as an unfortunate distraction or as a useful tool of foreign policy. As a prerequisite to such an analysis it is necessary to examine the most serious domestic political issues and to establish the domestic responses to foreign questions. Only then is it possible to suggest some tentative conclusions about the role of domestic politics in the formulation of German foreign policy on the eve of the First World War.

POLARIZATION, POLITICIZATION, PARALYZATION: THE POLITICAL CONTEXT

Germany had profound domestic problems. The most severe was the question of political reform, i.e., whether or not the country's political institutions would be adjusted to allow greater political power to the masses. The country was also plagued by economic problems, in particular the pressure of unions for improved working conditions and wages, tariff and tax reform, and inflation. Germans were likewise divided over the question of arms increases. In large measure, these problems were the result of Germany's rapid industrialization and urbanization, which caused the domestic political institutions established in 1871 to conform less and less with the aspirations of many Germans. In short, the problems and weaknesses were the result and cost of precisely those developments which had made Germany powerful. Power and problems were inextricably bound.

Political divisions were highlighted by the Reichstag elections of January 1912. At issue were two types of questions: economic problems—particularly inflation—were central, especially for the Social Democrats, and political problems—particularly conservative resistance to reform—agitated the parties of both Left and Middle. The Social Democrats ran on a platform of tax reform, inflation control, civil rights, and opposition to war, while the parties of the Middle—National Liberals and Center—allied on the question of tax reform against the

Right. In general, Left and Middle cooperated against the Right. The government expected and sought to deter a Social Democratic victory. Bethmann urged the supraparty goals of economic prosperity, political harmony, and national security. By criticizing the Social Democrats as a threat to national unity, the government unsuccessfully endeavored to disrupt cooperation between the parties of the Middle against the Right. Likewise, the government was disappointed in its hopes that foreign policy issues—particularly a success in the second Moroccan crisis— would favor the Conservatives. For their part, the Social Democrats had specifically postponed resistance to the government's policy during the crisis to avoid being cast as the scapegoat for failure. The election results in fact turned out to be a striking success for the Left, a moderate setback for the Middle, but a serious defeat for the Right.

The reactions to such results were predictable. The Social Democrats interpreted their victory as evidence of worker and middle-class impatience with the existing system and therefore demanded reform of taxes, tariffs, suffrage, social legislation, and working conditions. Representing the moderate wing of the party, Social Democratic leaders perceived the election both as proof of the wisdom of their gradualist policy of working within the parliamentary system and as a warning to the government against reactionary responses. The parties of the Middle were ambivalent. They regarded their tactic of cooperating against the Right as justified by the Conservative losses but were disturbed by their own loss of Reichstag seats. When the unifying impulse of opposition to the Right on domestic issues was replaced by the issues of foreign policy and arms increases during 1912 and 1913, the National Liberals and Center tended to gravitate toward the Right against the Social Democrats. The parties of the Right were understandably embittered. They perceived a threat to the monarchical system and anathematized democracy, liberalism, parliamentary government, the press, capitalism, the Jews, and the unpatriotic proletariat. Some demanded the reimposition of strictures on the Social Democrats and even advocated a coup d' état, while others criticized Bethmann for weakness in defending Conservative interests. Rather than encouraging an inclination to change the existing system, the election made the Conservatives even more determined to resist reform. The election made it increasingly difficult for the government to pursue its supraparty policy and Bethmann had to tack even more shrewdly between the extremes. He announced that he would take neither the radical nor reactionary alternative. He continued to support moderate social legislation and resisted reimposition of anti-Social Democratic laws, for which he was criticized by the Conservatives; at the same time, he urged incorporation of the Social Democrats within the existing system by encouraging mutual understanding of Left and Right. But he resisted fundamental change advocated by the Left and even moderate change advocated by the Middle, because it would divide the country. Instead, as a pragmatic conservative committed to preserving the existing system, he granted small concessions to discourage larger demands.[1]

The election raised the question of whether the Social Democratic victory presaged a leftward trend or merely a swing of the pendulum. Events of the following year and one-half (January 1912–July 1913) could be interpreted as a continued leftward trend, whereas the remaining year of peace (August 1913–August 1914) marked a return toward the right. The shift to the left seemed confirmed during the arms debate during which the Left and Middle disagreed on whether arms should be increased but reestablished their alliance on the question of how increases should be financed.[2]

The general method of financing arms increases was established by a demand of the National Liberals and Center in June 1912 for a property tax. Since this approach made it difficult to win approval of the conservative elements dominating the Bundesstaaten, the government decided in the autumn of 1912 that taxes on capital gains and inheritance were the only politically practical recourse. It soon became clear, however, that the Bundesstaaten could not agree on which of these alternatives was less undesirable. When the Prussian ministry opposed an inheritance tax which it feared the Social Democrats would use as a precedent, Bethmann managed to win the Ministry's begrudging approval of a capital gains tax. The other Bundesstaaten, however, favored an inheritance tax in preference to a capital gains tax, which they perceived as a threat to their autonomy from the imperial government. Bethmann found an escape in the recourse of a one-time arms tax on capital gains which received reluctant agreement from the Bundesstaaten in March 1913. But a new problem emerged when it was realized that the one-time tax would cover the large increases but not the regular running costs, and Bethmann again advocated a capital gains tax despite the opposition of the southern Bundesstaaten. He demonstrated a second time that he could not afford to alienate the Prussian Conservatives and the main supporters of the arms increases.

The funding problem was less serious in the Reichstag as long as some type of property tax was advocated, and it accepted the principle of a one-time capital gains tax to cover the increases. The regular running costs of the military, however, presented some difficulties. The Social Democrats unsuccessfully advocated an inheritance tax, as the Prussian Conservatives expected. Efforts of the Left and Middle to alter the details of spending were rejected by the government as an intrusion into the army's authority. A Social Democratic attempt to force the ruling families of the Bundesstaaten to pay taxes was also parried by Bethmann with the threat of dissolution. A Center party proposal for an imperial capital gains tax was finally passed on 30 June 1913, with the support of Left and Center. Bethmann then prevailed upon a reluctant Bundesrat to accept the method.

The funding issue and arms increases had different implications for the parties. Having supported both funding and increases, the parties of the Middle registered an unmitigated success. For the Social Democrats, who had opposed the increases but supported the funding, the result was mixed. In voting for the funding, the Social Democrats broke their tradition of opposing financial support of the existing system. They did so out of tactical considerations—the concern that new elections could increase the mandate of parties in favor of the arms increases and thus funding at the expense of the workers; the method decided upon in June 1913 at least had the virtue of making those most in favor of the arms increases—upper and middle classes—bear the largest financial burden. For the parties of the Right which supported the increases but opposed the funding, the result was also mixed. The Conservatives and conservative wing of the Center party (representing big agriculture and heavy industry) were alienated not by the details of funding—i.e., inheritance versus capital gains taxes—but by the principle of a Reichstag property tax altogether. They were bitter for precisely the reason that the Social Democrats had supported the funding, namely, that the rich bore most of the costs. More broadly, the Right perceived in the Reichstag's action an undesirable expansion of its powers, an extension of democracy and parliamentary government, and a defeat at the hands of the Middle and Left.

For the government, the arms increases and funding also had mixed results. Bethmann won passage of the increases which had not been certain at the start. The method of funding was basically what he had regarded as necessary and had therefore sought, since it was the approach desired by the Middle parties—a property tax—and avoided the least desirable method for the Prussian Right—an inheritance tax. But, because the Right was dissatisfied by any property tax whatsoever, Bethmann could not achieve his objective of avoiding their opposition. In the increases-funding issues, he was confronted with a dilemma. He could not win passage of the increases with the support of the Right alone and therefore had to gain the backing of the Middle parties, which, however, insisted on a property tax as the method of funding. In effect, the choice was both increases and property tax or neither. Bethmann opted for both but could not persuade the Right, which directed part of its bitterness at Bethmann and caused him to consider resignation during the summer of 1913. Despite the necessities of the situation, Bethmann was not happy himself with the outcome of the funding issue since, like the Conservatives, he felt that the Left and Middle parties in the Reichstag had become overbearing because of their victory in the funding issue. But he felt that the alternative of new elections was unacceptable since—unlike the Social Democrats—he feared that a new Reichstag would be even less disposed toward the Right. His only hope was that the embitterment which had been caused by the increases-funding issues would lessen after the Reichstag session ended in the summer of 1913.[3]

Tension rose, however, rather than fell after the summer of 1913. The victory of the Left and Middle in the funding question was followed not by further successes but by failures and frustrations. A reaction began to occur from the Right which had suffered setbacks since the elections of 1912. Accordingly, the summer of 1913 marked a turning point in German politics.

A Conservative reaction began in response to the elections of 1912 when efforts were initiated to consolidate the forces of the Right. The Conservatives represented the interests of industry by introducing anti-labor legislation into the Reichstag. The leaders of agriculture and heavy industry sought to establish cooperation by submerging their differences over agricultural tariffs and by agreeing on general objectives and opponents. They criticized the government, democracy, liberalism, and the masses, and advocated an association of agriculture, industry, the middle class, and nationalistically inclined labor which would favor industry and agriculture, as well as institute social legislation desired by the middle class. Although agriculture had traditionally been represented by the Conservatives, heavy industry had only a few supporters among the National Liberals and conservative wing of the Center party, who favored industry in economic and tariff questions but not in social legislation. Finding themselves isolated and insufficiently represented politically, agriculture and heavy industry moved closer together, although little formal cooperation had been established by the beginning of 1913. Meanwhile, the hypernationalistic Pan Germans were seeking contact with agriculture but had made it only indirectly by 1913. Despite these efforts, little was accomplished. The antilabor legislation introduced by the Conservatives was voted down overwhelmingly in 1912 and 1913 by the Reichstag, and the government continued to pursue its moderate policy in social questions.[4]

The Reichstag's behavior in the funding question during the summer of 1913 seemed to confirm Conservative concerns and galvanized the

Right into action. Agriculture and heavy industry criticized the property taxes as confiscatory and discriminatory since they affected only a small portion of the population. They claimed that the Reichstag's imposition of the tax constituted an augmentation of the Reichstag's power, encroached upon the independence of the Bundesstaaten, and demonstrated Bethmann's weakness in resisting parliamentary, democratic and Social Democratic elements. The passage of the arms increases favored by the Right had removed any reluctance in attacking their opponents in the Reichstag, and the funding vote seemed to indicate that danger was imminent and the necessity for action immediate.[5]

These pressures resulted in a coalescence of the Right. Representatives of the heavy industry, main agricultural, and middle-class pressure groups met at the end of August 1913. They demanded the preservation of the existing social system, more social legislation for the middle class, and, above all, a campaign against the Social Democrats. The meeting received considerable attention in the press, was regarded as an effort to politicize the middle class in a conservative direction, and was criticized by Social Democrats and middle class liberals as representing the interests of the rich. Heavy industry representatives sought to avoid the old stumbling block of agricultural tariffs by resisting the demands of agriculture for increases but by cooperating against the demands of the Middle and Left for reduction of tariffs. At the annual convention of the heavy industry pressure group (Central Organization of Industrialists) in September 1913, it was again argued that the dangers of continued democratization, mass pressures, "social struggle," and civil war could be resisted only if action were taken immediately by the government. Agriculture and heavy industry also cooperated in opposing an extension of social legislation—particularly unemployment insurance—and even argued for dismantling existing legislation. The first direct contact was established in the summer of 1913 between the main agricultural pressure group (Farmers' League) and the Pan Germans, who immediately agreed on the serious political situation and the need for a conservative alliance against democracy and socialism. Thereafter the League would support the Pan Germans on foreign policy questions, while the Pan Germans would support the League on agricultural tariffs, and they would cooperate on press propaganda. Although the agreement could not be announced openly, since it might alienate Pan German middle-class supporters in western and southern Germany, the Pan Germans thereby moved toward their objective of politicizing the economic pressure groups.[6]

While this sense of urgency and activism pervaded the Right, enervation spread on the Left. Paradoxically, the Right perceived the Left as a greater danger in its fantasies just when the Left became less of a threat in fact. The explanation for this paradox may lie in the Right's concern for old dangers rather than awareness of the doldrums in which the Left was languishing. Despite their great victories in the elections of 1912 and the funding debate of 1913, the Social Democrats had won few practical successes. Reform had been deterred not only by increased conservative resistance but also the inconducive circumstances produced by the Balkan wars. Military expansion diverted energies and transformed other issues. The Balkan wars caused a recession which created economic conditions disadvantageous to labor. Unemployment and increases in the cost of living reduced union funds and made unions less inclined to strike. Repercussions were felt in the autumn of 1913. The discovery that the rate of increase in party membership had fallen off for the first time in history caused a shock within the party. Election setbacks in October 1913 and declining appeal to traditional Social Democratic groups reinforced the fact of failure. The resulting despondency caused demands for action in the form of a moderate proposal for increasing membership and a radical demand for a mass strike. The debate over what was wrong with the party culminated during the annual convention of September 1913 in a cleavage between the moderates (including the executive) and the radicals. The effects of these events on German politics were twofold: at once Social Democratic energies were vitiated by internecine disputes rather than concentrated on reform, but the Left became more radical and thus reinforced the polarization of German politics.[7]

While the radical Left advocated a mass strike against the state, some members of the radical Right demanded an elitist strike against the state. In order to weaken or paralyze the Reichstag, some Conservatives urged reduction of Reichstag suffrage and others establishment of an upper house on the basis of economic groups. Both proponents and opponents of such changes recognized that they could be instituted only in a crisis and would risk revolution. More ominous was the agitation for a coup d'état which centered around the crown prince and was urged by the Pan Germans. The Pan Germans had been in indirect contact with the crown prince at least since 1912 and aware of his opposition to Bethmann at least since the second Moroccan crisis. Direct contact was established when the crown prince demonstrated his sympathy for the Pan Germans by sending a greeting to their annual congress in September 1913. Meanwhile, relations between the crown prince and the chancellor became increasingly strained. The Pan Germans had sought since 1912 to win the crown prince over to their idea of a coup d'état, but their most notable attempt was a memorandum by the Pan German General Gebsattel which the crown prince received in the autumn of 1913. Perceiving suffrage, Jews, and the press as Germany's three basic problems, Gebsattel demanded a coup which would require either a successful war or, preferably, a move against the Reichstag. Although haste was required because the army might become unreliable, Gebsattel doubted that the government was capable of the necessary decisiveness. The crown prince forwarded the memorandum with his approval to the kaiser and Bethmann. Since new efforts were being made by the Right to force Bethmann's resignation, the crown prince may have hoped either to force Bethmann to the right or to alienate him from the kaiser.

Bethmann reacted immediately and lengthily. He admitted that criticism of his government had been widespread but sought to disarm it by denying Gebsattel's assertions that the government had capitulated to the Reichstag. He nonetheless opposed a move against the Reichstag, Jews, and press both because the German federal system was inconducive to a coup and because a coup would risk revolution. Bethmann also sought to deflect Gebsattel's criticism that the government was determined to preserve peace at any price by cautioning the crown prince that a European war would risk not only the dynasty but also "the future of Germany" and would be both "foolhardy and criminal" unless the "honor, safety and future of Germany" were at stake. The kaiser's reply to the crown prince departed from Bethmann's in detail and style but not in essence. He granted Gebsattel's criticism of universal suffrage, the Reichstag, Jews, and press but rejected his pessimism. He also agreed with Gebsattel's complaints about the government's lack of energy in domestic affairs but saw no better candidate than Bethmann and defended his foreign policy. Above all the kaiser rejected Gebsattel's suggestion of a coup d'état as more dangerous than a revolution. Although Gebsattel's initiative failed because of the kaiser's refusal, it was not without importance in the polarization of German politics. As the rejection of a mass strike by the moderate Social Democrats forced its advocates to seek more radical means, the opposition to a coup d'état made the extreme Right more desperate. A unifying point for radical dissent on the Right, the crown prince remained a potential political power and warning to Bethmann and indeed the kaiser. The incident therefore made Bethmann and the kaiser aware of conservative bitterness and may in fact have affected Bethmann's policy in the events which followed.[8]

Bethmann and the kaiser were forced by the so-called Zabern (Saverne) affair of October–December 1913, to take public stands on some of the general issues raised by Gebsattel. Since the specific incident—excesses of German soldiers toward Alsatian civilians—was insignificant, its conversion into a serious political crisis was an indication of existing tensions. The affair was complicated by the efforts of different groups to exploit it for their own purposes. The Conservatives sought to use it to defeat the Reichstag and dismiss Bethmann, while the parties of the Middle and Left tried through it to extend parliamentary control over the army. Where the majority of Germans stood is open to debate but probably most supported the Reichstag against the army. When the issue became Reichstag versus army, the kaiser sided with the army and rigidly rejected Reichstag criticism as an encroachment on his power. Opinion among conservative bureaucrats was not monolithic but generally supported the army. Although convinced that the army was wrong and expected by some civilian bureaucrats and the Reichstag to support them, Bethmann opted for the army and the kaiser. His behavior has understandably been interpreted by liberal historians as a betrayal of Reichstag and nation. But, while his conservative temperament may have been a factor when confronted with an unavoidable choice between conservative and parliamentary systems, the decision was probably necessary if he was to retain the kaiser's support against conservative criticism.

The affair had important implications for German politics. It clarified the nature of parliamentary government in Germany. In joining together against the Right as they had done during the funding debate of the previous summer and in defending the Reichstag's powers, the Middle and Left identified themselves with the Reichstag. When they equated the Reichstag with the nation, they deepened the rift between ruled and conservative rulers. By seeking a renewed Reichstag success but suffering a setback, the parties of the Middle and Left demonstrated the limits of Reichstag power. The Middle made clear the limits of its commitment to parliamentary government by not supporting the Left's demand that Bethmann resign as if he were responsible to the Reichstag. The parties of the Middle were ambivalent and preferred to accept the fact of limited parliamentary government rather than the risks of genuine democracy. The affair marked a turning point in favor of the Right which had been gathering its forces since the defeat of the previous summer. The event constituted a victory of military over civilians not only in the Reichstag but also in the bureaucracy—an ominous result in a period of increasing armaments—and gave the impression to other powers that Germany was more than ever in the hands of reactionaries and militarists. Finally, the affair altered Bethmann's position. In opting for the kaiser and army, Bethmann alienated the Middle and Left but was unable to win the support of the Right and thereby became more dependent than ever on the kaiser. Paradoxically, his tenure of office may actually have become more secure since the crown prince's influence was slightly reduced after the affair. But the basic fact remained that

Bethmann had been forced to move right and his maneuvering room had been further narrowed.[9]

The conservative success in the Zabern affair was reinforced by events during the first half of 1914. The Right continued to consolidate. By the spring of 1914, the Pan Germans and Farmers' League openly supported one another. Planned since mid-1912 in response to the election of 1912, the Prussian League (*Preussenbund*) was founded in January 1914 by representatives of heavy industry, conservatives, churches, and military to maintain the status quo in Prussia as a bulwark against democracy and liberalism; it advocated alterations in the Reichstag, was hostile to Bethmann, and was perceived by Social Democrats as sympathetic to a conservative coup d'état. The crown prince remained a potential political force as the openly acknowledged rallying point for reactionary elements. The Right, meanwhile, increased its pressure for discontinuation of the government's social policy and succeeded when the government announced in the Reichstag at the beginning of 1914 that no further social legislation would be introduced, although existing legislation would be maintained. Bitterness aroused by social questions was intensified by economic problems. Increasing inflation and unemployment made more social legislation desirable to the Left, whereas shortages of capital and predictions of recession made employers resist greater expenditures. Although it won no further resounding success, the Right was probably in a more favorable position in the spring of 1914 than it had been since the elections of 1912.[10]

The German political situation considerably reduced the government's power. Bethmann is perhaps better understood as a symptom than cause, as acted upon more than actor. His choices were severely limited by the forces and conflicts which neither he nor any other politician could have altered. In a general sense, his policies were a common denominator of these forces, at least in the negative sense of what he could not do. It has been argued that his main consideration was to preserve national unity for the specific purpose of preparing for war.[11] But his motives were probably less specific or self-conscious—he was probably less a planner than a pragmatist and realist. He certainly had the bureaucrat's distaste for politics and later complained about a kind of "imperial enervation" caused by the parties' anachronistic programs, sensationalism, materialism, and fear of reform. This politics of enervation seemed to necessitate his "policy of the diagonal," namely navigation between extremes and neutralization of conflicting elements.[12] Such a tactic was facilitated by the conflicting interests of the parties and groups. On domestic questions, the Middle and Left cooperated, while the Middle and Right cooperated on foreign and military questions.

Bethmann's was a policy of tactics rather than strategy, of accommodation rather than achievement, of conservation rather than change. But just as the politics of enervation required the policy of the diagonal so the policy of the diagonal also presupposed the politics of enervation. The policy of the diagonal and indeed Bethmann's political survival altogether were possible only as long as German politics were impacted and neither extreme prevailed; he was successful in the sense that no open breach occurred before the war. But what made his policy both necessary and successful also precluded any reconciliation and genuine national unity. He could play off opponents precisely because they were irreconcilable; had they been reconcilable, his policy and perhaps his tenure in office would have been neither necessary nor possible. Consequently, the government could seek to conceal, divert, or neutralize but could not remove domestic conflicts.

German politics were therefore characterized by paralysis, polarization, and politicization. The pressures for reaction and revolution had been neutralized and neither was probably likely without war. German problems were, however, no more or less severe than those of the other powers. French politics was embittered by a struggle over national priorities; the Irish question caused serious tensions in Great Britain; and the Austro-Hungarian subnationalities became increasingly restive. Although Russian domestic politics were not particularly unsettled during the spring of 1914, it was one of the common assumptions from ruling chancelleries to revolutionary cells that revolution would erupt again in Russia. The general prewar European domestic immobility was consequently the result of a tense impasse rather than tranquil stability, a condition inconducive to calm evaluation of international politics.

THE DOMESTIC IMPULSES: POLITICAL RESPONSES TO FOREIGN AND MILITARY ISSUES

An evaluation of the influence of domestic politics on foreign and strategic policies involves two aspects: domestic responses to diplomatic-military questions and government reactions to these domestic responses. The responses of the German public to diplomatic and military questions are examined in this section, the government's reaction to public opinion in the next. From mid-1911 to mid-1914, the German public was confronted with a series of diplomatic and military incidents (international crises, arms bills, and colonial negotiations) which stimulated responses to the general issues of imperialism, Germany's role and aspirations in the world, war, perception of Germany's allies and opponents, and the relationship between domestic and diplomatic questions.

The second Moroccan crisis (July-November 1911) focused the public's attention on foreign affairs. Response to the government's initiative was enthusiastic from the Right, Pan Germans, National Liberals, and heavy industry; moderately enthusiastic from the Center; mixed from the Progressives; and outspokenly critical only from the Social Democrats. Even moderates—such as the shipping magnate Ballin—applauded the government's activism. When it appeared, however, that the government was seeking concessions from the French outside rather than inside Morocco as they had been led to expect, the Pan Germans, National Liberals, and industrialists involved in Morocco protested and accused the government of weakness. Although less wed to concessions in Morocco and critical of the hard liners, the moderates nonetheless insisted on some concessions. After the government acceded to a British warning against demands in Morocco, criticism from the Right and Pan Germans intensified. The mass of Social Democrats and particularly the party executive remained staunchly opposed to concessions in Morocco or elsewhere; they nonetheless sought to avoid being placed in the position of antipatriotic opposition by arguing that Germany had a right to participation in world trade and therefore advocated an open door policy. When the crisis reached its acme (in September 1911), the press of the Right, Middle, Pan Germans, and even the Lutheran church assumed the hard line, while the Center and government-inspired press was more cautious but still firm. The left liberal press was critical of the Middle, Right, and Pan Germans for their talk of war and urged an understanding with France. The Social Democratic leaders considered but rejected the possibility of a strike during the crisis. The conflict of views was illustrated clearly when it was rumored that the kaiser and Bethmann were restraining Kiderlen: the conservative and Pan German press (possibly with encouragement of Kiderlen) criticized the kaiser, while the Middle and Left press defended him.[13]

The concessions won from the French (in November 1911) were regarded by the German public in general as unsatisfactory. Those groups which had had the greatest expectations—Right, Pan Germans, heavy industry, military, National Liberals, and some members of the Center—were particularly bitter and even groups which traditionally supported the government were critical. Only the Social Democratic press applauded the outcome and enjoyed the disappointment of their opponents. The government sought to dampen the criticism by presenting the agreement with France as a success. The critics remained unappeased and anxious for Bethmann's displacement but moderated their opposition because of domestic reasons—namely, the need to present a united front against the Social Democrats in the elections of January 1912. The Social Democratic electoral victory can be seen as a vindication of their policy and an indication of mass opposition to the Moroccan venture, but their own strategy argues against this interpretation. The Social Democrats perceived the affair as a government effort to influence the elections with a foreign success. They therefore played down the crisis in order to minimize mass involvement and avoided the role of antipatriots who would be cast as scapegoats for failure. Thus the elections of January 1912 were probably not so much a vote against imperialism as a demonstration that many Germans were less interested in imperialism than the domestic problems (particularly inflation) emphasized by the Social Democrats. Nonetheless the electoral failure of the Right and Middle can be regarded as an indication that their hard line during the crisis and nationalistic slogans during the election were not appealing to the masses.[14]

The debate over arms increases (February–July 1913) raised foreign issues in a more general sense. The Right, Pan Germans, National Liberals, and nationalist press strongly favored increases for which they propagandized by establishing an organ, the Army League (*Wehrverein*), in part in reaction to the failure of the second Moroccan crisis; when the increases were finally passed, they claimed it as a success and vindication for the Army League's activities. The Center was typically ambivalent, criticizing the cost but regarding the increases as necessary. The liberal press was initially critical but gradually became less so. The Social Democrats in general opposed the "arms madness" and issued a joint protest with the French Socialists against the actions of the ruling classes of both countries. The German Social Democrats were hardly monolithic, however. Although they resisted large increases, the moderates were not opposed to increases in principle. The party decided that it could not stop the increases and therefore sought to minimize their undesirability by placing the financial burden on those who were most anxious for them, the rich. Thus the Social Democrats voted alone against the increases but were joined by the Middle parties in determining the method of funding. The alignment on the increases indicated fundamentally divergent views of international relations. The parties of the Right and Middle generally regarded international relations as competition and potential conflict which necessitated military strength, whereas the Left viewed this approach as dangerous and most remained critical of the government's foreign policy.[15]

These divergent views of international relations were reflected in perceptions of German imperialism. Proponents—generally the parties of the Right and Middle—perceived it as the result of compelling or commendable impulses. The economic impulse—need for markets and raw materials but only infrequently for investment opportunities—was commonly seen. Although it was often argued that Germany needed space for its excess population, land was generally not demanded. The political claims of national power and prestige were offered as frequently as economic arguments. Cultural, spiritual, and racial superiority were common. Determinist arguments—social Darwinism, historical or economic necessity—were used alongside assertions of justice. The validity and consistency of these demands were less important than was the fact of their wide currency among members of the upper and middle classes.[16]

The parties varied in their attitudes toward Germany's international role and aspirations. The Right generally favored imperialism. Although they usually supported imperialism and took a strong stand in instances like the second Moroccan crisis, the conservatives and agricultural organizations were criticized by more-committed imperialists as being insufficiently fervent. The Pan Germans and Army League were the most outspoken imperialists and advocates of German international activism. Heavy industry which frequently had connections with the Pan Germans and National Liberals was largely imperialist. The Lutheran church likewise favored imperialism. The Middle parties were less monolithic. The National Liberals were overwhelmingly imperialist. The Center party was more cautious but in general supported imperialism. Although Progressives were more reserved, they were not openly opposed and there was a vocal group of liberal imperialists. The only opposition to imperialism came on the Left yet even there divergence existed. General criticism but qualified acceptance under certain humanitarian conditions characterized the moderate Social Democratic position. The only outright opposition occurred on the extreme Left. Thus there were differences of detail which seemed considerable at the time and constitute the stuff of which political conflict is usually made. There was, however, little disagreement on the general issue of German expansion and international activism.[17]

The issue of German imperialism became more immediate on the eve of war. The rapid rise of German economic power after 1870 was accompanied by a corresponding increase of German international trade and penetration into the Balkans, Near East, and even developed states such as France and Belgium. This increase had continued until the end of the first decade of the twentieth century, at which point German international trade and imperialism began to meet with increasing complications. German problems were due in part to a shortage of capital for international investment. In contrast with the British and French economies whose earlier development freed greater capital for foreign investment, the German economy absorbed most of the available capital itself. Consequently, the Germans had greater difficulty competing for commercial influence in the underdeveloped areas of the Balkans, Near East, and Africa which were still available for competition. But German difficulties were caused also by exclusion from markets in Europe—especially in France and Russia—and the colonies of their competitors. Both these considerations seemed to augment the importance of a colonial empire from which Germany could not be excluded either by dictum or financial competition. Although negotiations with France and Britain over colonies in Africa produced formal agreements, little tangible success accrued as far as committed German imperialists were concerned. Worse yet, Germany's hold on its traditional spheres of influence—especially Turkey—seemed to be jeopardized. Markets and raw materials seemed less available at a time when they appeared more necessary. Whether the situation can be described as a crisis in German imperialism is debatable, but the prospects for a continued rise of German international economic influence at the previous rapid rate were clearly unpromising. These disappointing prospects caused increasing criticism of the government from the imperialists. Thus imperialism had become not only more prominent but also more problematical by 1914.[18]

The attitudes of the various elements of German society toward foreign affairs were determined not only by foreign but also by domestic considerations. In rare agreement, Right and Left perceived foreign and domestic politics as competitive. Conservatives, Pan Germans, heavy industry, and some National Liberals sought to obscure domestic problems and maintain the existing social order by achieving foreign successes; the prosperity and prestige thought possible through imperialism might defuse demands for domestic reform. The Social Democrats sought to resist this tactic—the "export of social problems"—by concentrating the masses' attention on domestic problems. In contrast to Right and Left, the Middle parties perceived foreign and domestic questions as compatible if not complementary and advocated both imperialism and liberalism. In arguing their positions, all parties naturally claimed to represent the "nation" and "people." The Right argued that the people preferred imperialism to reform, the Left reform to imperialism, and the Middle, both. Although these assertions had little to do with the actual attitudes of the masses who were not consulted, they did indicate that the parties felt compelled to speak in the people's name. Consequently, as in the case of domestic politics on the eve of war, the discussion of foreign issues became increasingly polarized and politicized.[19]

The German public's perception of the other powers varied with the circumstances. Its attitude changed less in regard to France than the other powers. During the second Moroccan crisis, which began as a Franco-German confrontation, some German papers (particularly on the Right) spoke of the possibility of a conflict and mutual animosities persisted after the crisis, but most bitterness was diverted to Britain after its intervention. Economic rivalries in the Balkans and Turkey, as well as difficulties for German firms in France, precluded improvement in the German public's view of France. During the debate over arms increases, France and Russia were presented by proponents as a threat to Germany and anti-French feeling was reinforced by French financial support for Russian arms increases in 1914. Antipathy toward France consequently remained during the prewar years but it was mitigated by perceptions of French weakness, decadence, and even pacifism such that France was seldom seen as the main enemy.[20]

The view of Britain shifted radically between 1911 and 1914. Seen by many Germans as the cause of their failure during the second Moroccan crisis, Britain was regarded as Germany's main enemy and the possibility of an Anglo-German war was frequently discussed in the press. This bitterness was perpetuated by incidents after the crisis had passed and by propaganda for naval increases. But Anglophobia declined during the debate over arms increases, when Germany's continental foes were perceived as the main enemies. This decline of Anglo-German tension in the German press was reinforced by Anglo-German cooperation during the Balkan wars, negotiations over colonial questions, and lack of direct conflicts. Although Britain was frequently used as the scapegoat for German colonial failures by German imperialists, the animosity felt widely toward Britain during the second Moroccan crisis had largely dissipated by the spring of 1914.[21]

German opinion of Russia and Britain followed reverse patterns between 1911 and 1914. Hardly mentioned during the second Moroccan crisis, and only an indirect opponent in the Balkan wars, Russia was perceived along with France as the main enemy during the debates over arms increases. The Sanders episode increased Russo-German tensions and was presented in the German press as a German defeat. But the real turning point in the perception of Russia by the German press and parties seems to have been the so-called press feud of the winter of 1914, during which bitter and belligerent statements by the press of both countries were widely circulated, and some German papers predicted that Russia would become more aggressive in several years when its arms increases had been completed. The Right and Middle press continued to discuss the Russian danger during the spring, and the Pan Germans urged new German arms increases because the Russians and French were planning to attack Germany. The perception of Russian opinion changed as a result of the incident: whereas in March the German press had viewed Russian bellicosity as limited to a few chauvinists, it tended to blame the government and Russian opinion in general by the spring of 1914. Russo-German tension was reinforced by simultaneous disagreements in negotiations over a commercial treaty. Although generally anti-Russian, the Left press sought to dampen the tension, and the principal Social Democratic paper, *Vorwärts*, even laid the blame on the German press. Russia had evolved between 1911 and 1914 in the perception of the German press and parties from least to most dangerous opponent.[22]

Incidents such as the second Moroccan crisis, arms increases, the Balkan wars, and the Russo-German press feud necessarily raised the issue of war. The most outspokenly militant in their advocacy and indeed idealization of war were the Pan Germans. The Conservatives, Lutheran church, National Liberals, and heavy industry romanticized war somewhat less but used it freely as a threat during crises. The Middle parties' press tended to speak of war in more abstract and vague terms but nonetheless as the necessary *ultima ratio*. Only the Left press consistently opposed war and criticized those who threatened or idealized it. It is difficult to know where the mass of Germans stood. Since it was discussed increasingly in the press after the second Moroccan crisis, war was probably seen as a more real possibility, but even the Pan Germans recognized that the masses probably regarded it as undesirable. It is clear, however, that the majority of the parties and press from Right through Middle—i.e., the articulate and powerful—increasingly discussed the eventuality of war as 1914 approached.[23]

This acknowledgement of war is susceptible to contradictory interpretations. There is much evidence of confidence in the widespread acceptance of war among leading Germans and the assertion of German political and military power, economic success, and spiritual, racial, and cultural superiority can even be viewed as arrogance. But there is also considerable evidence of anxiety. All the complaints about German imperial failures and frustrations demonstrated concern about Germany's future. Encirclement and Franco-Russian arms were seen as threats. Predictions of massive growth by new world powers such as Russia and the United States boded poorly for Germany's future economic position. Such weaknesses as the shortage of capital even indicated that Germany might have trouble competing with the old European powers like France. Germany's domestic political problems were interpreted in different ways by all parties but by none as optimistic. Indeed, the Pan Germans and other propagandists of the Right and Middle frequently justified their assertions of German power as necessary to counter increasing popular pessimism. It is correctly argued that some of these statements of anxiety were only tactics to achieve immediate purposes, such as arms increases, but most were expressed in ways and moments which indicate real concerns and even pessimism espoused for tactical purposes probably had a permanent and cumulative effect. Therefore, German public opinion was characterized by both arrogance and anxiety. Indeed, the striking feature of German public opinion on the eve of war is precisely its duality. Frequently, both arrogance and anxiety are expressed in the same statement, particularly from the Right and Middle. For the Pan Germans, the choice was simply between world power and defeat. The National Liberal Stresemann wrote in 1914 that any nation which did not grow would decline. Another National Liberal leader, Bassermann, claimed that Germany had to expand or get bogged down in Europe. Former Chancellor Bülow perceived similar alternatives, as did intellectuals like Hans Delbrück and Max Weber. This polarization of alternatives became increasingly typical of German public opinion, as it did of German leaders. Thus, neither arrogance nor anxiety but ambivalence and oscillation between the two characterized German attitudes on the eve of war.[24]

It is often argued—particularly by liberal historians—that greater liberalization of German society might have prevented some of the excesses of German international behavior. This contention is based on the assumption that German anxiety and aggressiveness were due to the influence of the monarchy, bureaucracy, army, and conservative upper class, especially the Junkers. It assumes conversely that greater influence by the middle and lower classes would have significantly modified German foreign policy. The ruling classes undoubtedly ruled in prewar Germany and had a high degree of control over the conduct of foreign policy. But it is not certain that German international behavior was due exclusively to their influence and would have been altered by greater liberalization. The leading beneficiaries of greater liberalization—the National Liberal and Center parties—were no less nationalistic than the Conservatives and indeed more imperialistic. A factor only after the first decade of the twentieth century, the Social Democrats were certainly opposed to war and military expansion but, as has been shown above, were willing to subordinate this opposition to domestic objectives. More important, the Social Democrats in Germany, as elsewhere, were also patriots and would place national survival over peace when confronted with the choice in August 1914. Greater Social Democratic control over foreign policy might have moderated German policy in style and degree but probably not in kind. Ultimately it might only have forced the Social

Democrats to take greater responsibility for what was in general outline the same policy.

POLICY AND POLITICS: THE RELATIONSHIPS AMONG FOREIGN POLICY, DOMESTIC AFFAIRS, AND PUBLIC OPINION

It remains to examine the relationship between foreign policy and public opinion. Several types of relationships are possible. Policy and opinion can be closely, vaguely, or little related and, if related, then directly or inversely. During the period from 1911 to 1914 German policy was generally similar to Right-Middle opinion and departed from Left opinion on the major events and issues. In the second Moroccan crisis, government and Right-Middle opinion perceived France and particularly Britain as the main opponents and Russia as less threatening. Public opinion in general accepted the prospect of better relations with Britain as pursued by the government after the crisis. During the debate over arms increases, Russia and France were perceived as the main opponents by Right-Middle public opinion and the government. In the Liman von Sanders incident and the Russo-German press feud which followed it, Russia was seen as the main enemy and France a lesser threat by most public opinion and the government. Thus public opinion of the Right and Middle were directly related to policy, whereas Left opinion was generally inversely related.

This relationship can be regarded as coincidental, causal, complementary, congruent, or complex. If it is asserted that the relationship is coincidental, it must be assumed that opinion and policy were essentially isolated and ran parallel during this period only by chance. If it is asserted that the relationship is causal, several possibilities exist. At one extreme, it can be argued that government policy was the determinant which created, controlled, or at least manipulated public opinion as a tool. At the other extreme, policy can be seen as determined by opinion. In between these extremes, it can be argued that the relationship alternates: first opinion determines policy, then policy determines opinion. It can be asserted that the relationship is complementary in the sense that opinion sets the limits within which policy operates more or less freely. The relationship can be seen as congruent, i.e., policy and opinion either are essentially the same or respond to similar impulses. Finally, one can claim that the relationship between opinion and policy is so complex that it cannot be analyzed in detail or explained but only described in general terms. Evidence can be found for all of these interpretations.

The influence of public opinion on foreign policy is determined in part by the government's conception of public opinion, i.e., whose opinion counts. The German leaders' frequent mention of the "nation" or "people" was a significant indicator that they felt compelled to use the phraseology of mass-nationalist society. In actual fact, they seldom knew or genuinely cared what the nation as a whole felt. At most their concern was usually for the articulate, educated, and affluent segment of society whose opinion was reflected by the parties and press of the Middle and Right. Even toward this segment of opinion, however, the attitudes of German leaders varied.[25]

There is considerable evidence that German leaders regarded public opinion on foreign policy as essentially passive and unimportant. This perception took one of two general forms: public opinion was either disregarded, or it was considered but rejected and even denigrated. The first attitude is reflected in the fact that public opinion was not consulted on the major policy decisions of the period from 1911 to 1914—the second Moroccan crisis, naval *détente* with Britain, Balkan wars, negotiations with Britain over colonies, the Sanders affair and the press feud with Russia, and alliance questions. Like most governments, the German government made these decisions in virtual isolation from public opinion, which is not to say without any consideration of public opinion. On some occasions, public opinion was recognized but rejected, as when Bethmann asserted that "the German people" (which meant primarily the Right and Middle in this instance) had played irresponsibly with the idea of war during the second Moroccan crisis and pledged himself to oppose it even at the risk of unpopularity. On other occasions, the aspirations of special—usually economic—interest groups were disregarded, for instance, when Bethmann condemned war for the sake of German companies in Morocco as a "crime." In several instances, the government subordinated private financial interests to political objectives, especially in regard to Austria-Hungary, the Ottoman Empire, the Balkans, and colonial questions. If the Reichstag is regarded as a reflection of public opinion, it was rejected at several junctures (most notably during the Zabern affair). German leaders specifically denigrated public opinion, the press, and Reichstag frequently (but always privately) as overrated, irresponsible, negligible, or worse.[26]

The conclusion that German leaders viewed public opinion as passive but important is suggested by their efforts to mold it. The Foreign Ministry and particularly the Admiralty were in continual contact with the press. During the second Moroccan crisis, Kiderlen sought to arouse public interest (partly by encouraging the Pan Germans) and probably used public opinion to extract support from the kaiser and Bethmann; but, when its usefulness had passed, Kiderlen and later Bethmann sought to restrain public opinion during and after the crisis. By public statements, Bethmann sought to reduce the animosity engendered during the second Moroccan crisis toward Britain in order to facilitate an Anglo-German naval *détente* and perhaps even draw Britain away from its allies. To the same end, he used the press to limit the demands of the kaiser and Tirpitz for naval expansion, even while Tirpitz manipulated the press to arouse support for naval increases. The most notable and consistent efforts by German leaders to influence public opinion were during the debates over arms increases. Bethmann was typically ambiguous in opposing bellicosity—particularly toward Britain—but nonetheless discussing the possibility of war in order to arouse support for arms increases. The kaiser, Moltke, and Ludendorff were more specific and less qualified when they demanded that Bethmann and Tirpitz apply all means at their disposal to persuade the German people of the necessity for arms increases. The most active and probably most successful propaganda for the increases was conducted by the Pan Germans and the recently founded Army League, which was not officially backed but expressed views held by the kaiser and Moltke. The government's role in the so-called Russo-German "press feud" (winter 1914) is not entirely clear. It is possible but not proven that the German press's bitterness toward Russia was encouraged by the government; this result certainly conformed to German leaders' attitudes toward Russia and may have suited their diplomatic goals. All of these efforts to influence the public may have constituted a concerted governmental campaign to prepare the German people for an imminent war. The kaiser and Moltke advocated such a campaign, but Bethmann again seems to have been ambivalent. He made public statements implying war but deplored bellicosity in private, hoped to discontinue public discussion of war after the Reichstag had approved arms increases, and claimed that he did not regard war as unavoidable. However consistent and conscious these efforts may have been, they implied an assumption on the government's part that public opinion could and should be manipulated.[27]

Some evidence implies that the government regarded public opinion as a useful tool of diplomatic policy. Before the second Moroccan crisis, Kiderlen arranged for German companies in Morocco to request assistance and had the Pan Germans demand a hard line from the government so that he could then claim to the French that concessions were necessary because of public opinion. Himself skeptical of the viability of Albania, the kaiser resisted Austro-Hungarian requests during 1913 for support there by arguing that German public opinion was opposed. In favor of German involvement in the Ottoman Empire, Jagow and Bethmann asserted that German public opinion desired it. Bethmann used German (and Ottoman) public opinion as a justification for his hard line during the Sanders crisis. In negotiations with the French and British during the winter of 1914, Bethmann and Jagow contended that public opinion forced them to demand colonial concessions. Like the kaiser a year earlier, Jagow used public opinion in early 1914 as his reason for not supporting Austria-Hungary in Albania. In his effort to torpedo an Anglo-Russian naval agreement during the spring of 1914, Jagow aroused public opinion by leaking reports of negotiations to the press; he and Bethmann then claimed that the German people opposed such an agreement but assured the British that they had sought to restrain public opinion. Yet on other occasions, German leaders found it convenient to contend that public opinion—particularly the press—was unimportant and to employ it as a scapegoat. In order to encourage an Anglo-German *détente*, Bethmann sought to shift responsibility for Anglo-German tension during the second Moroccan crisis to the press. Domestic considerations were sometimes quite consciously subordinated to diplomatic objectives, as when the kaiser justified retention of Bethmann as chancellor despite his domestic political shortcomings on the grounds of diplomatic considerations, particularly the improvement of relations with Britain. All these instances indicated a willingness to manipulate opinion for diplomatic objectives.[28]

Yet, while these instances suggest that the government perceived opinion as weak, other evidence indicates that German leaders may have viewed it as strong. Some governmental claims that public opinion was potent were made to opponents or allies and are therefore suspect as diplomatic tactics, and retrospective statements can be interpreted in contradictory ways. Contemporary confidential statements are, however, more reliable and less ambiguous. When the kaiser and Bethmann criticized the German press to the crown prince, they were probably reflecting genuine distaste and perhaps even a fear which implied that they were affected by public opinion. Bethmann complained in December 1911 of "resistance from all sides" to his policy of restraint toward England, by which he probably meant not only the kaiser and Tirpitz but also the Pan Germans, Army League, and heavy industry. Lichnowsky's claim that the importance of German public opinion was exaggerated implied that some German leaders—probably his superiors at the Foreign Ministry and Bethmann—did in fact take opinion seriously. The government seems to have been genuinely concerned that the public would not support a war over a Balkan question and therefore restrained Austria-Hungary during the Balkan wars. They also worried that a considerable segment of opinion—the Social Democrats and possibly the workers—would not support any war.[29]

German leaders not only spoke but also acted in ways which indicated that public opinion may in fact have influenced foreign policy. The government's ability to negotiate during the latter stages of the second Moroccan crisis was limited and the eventual agreement severely criticized by the very bellicose elements whom the government had encouraged during the early stages. The tendency of German leaders toward bellicosity during the debate over arms increases may have been necessary to insure passage by the Reichstag. It is more likely, however, that those parties which voted for the increases—Middle and Right—would have done so without encouragement from the government. The government's bellicosity may have been instead a response to the general chauvinism of the proponents, particularly such groups as the Army League, Pan Germans, and heavy industry. Thus the government's language can be perceived as a necessary formality but insignificant in the sense that it did not alter the eventual vote. Since it is not proven that the government arranged the Russo-German press feud (winter 1914), it is possible to see the incident as an outburst of genuine anti-Russian feeling which the government could not resist. If the difficulties and frustration confronting German imperialism by early 1914 are perceived as a crisis, then the government can be regarded as compelled to greater activism by public criticism. The government's diplomacy was also influenced on several occasions by domestic political questions. Kiderlen and probably Bethmann hoped that a diplomatic success during the second Moroccan crisis might favorably affect the elections of January 1912. Conversely, German leaders feared that the Social Democratic success in these elections (which was probably due in large measure to economic and domestic rather than foreign considerations) would affect passage of arms increases. Some conservatives apparently saw diplomatic questions primarily in domestic terms and favored war as a means of preserving the existing social structure. There is, however, little evidence that German leaders agreed and much evidence that they specifically rejected a decision for war on such grounds. The totality of these influences—i.e., public opinion on diplomatic-military issues and domestic political questions—can be perceived as proof of the argument that foreign questions were subordinate to domestic considerations for the German government.[30]

The statements of German leaders in regard to public opinion on specific international issues were ambiguous. Although German leaders officially favored imperial expansion and world power, the government's commitment to imperialism was qualified, and Bethmann asserted that colonial concessions were not worth a war. The basic complaint of all groups—whether favorably or unfavorably disposed toward concessions—during the second Moroccan crisis and on frequent occasions thereafter was that the government failed to make its colonial objectives clear.[31] The government's public comments on the question of war were likewise mixed. Some leaders—the kaiser and Moltke, in particular—urged a campaign to convince the German public of the necessity of war, and the government made many pronouncements— especially during the debates over arms increases—which increased tension and even encouraged the expectation of war. Sometimes on the same occasion, they sought to reduce tension and discourage the view that war was unavoidable. The government was in fact ambivalent on the public's attitude toward war. In some confidential and public statements German leaders implied that they felt the people were convinced of the possibility, necessity, or even desirability of war, while other comments suggested that the government believed many Germans were opposed to or unprepared for war under some or all conditions. Hence, there was no consistent relationship between policy and opinion on the questions of imperialism and war.[32]

Neither the government's public statements nor its perceptions of opinion were consistently arrogant or anxious. Some official pronouncements implied ambition, optimism, and even arrogance, while others seemed defensive, fatalistic, or even anxious. Sometimes opinion appeared arrogant and aggressive to the government, but at other times, the public looked anxious and pessimistic. In short, both public opinion and official statements were contradictory.[33]

The government's public comments on other states were likewise ambiguous, changing, and infrequent, except at particular moments. Pronouncements on Britain were reserved and indirect but unfriendly during the second Moroccan crisis. When the crisis passed and the government—particularly Bethmann—became anxious to encourage an Anglo-German naval *détente* or even British neutrality in case of war, German statements became more friendly. This tendency was reinforced by Anglo-German cooperation during the Balkan wars. On occasion, German leaders even expressed publicly the hope that Britain would remain neutral, at least initially, in an eventual war. On the eve of war, German official statements regarding Britain were friendly but infrequent. Official German statements on France likewise fluctuated. During the second Moroccan crisis, France was seen as hostile but less so than Britain. France and Russia were presented as the main enemies during the debate over arms increases. After the arms bill had been passed, France appeared in government statements as less hostile than Russia but more so than Britain. Despite the Russo-German tension caused by the Sanders episode and the Russo-German press feud of the winter of 1914, Russia is only infrequently mentioned by German leaders in public statements. In fact, in their official statements to the Reichstag during the arms debate of the spring of 1913 and again in the spring of 1914 soon after the press feud, German leaders spoke of official relations with Russia as good. Official German statements on relations with other governments were therefore mixed and minimal.[34]

The German government's attitude toward foreign public opinion and press was more hostile but no more consistent than it was toward its own people. German leaders were uncertain of the relationship between the British government and its public opinion. They hoped that domestic problems such as the Irish question would distract the British government and reinforce the tendency toward neutrality in case of war. German leaders had stronger opinions on the relationship between the French government and the public. They tended to agree on the distinction between the two but not on which was the determinant. Some saw public opinion as the critical element, particularly during the crisis over the Three-Year Law in the spring of 1914; the kaiser anticipated another French Revolution and believed that the French (and Russian) press determined French policy during the Sanders episode. But on other occasions German leaders regarded the French government as the driving force behind a bellicose French policy, while the French public was largely peaceful and passive. Similarly, in the case of Russia, German leaders agreed on the distinction between public and leaders but not on which determined policy. Frequently it was claimed in public German statements that the Russian government was friendly but that the Russian press and elements of the public (especially Pan Slavs) were chauvinist. Some German leaders perceived the possibility of revolution in Russia as a factor influencing the diplomatic calculations of Russian leaders. In confidential discussions, however, German leaders were less agreed. Some still saw the Russian government as peaceful though weak and the public as bellicose and strong, while others—especially the kaiser— reversed the proposition and saw the government as the driving force. Hence the perceptions of German leaders toward the governments and publics of their opponents were unclear and inconsistent.[35]

This ambiguity was in fact typical. The British government's attitude toward opinion at home and abroad varied. As elsewhere, domestic problems, particularly the Irish question, existed in Britain and could distract the government's attention from foreign questions. British leaders generally claimed that public opinion influenced their policy, but these claims were adjusted according to the circumstances. They told the Germans that British opinion would not allow France to be defeated but informed the French that public opinion would not condone a commitment to France. Grey may have been influenced by public opinion in postponing naval talks with Russia during the spring of 1914, but he probably favored postponement himself. Each of these instances is in fact amenable to the interpretation that British leaders were either in agreement with public opinion as they saw it or even using opinion as an excuse. Grey's attitude toward public opinion in other countries was similarly ambiguous. He dismissed the Russian press as insignificant because it did not represent the government's policy. He used German public opinion as an excuse to drop unprofitable naval negotiations with the Germans but did not distinguish between the German press and official policy during the Russo-German press feud.[36]

The French government's ability to make diplomatic and strategic decisions independent of politics and public opinion may have been more limited than that of any other government. The issue of French military expansion and related diplomatic problems was involved in the domestic political crisis over the Three-Year Law during the spring of 1914. Nonetheless, the government's policy was relatively unaffected because it was able by extensive manipulation to maintain the law and thus its plans for military expansion. Indeed, French leaders used public opinion as a justification for pursuing risky policies and saw the German government as doing the same by arousing its press during the Russo-German feud.[37]

Russian leaders were perhaps the most cynical toward public opinion. Although the danger of revolution in Russia was mooted by some (particularly those who had the most to gain from it), the possibility does not seem to have affected the conduct of Russian foreign policy. Russian leaders presented their public opinion variously in dealing with other governments. Sazonov claimed that opinion demanded his strong line during the Balkan wars, support of Serbia against Austria-Hungary, opposition to the Sanders mission, and concessions from the British in Persia. But he disavowed the Russian press during the Russo-German press feud and disregarded the public demands for concessions from the British in Persia when he himself offered them in exchange for negotiations with the British for a naval agreement. Sazonov's dismissal of Russian public opinion was probably as valid as his disavowal of official responsibility for bellicose articles in the press during the feud was invalid. The Russian minister of war, Suchomlinov, had in fact written the articles which sparked the feud in March 1914 and revived it in June. The other powers' public opinion was treated as cavalierly by Russian leaders. Although the German press during the Russo-German feud was seen as government-inspired, Sazonov was quite willing to dismiss the German press as insignificant in order to reestablish good official relations with Germany. The Suchomlinov articles during the feud were designed to influence Russian opinion but probably even more to force

French public opinion to support the Three-Year Law. In short, Russian leaders seem to have disregarded or manipulated, rather than reflected, public opinion.[38]

Similar variety existed in the Austro-Hungarian government's attitude toward its public opinion and politics. The subnationalities involved Austro-Hungarian political problems deeply with international questions and on occasion the Austro-Hungarian government claimed that these groups—particularly the South Slavs—as a consideration but may have done so only to win German support for a move against Serbia. In general, however, Austro-Hungarian leaders did not seem to consider the opinions of the subnationalities or indeed to have been aware that any such opinion existed, and they were hardly more responsive to their own constituents, i.e., Austrian and Hungarian opinion. While it was diplomatically useful to play down Austro-Italian frictions, the Austro-Hungarian press was amiable toward Italy but, when Berchtold took a hard line against Italy in June 1914, the Austro-Hungarian press and opinion were aroused and used against Italy. The German government's perception of Austro-Hungarian opinion was contradictory in dismissing it to Austro-Hungarian leaders but in discussing it seriously in private.[39]

As in the case of all states with conationals inside the Habsburg Empire, the Italian government had to reckon with some irredentist pressures for a hard line against Austria-Hungary which probably precluded a genuine Austro-Italian rapprochement. In fact imperialism may have constituted a greater stumbling block in their relations than irredentism. The Italian government claimed that it was forced by public opinion to take a hard line against Austria-Hungary in Albania. This may have been a case of one faction among Italian leaders manipulating public opinion against another, as in the case of Kiderlen's tactics against the kaiser during the second Moroccan crisis. Alternatively, the Italian government may have used public opinion as an excuse to pursue the objective of Albanian dissolution and expansion of Italian influence. This was quite understandably the interpretation favored by Berchtold in June 1914, and, after initially minimizing Italian and Austro-Hungarian public opinion in order to facilitate an Austro-Italian rapprochement, German leaders accepted Berchtold's view in June 1914.[40]

Rumanian opinion was described by the king alternately as irresistible and appeasable. The Austro-Hungarian envoy in Bucharest, Czernin, saw Rumanian public opinion as a serious threat, whereas Tisza claimed that it was a passing phenomenon. German leaders took Rumanian public opinion seriously in private but dismissed it in Vienna as an artificial creation of Russian and French propaganda. German leaders claimed that Turkish public opinion was important as long as they took a hard line toward Russia during the Sanders episode but disregarded it when they forced concessions on the Turks at the end of the crisis.[41]

Contradictory conclusions can be drawn from this evidence. As suggested at the beginning of this section, the relationship between opinion and policy can be perceived as coincidental, causal, complementary, congruent, or complex. If the similarities and differences between opinion and policy are seen as coincidental, it must be assumed that they are separate but unrelated. The argument for separateness can be supported with considerable evidence, in particular, the disagreements and mutual criticism between elements of the public and government. But it is more difficult to demonstrate that opinion and policy were unrelated, since the frequent efforts to influence each other and responses to pressures suggest the opposite. Hence, the case for coincidence is difficult to make.

The case for causality is better but more complicated. It assumes that opinion and policy were separate but related, an assumption supported by all the evidence of mutual criticism and influence. But it is less clear how opinion and policy influenced each other. There is considerable evidence for both views that opinion influenced policy and that policy influenced opinion. One of these interpretations can be applied generally and the other rejected only if much evidence is neglected or dismissed. If the evidence for both views is accepted, however, neither can be put as a total explanation.[42]

The case for alternating causality can be made more persuasively. It assumes that opinion and policy were separate and related but constantly changing. In one instance, policy influenced opinion; in another, opinion influenced policy. The degree and duration of this influence varied. This interpretation has the advantage of accommodating much of the evidence but involves the disadvantage of suggesting causality only at the level of immediate events but not in more general terms. In effect, it can provide an explanation for a single event, such as a crisis, but is less satisfactory in explaining the general relationship between opinion and policy.

Opinion and policy can be regarded instead as complementary. This interpretation assumes that opinion and policy were not only distinct but also operate in different areas or at different levels. Thus, public opinion sets the limits within which policy is conducted more or less independently. Opinion establishes these limits by taking a position on general issues such as national interest, aspirations, and prestige. Public interest in these questions varies in intensity and character: the more intensive it is, the more the government's mobility is limited. The available evidence can be interpreted in this sense. Articulate German public opinion—i.e., primarily of the Middle and Right—made its views on these questions amply known to the government on the eve of war. In general it perceived Germany as at once powerful and threatened. Finding it difficult to act in any manner which seemed to neglect this view, German leaders were limited in a general sense. But on many foreign policy issues the government took the initiative and did not—indeed, could not—consult opinion. This was especially true in questions of tactics, timing, and specific or immediate diplomatic objectives, such as Bethmann's efforts to separate Britain from France and Russia. This type of interpretation has the advantage of simplifying the question by separating policy and opinion into two distinct areas. The general objectives of policy are accordingly defined by opinion, whereas the details are explained in terms of strictly diplomatic considerations. It has the disadvantage of leaving the essential question open to interpretation: where does public opinion draw the limits for policy at any particular moment?

Another possible interpretation is congruency. It assumes that the difference between policy and opinion is only apparent since leaders and led are motivated by fundamentally similar assumptions and respond to the same basic impulses. The variety of views on foreign-policy questions among the German people and leaders can be interpreted as evidence disproving this view but whether it does so depends on how these disparities are perceived. If they are seen as fundamental, public opinion and policy cannot be regarded as essentially monolithic, whereas opinion and policy can be perceived as essentially homogeneous if these disparities are regarded as superficial. The congruency argument suggests that the German public and leaders perceived international questions in the same way because they were responding to the same impulses of national interest, aspirations, and prestige. This interpretation suffers from the double disadvantage of depending on such ill-defined terms and minimizing disagreements and deviations in German policy, but it offers the advantage of explaining the general direction of German opinion and policy.

Finally, the relationship between opinion and policy can be regarded as so complex that no explanation is satisfactory. This interpretation assumes that opinion and policy can be neither isolated nor identified well enough to establish their relationship but can only described in a general way. The great variety of evidence available can be regarded as support for this interpretation. It has the advantage of conforming most closely with the evidence but the disadvantage of leaving the policy-opinion problem largely unresolved.

Since most of these interpretations can be applied with some persuasiveness, the question ultimately reduces to which is preferable. A combination of congruency and complementarism would seem to be the most convincing. Congruency is appealing because it explains the general character of German policy. The disputes among Germans seemed significant at the time and must be comprehended if contemporary politics is to be understood, but these arguments obscured the fact that general agreement existed among most Germans on the fundamental issues of national interest, aspirations, and prestige. Most Germans were at once arrogant and anxious in viewing Germany as both powerful and threatened. While the basic thrust of German policy is thus explained by congruency, the specifics would seem to be understood best by seeing policy and opinion as complementary. Accordingly, although limited in general outline by opinion, the government acted with considerable freedom in pursuing its immediate objectives. The relative importance of the congruency and complementary theories depends on an interpretation of international affairs. If the course of international affairs is seen to be dependent on chance events and/or personal whims of policy makers, then the complementary interpretation is emphasized. But, if international affairs are viewed as determined by forces largely unaffected by the details of diplomatic relations, then the congruency theory is more applicable. Since the present analysis takes the latter position that international affairs are dominated by such forces, the congruency model appears more apt. The German public and leaders held basically identical views which determined the course of German foreign policy.

NOTES

1   Rosenberg, *Birth*, pp. 55–56; Schorske, *Democracy*, pp. 250–60; Zmarzlik, *Bethmann*, pp. 50–62; Fischer, *Krieg*, pp. 145–59.

2   For details of the debate over arms increases, see p. 101 above.

3   Zmarzlik, *Bethmann*, pp. 62–73; Ritter, *Staatskunst*, 2:279–80; Strandmann, *Erforder-lichkeit*, p. 14; Westarp, *Politik*, 1:238–72; Fischer, *Krieg*, pp. 257–69, 387; Fischer, *Griff*, pp. 38, 43; *Kriegsrüstung*, 1:188; Karl Bachem, *Vorgeschichte, Geschichte und Politik der Deutschen Zentrumspartei* (Cologne, 1928), 4:250; Bethmann, *Betrachtungen*, 1:87; Schorske, *Democracy*, pp. 260–63, 268; Johanna Schellenberg, "Die Herausbildung der Militärdiktatur in den ersten Jahren des Krieges," in *Politik im Krieg, 1914–1918* (Berlin, 1964), p. 30.

4   Fischer, *Krieg*, pp. 384–98; Westarp, *Politik*, 1:343; Hans Jürgen Puhle, *Agrarische Interessenpolitik und Preussischer Konservatismus im Wilhelminischen Reich* (Hanover, 1966), p. 317.

5   Fischer, *Krieg*, pp. 387–88; Westarp, *Politik*, 1:267–72.

6   Fischer, *Krieg*, pp. 388–95, 398–400; Westarp, *Politik*, 1:345–46, 365; Class, *Strom*, pp. 267–79; Zmarzlik, *Bethmann*, p. 74.

7   Schorske, *Democracy*, pp. 267–84.

8   Strandmann, *Erforderlichkeit*, pp. 16–26; Fischer, *Krieg*, pp. 401–7; Stenkewitz, *Bajonette*, p. 290.

9   Fischer, *Krieg*, pp. 407–12; Herre, *Wilhelm*, p. 35; Wehler, "Fall," pp. 31–35; Zmarzlik, *Bethmann*, pp. 116–39; Rosenberg, *Birth*, pp. 57–58; Bethmann, *Betrachtungen*, 1:86–95; Schorske, *Democracy*, p. 259.

10 Strandmann, *Erforderlichkeit*, pp. 30–31; Fischer, *Krieg*, pp. 401, 407, 412, 516–26, 651–52; Class, *Strom*, p. 279.

11 This is Fischer's contention (*Krieg*, pp. 269–70, 409).

12 Bethmann, *Betrachtungen*, 1:86–95.

13 Wernecke, *Wille*, pp. 32–36, 43–46, 48–49, 70–82, 85, 90; Fischer, *Krieg*, pp. 118, 121–22, 127–30, 136–37; Class, *Strom*, p. 178.

14 Wernecke, *Wille*, pp. 62, 90, 102–18, 122–23, 128; Fischer, *Krieg*, pp. 137, 142–44, 147; *GP*, 29:413–22.

15 Wernecke, *Wille*, pp. 174, 190–93, 227–28; Fischer, *Krieg*, pp. 146, 152, 159–62, 164, 175, 265, 357, 378; Fischer, *Griff*, pp. 38, 43.

16 Wernecke, *Wille*, pp. 33, 42, 49, 67, 79, 82, 90, 157, 190, 304–9; Fischer, *Krieg*, pp. 162, 324–54, 362–74, 442–52, 458, 641, 650–53.

17 Wernecke, *Wille*, pp. 30–37, 41–49, 77, 80, 141, 152, 168, 289–94, 307–12; Fischer, *Krieg*, pp. 162, 294, 301–3, 325–57, 368, 373–83, 640–44, 648, 658.

18 Wernecke, *Wille*, pp. 33, 36, 42, 49, 67, 72, 79, 82, 90–91, 102–38, 190; Fischer, *Krieg*, pp. 120–22, 136, 139, 370–81, 414–78, 527–29, 541, 640–41, 650.

19 Wernecke, *Wille*, pp. 32–36, 41, 45–48, 52, 68, 72–73, 77–78, 85–90, 245–47, 269, 312; Fischer, *Krieg*, pp. 121, 151–52, 325–33, 342, 352, 354–57, 359, 366–67, 392–93, 404, 444, 640–41, 651–52, 658–59.

20 Wernecke, *Wille*, pp. 33, 46–51, 65, 76, 87, 90, 97, 102, 198–209, 216–17, 223–43, 259, 273–75, 285; Fischer, *Krieg*, pp. 471, 651, 655.

21 Wernecke, *Wille*, pp. 55–61, 68, 84, 92–97, 103, 131–37, 144, 151, 158–71, 199, 261–87; Fischer, *Krieg*, pp. 126–27, 139–42, 655–56.

22 Wernecke, *Wille*, pp. 184, 216–17, 244–73, 287; Fischer, *Krieg*, pp. 342, 358, 373, 527–35, 648, 651–56.

23 Wernecke, *Wille*, pp. 33, 44, 48–52, 61, 67–72, 77–91, 97–102, 110, 121–33, 157, 161, 164, 185, 192–93, 210, 219–23, 228, 249–66, 271–72, 304, 308, 311, 441; Fischer, *Krieg*, pp. 132, 151, 262, 328–42, 352–62, 372, 375–83, 402–6, 648, 651–59.

24 Fischer, *Krieg*, pp. 33, 161–63, 329–31, 335–37, 344–49, 354, 359, 373–79, 383, 393, 416, 420, 439–43, 640–42, 648–53; Wernecke, *Wille*, pp. 33, 46–47, 82, 155–58, 166, 174, 176, 193, 195–99, 217, 222–24, 308.

25 Fischer, *Krieg*, pp. 123, 142, 145, 640, 642.

26 Ibid., pp. 142–45, 423, 433, 442, 449; *GP*, 37:58–59; Strandmann, *Erforderlichkeit*, pp. 23–26, 43; Stenkewitz, *Bajonette*, p. 112; Bethmann, *Betrachtungen*, 1:86; Wolff, *Eve*, p. 342.

27 Class, *Strom*, p. 178; Erdmann, "Beurteilung," p. 534; Müller, *Kaiser*, pp. 101–2, 105–7; *Kriegsrüstung*, p. 138; Tirpitz, *Aufbau*, pp. 282, 286; Huldermann, *Ballin*, p. 272; Conrad, *Dienstzeit*, 3:146–52; Stenkewitz, *Bajonette*, p. 190; Anton Jux, *Kriegsschrecken* (Berlin, 1929), pp. 34–67; Alfred Schroeter, *Krieg-Staat-Monopol 1914 bis*

1918 (Berlin, 1965), p. 51; Bethmann, *Betrachtungen*, 1:90–91; Ritter, *Staatskunst*, 2:268; Fischer, *Krieg*, pp. 118–20, 124, 138–39, 142, 145–48, 158–64, 169, 178–88, 261–62, 265–67, 270–78, 542–52, 561–63; Fischer, "Weltpolitik," pp. 330–36; Fischer, *Griff*, pp. 44–45; Wernecke, *Wille*, pp. 8, 29–31, 39, 49, 114, 138, 187–228, 249–85; *GP*, 29:142–49; *GP*, 34:351–53; *GP*, 39:9–11, 177–78, 544–69.

28   Wernecke, *Wille*, pp. 29, 39, 49, 53, 138; Fischer, *Krieg*, pp. 118–20, 122, 128, 139, 204, 642; Strandmann, *Erforderlichkeit*, p. 38; *GP*, 33:302–4; *GP*, 34:50–52, 54–56, 227; *GP*, 39:617–20; *BD*, 10:791–94, part 2.

29   Bethmann, *Betrachtungen*, 1:2; Strandmann, *Erforderlichkeit*, pp. 32–39; Fischer, *Krieg*, pp. 145–46; *GP*, 38:227; *Documents diplomatiques francais (1871–1914)* [*DDF*], ed. by Commission de publication des documents relatifs aus origines de la guerre de 1914 (Paris, 1929), Series 3 (1911–14), 9:117, 129; *IB*, 1:434.

30   Wernecke, *Wille*, pp. 29–30, 46, 66, 78, 89, 115–37; Fischer, *Krieg*, pp. 12–13, 117, 121, 127, 137–41, 149, 154, 158, 163, 329, 439–43; Fischer, "Weltpolitik," p. 322; Ernst Jäckh, *Kiderlen-Wächter: Der Staatsmann und der Mensch* (Berlin and Leipzig, 1925), 1:122, 171; *Kriegsrüstung*, 1:141, 472, 491, 497, 503; *IB*, 1:434; Müller, *Kaiser*, p. 88; *GP*, 37:115–18, 121–28, 133–35; Tirpitz, *Aufbau*, p. 404; Strandmann, *Erforderlichkeit*, pp. 26–39; *Bayerische Dokumente zum Kriegsausbruch und zum Versailler Schuldspruch*, ed. by Pius Dirr (Munich and Berlin, 1925), p. 113; Erdmann, "Beurteilung," pp. 526, 536.

31   Fischer, *Krieg*, pp. 139, 370, 650; Wernecke, *Wille*, pp. 289, 307–8; *DDF*, 9:129, 177; *DDF*, 10:102.

32   Wernecke, *Wille*, pp. 114, 197–99, 208; Fischer, "Weltpolitik," pp. 335–36; Fischer, *Griff*, p. 42; Fischer, *Krieg*, pp. 139–40, 261–80, 378–81; *GP*, 33:302–4; *GP*, 38:50–56; *GP*, 39:9–11; *Kriegsrüstung*, 1:155–58, 253–57, 287; Schroeter, *Krieg*, pp. 38–51; Baernreither, *Weltbrand*, pp. 195, 298; Müller, *Kaiser*, pp. 125–26; *Julikrise und Kriegsansbruch 1914*, ed. by Imanuel Geiss (Hanover, 1963), 1:45; Conrad, *Dienstzeit*, 3:144–55; Stenkewitz, *Bajonette*, p. 109; *DDF*, 9:129, 177; Erdmann, "Beurteilung," pp. 526, 536; Tirpitz, *Aufbau*, p. 203; Huldermann, *Ballin*, p. 272.

33   Wernecke, *Wille*, p. 217; *DDF*, 9:129, 177; *IB*, 1:434.

34   Fischer, "Weltpolitik," p. 330; Fischer, *Krieg*, pp. 265, 276–80, 542–64; Bethmann, *Betrachtungen*, 1:90–91; Ritter, *Staatskunst*, 2:268; *GP*, 39:177–86, 634–36; Wernecke, *Wille*, pp. 198–99.

35   *GP*, 33:228–32, 463–65; *GP*, 38:284–86, 293–97; *GP*, 39:248–51, 260–66, 284–86, 293–97, 544, 547–54, 558–60, 578–79, 587, 632, 634.

36   *GP*, 39:74–76, 619–20, 623–26, 630–33; *IB*, 1:421.

37   *GP*, 39:256–58, 266–74, 582; Fay, *Origins*, 1:522; *DDF*, 9:402, 460, 461.

38   *GP*, 33:189–93; *GP*, 38:225–27, 309–10, 313–17; *GP*, 39:260–66, 540–44, 547–50, 554–56, 567–69, 580, 586–87; Fay, *Origins*, 1:499–500, 599–600; *IB*, 1:442.

39   *GP*, 35:115–16, 122–24, 128–30, 146–48, 166–70; *GP*, 39:333–38, 348–51, 361–70, 402–4.

40   *GP*, 39:342–43, 348–51.

41   *GP*, 38:227, 284–86.

42   Fischer provides a good example of the contradictions involved in seeking to reconcile all the evidence. He argues on occasion that German leaders conducted a propaganda campaign to prepare the German people for war (*Krieg*, pp. 270–71, 276–78, 639) and that the campaign had succeeded by the beginning of 1914 (*Krieg*, pp. 273, 279, 542, 546–52, 561–63). Elsewhere he contends that the campaign was conducted in fact by groups beyond the control of the government, such as the Pan Germans and the Army League (*Krieg*, pp. 274, 367, 641). In other instances he asserts that the government was forced to be bellicose by nationalists ("Fronde," "breakthrough of the nationalist opposition"; see *Krieg*, pp. 12–13, 135, 138–39, 143–44, 362, 377–78, 641–62). The di-

lemma involved in seeking a consistent theory is particularly evident in his evaluation of the Russo-German press feud during the winter-spring of 1914 which he regards a¹ once as a government propaganda campaign and a demonstration of popular bellicosity (*Krieg*, pp. 542–63).

VI / THE MILITARY ALTERNATIVE:

The Relationship Between German Diplomatic Policy and Military Strategy (1912–June 1914)

THE RELEVANT ISSUES: PLANS, PREPARATIONS, AND PREDICTIONS

An analysis of German foreign policy is incomplete without consideration of the military alternative. The central question is how the possibility of war affected diplomatic policy. This general problem must be subdivided into several subordinate areas—strategic plans, military and economic preparations, predictions and perceptions of war, and general attitudes toward the prospect of war.

STRATEGY AND POLICY: CONFLICTING, CONTRADICTORY, OR COMPLEMENTARY?

German strategy remained basically unaltered on the eve of war. As the blueprint of German military success, the Schlieffen plan assumed that Germany would face a Franco-Russian alliance. German victory against this alliance was possible only if one opponent were defeated rapidly. Considerations of space and mobilization speed made it seem that only France could be defeated speedily. France could be defeated quickly only if the French army were encircled and annihilated as a military force. The French army could be encircled only if the war remained mobile. It would remain mobile only if the Germans avoided French frontal attacks and forts. They could do so only if they advanced west through Belgium and then turned south into the broad northern French plains. This advance through Belgium and subsequent encircling movement could succeed only if the Germans concentrated the mass of their forces on the attacking wing. They could do so only if they were not threatened by a Russian attack. This Russian threat could be avoided by a combination of rapid German mobilization, slow Russian mobilization and/or attack, and Austro-Hungarian diversion of Russia. Accordingly, German success seemed to depend on rapid German mobilization and concentration for the advance through Belgium, slow Russian mobilization and/or attack, and Austro-Hungarian diversion of Russia.

Several of these conditions of success seemed endangered on the eve of war. Although the crises of 1905–11 had cast some doubt upon the Franco-Russian alliance, its consolidation after 1912 seemed to validate the assumption that Germany would face a two-front war. The assumption that France could be defeated rapidly was jeopardized by the increase of French forces as a result of the Three-Year Law (extending conscription from two to three years) and by the probability of British support, as demonstrated in the two Moroccan crises. On the other hand, the possibility that the French army would be encircled was increased in 1912 by its adoption of an offensive strategy which would expose its northern (left) flank facing the German advance through Belgium in order to concentrate and attack rapidly with the center. The German advance through Belgium was threatened by Belgian resistance but this prospect was not altered radically on the eve of war, except perhaps by the increased likelihood of British entry. German ability to concentrate in the west for the advance through Belgium was, however, jeopardized by the possibility that German troops would have to be diverted to the east. Increases and improvements in the Russian army, as well as the building of railroads in Poland, made it likely that the Russians would be able to impose pressure more rapidly on Germany. At the same time, Balkan developments and domestic problems within the Habsburg Empire made it possible that Austria-Hungary would be distracted and thus less able to divert Russia. In short, the prospect of German military success on the eve of war appeared to be dimming.

The German response to these developments is revealing. They retained the Schlieffen plan but sought at once to remove the obstacles and to encourage the preconditions for its success. They not only made no basic change in the Schlieffen plan but in fact renounced the one alternative—an offensive against Russia—in April 1913. This was a logical decision in terms of the German assumption that France and Russia would fight together. Since they assumed that only France could be defeated quickly, they would not attack Russia first in a two-front war. Since they assumed that Russia would not fight alone, they would not have to attack Russia in a one-front war. The Germans demonstrated that they acted upon these assumptions when they did not consider attacking Russia during the Bosnian crisis of 1909, at which point France was not openly supporting Russia and Germany still had its plans for an offensive operation against Russia. It is less surprising that the Germans dropped the plan for an attack on Russia than that they had such a plan which they would never use as long as their basic assumptions existed.[1] The Germans meanwhile sought to compensate for the increasing disadvantages by an emphasis on efficient mobilization. Although no important change was made in fact on the eve of war, there may have been one of attitude in that the greater need for speed made German generals even more inclined to equate mobilization with war—a logical conclusion, considering German assumptions about the Franco-Russian alliance. The only actual and indeed radical change was the increase of German forces.[2]

The Germans did, however, seek to meet the emerging disadvantages by affecting the behavior of their allies and enemies. A German concentration against France depended in part on an Austro-Hungarian diversion of Russia which presumed Austria-Hungary was willing and able to concentrate against Russia. Austro-Hungarian willingness depended on the alliance with Germany. Austro-German relations had been rocky during the Balkan wars but were improved from the autumn of 1913 onward by increased German willingness to support Austro-Hungarian aspirations in the Balkans. Yet Austro-Hungarian ability to concentrate against Russia required removal of outside threats, especially from the Balkan states, and German policy in this respect oscillated between denials of the Serbian threat and encouragement of Austro-Hungarian decisiveness. From the autumn of 1913 onward, the Germans urged Austro-Hungarian resolution of the Serbian problem, although they never opted clearly for either denial or decisiveness until the July crisis. German ambivalence in this regard was due in large measure to Germany's simultaneous efforts to encourage British neutrality which seemed to require presenting Russia as aggressive and therefore precluded encouragement of Austro-Hungarian action against Serbia. Austro-Hungarian ability to concentrate against Russia was also jeopardized by internal threats which concerned many German leaders increasingly by 1914. As in the case of the outside dangers, the German government pursued the ambivalent policy of denial and decisiveness. The kaiser essentially denied the seriousness of the problem to Tisza and Francis Ferdinand but at the same time encouraged greater determination on the part of the ruling Magyars and Austrians. The Germans also encouraged Austro-Hungarian willingness to concentrate against Russia by presenting war with Russia as an unavoidable racial struggle and by promising vague military support. In the final analysis, the Germans were apparently concerned less to increase than to avoid decrease of Austro-Hungarian support.

Their objective was similar in regard to Italy. The military clauses of the Triple Alliance between Germany, Austria-Hungary, and Italy called for Italian support of Germany against France and Austro-Italian naval cooperation against Anglo-French naval forces in the Mediterranean. The prospect of this cooperation was apparently improved by the renewal of the alliance at the end of 1912 and negotiations between the three members on military and naval cooperation during 1913 and 1914. But differences between Austria-Hungary and Italy increased over Italians within the monarchy and conflicting aspirations in the Balkans, especially in Albania. As in the case of their campaign to encourage British neutrality, German efforts to smooth over Austro-Italian differences were contradicted by German attempts to maintain good relations with Austria-Hungary by supporting its Balkan aspirations. As a result, German policy toward Italy and Austro-Italian frictions was an ambiguous mixture of negation and encouragement of negotiation. In fact, this was not inconsistent with German attitudes toward Italy. German leaders probably expected little from Italian support since it would arrive too late to help defeat France and was unlikely against Russia. The main consideration was to avoid Italian intervention against Austria-Hungary which would divert Austro-Hungarian troops from Russia and thus jeoparadize the German concentration against France. As they were with regard to Austria-Hungary, therefore, the Germans were probably more interested in avoiding new disadvantages than in seeking new advantages.[3]

The Germans made few efforts to alter the behavior of France and Russia on the eve of war. Berlin had sought to shake the Franco-Russian alliance during the Moroccan and Bosnian crises with the appearance of limited success at least in the sense that neither of its opponents supported the other strongly during those incidents. Franco-Russian cooperation was neither unblemished nor entirely satisfactory to either partner on the eve of war, but it increased after 1912, and the Germans correctly assumed that the Franco-Russian alliance would persist in a war. They did little to alter this eventuality by their diplomacy or strategy. They might hypothetically have sought to lure Russia away from France by restraining Austria-Hungary in the Balkans and acceding to Russia at the straits but instead tended to confirm the Franco-Russian alliance by supporting Austria-Hungary and opposing Russia. Characteristically the kaiser rejected Francis Ferdinand's suggestion of a revived Three Emperors' League with the assertion that Slav-German hostilities were insurmountable. German leaders spoke occasionally before the war of the possibility of social revolution in Russia and France but they did little to encourage it.[4] Hence the Franco-Russian alliance and a consequent two-front war were accepted by German leaders as a given in the situation.

Their perception of Belgium was less fixed. The success of the campaign against France depended in part on the rapidity of German passage through Belgium, which would be insured by force, namely, the strength of the German right wing. But it would be achieved more efficiently—i.e., more quickly and at less cost—if the Belgians could be persuaded to allow German passage without resistance. Such an arrangement might have had the additional benefit of reassuring the British on Belgium and thereby persuading them to remain neutral. Consequently, the Germans sought Belgian neutrality in conversations of the kaiser and Moltke with Belgian King Albert at the end of 1913. But their carrot (reassurance that Germany would not invade Belgium) and stick (claims that Russia and Britain would leave France to be defeated alone by Germany) proved unsuccessful when Albert asserted that Belgium would defend itself against invasion from any quarter.[5] The Germans were not entirely persuaded, however, and would repeat their offer of guarantees in exchange for passage in August 1914.

The most concentrated German effort to improve the chances for military success were made in regard to Britain. It is not entirely clear how the Germans expected British neutrality to affect the military conflict. Moltke seems to have been unconcerned about British troops during the opening campaign against France. The objective may in fact have been diplomatic, namely, to discourage the French, Belgians, and/or Russians sufficiently to make them surrender after military setbacks. The Germans pursued the objective of British neutrality by both diplomatic and military means. After the Anglo-German tensions of the second Moroccan crisis, Bethmann, Kiderlen and then Jagow sought to improve relations with Britain by negotiations over colonies and cooperation in the Balkans. Bethmann, meanwhile, tried to cash in on Tirpitz's risk theory by offering a naval agreement in exchange for a promise of British neutrality. To smooth the way for such an arrangement, he presented German naval increases in a manner least inclined to alienate the British. The most revealing episode in these efforts was perhaps the suggestion of Jagow (and probably Bethmann) that German strategy should be altered to encourage British neutrality. Jagow asked Moltke during the winter of 1913 whether it was possible to avoid violating Belgian neutrality in order to keep Britain neutral. Moltke argued that the violation of Belgian neutrality was essential to a rapid defeat of France, whereas British entry was unavoidable in any case but would not preclude victory over France. Jagow and presumably Bethmann accepted this verdict and made no further recorded protest.[6]

Both military and civilian leaders were aware of the interrelationship of strategy and policy and even specifically said so on occasion. Acceptance of British entry as the result of violating Belgian neutrality was not proof of the subordination of policy to strategy in general. Instead, it is a case of the subordination of one policy consideration to a basic strategic consideration, which in turn was based on a general policy consideration. British neutrality was desirable but not worth the price of renouncing the passage through Belgium, which seemed essential to a rapid defeat of France. A quick French defeat seemed necessary because the Germans expected a two-front war which was based ultimately on the political assumption that the Franco-Russian alliance would persist in war. In short, British neutrality did not justify the risk of a long war against France and Russia. British neutrality might have been worthwhile if the Germans had expected British entry to preclude German victory, but they did not. Alternatively, the Germans might have renounced an attack on either France or Russia and accepted the prospect of a protracted defensive war, but doing so would have contradicted their political assumption that Austro-German power would decline relative to the Franco-Russian alliance. Accordingly, German strategy and policy were not contradictory but consistent and complementary. Like all policy makers, German leaders had to opt between contradictory objectives. Their choices were generally consistent with their assumptions. The Schlieffen plan was retained because it was logical in terms of German policy. It would have been logical to renounce it if German leaders (and people) had felt that Germany was either strong enough to stand on the defensive against the Franco-Russian alliance or too weak to fight such a war. Instead, the Germans felt too weak to win a long, defensive war but strong enough to win a short, offensive one. Thus, precisely their ambivalence—the mixed sense of anxiety and arrogance—made the Schlieffen plan appropriate.

The striking fact about German strategy on the eve of war was, therefore, that it remained unchanged. This constancy was attributable to a basic continuity of objectives and assumptions in German policy. But there were general strategic changes which seemed to make German military success less likely as time went on. Hence, the adjustments were not in German strategy but in the prospects for its success, i.e., in German attitudes toward German strategy. The choice seemed increasingly polarized as the option of "later" tended to disappear and only "now" or "never" remained.[7]

Vienna's strategy also remained basically the same on the eve of war. Austro-Hungarian planners foresaw the two possible eventualities: a war with Serbia alone or a war with Russia and Serbia. The war with Serbia would be possible only if Russia renounced Serbia because of fear of Germany, revolution, or doubts about French support; it would be a punitive, offensive, and probably short and successful war, the results of which would be not only protection of Austro-Hungarian integrity but also probably establishment of Austro-Hungarian predominance in the western Balkans. The war with Russia and Serbia would occur if Russia did not renounce Serbia and would be basically defensive, with less-certain results and duration. Although the initial objective was defensive—namely to hold against Russia until the Germans had defeated France—Austro-Hungarian strategists planned an offensive against the Russian forces in the Polish salient. One consideration was military, namely, to deal the Russians a rapid setback before reinforcements arrived from central Russia. Another may have been the political one of carrying the war into Polish territory under Russian rule rather than letting the Russians launch it into Polish territory under Austro-Hungarian rule or even into Austria and/or Hungary. The Austro-Hungarians, consequently, had not one but two strategies between which they would choose depending on the conditions.

The conditions altered during the last two years of peace. Events in the Balkans seemed to increase the threat of war with the monarchy's southern neighbors and thus made the Austro-Serbian war and distraction from a war with Russia more likely. But contemporary Russian military reforms and increases made a war with Russia more unavoidable and necessary. Domestic political difficulties threatened to make any war at all unfeasible. In response to these developments, Austro-Hungarian leaders might have altered their strategy. They might have assumed a genuinely defensive posture against both Serbia and Russia. But doing so would have assumed that their offensive against Russia and/or Serbia was unpromising and that the defensive was more promising, whereas in fact Austro-Hungarian strategists believed that their offensive might succeed and that the defensive would not. They could hypothetically have renounced war altogether and thrown themselves on the mercy of the Entente powers, but Austro-Hungarian leaders were still too confident to consider this option seriously. A more serious possibility was to drop one of the two existing alternate strategies and concentrate on the other, i.e., either against Serbia or against Russia. Ultimately this recourse depended on a political decision, namely, whether Austro-Hungarian strategists believed Russia would support Serbia. If they assumed that Russia would not, they could afford to drop the strategy for a war with Russia; if they assumed that Russia would, they could drop the strategy for a war against Serbia. Since they never accepted one of these assumptions, they did not alter their strategy although they augmented their forces.[8]

Austro-Hungarian strategists, however, did seek to improve the strategic conditions by affecting the behavior of their allies and opponents. On the assumption that Russia's decision to back Serbia was alterable, Austro-Hungarian strategists and statesmen requested German promises of diplomatic and military support which might make Russia renounce Serbia. They also asked German guarantees of assistance even if Russia declared war so that Austria-Hungary might fight Serbia at the same time. These Austro-Hungarian appeals were designed to increase the chances for a war against Serbia. Meanwhile Austro-Hungarian leaders sought to shore up the alliance with Italy. In doing so, they were probably less anxious to win Italian military or even naval support than to avoid the threat which dissolution of the alliance with Italy would imply. To the extent that Italian aid might be forthcoming, it would be indirect: Italian support of Germany against France might release German troops for the campaign against Russia and thus aid Austria-Hungary. Vienna, meanwhile, tried to affect the strategic dispositions of their enemies. The efforts to create a Balkan alignment which would distract and ideally negate Serbian military power were designed to allow Austria-Hungary to defeat Serbia or to concentrate its forces against Russia. The desired promise of German support against Russia might divert Russian forces from Austria-Hungary. Little concern was paid to the strategic dispositions of France and Britain. The minimal goal of these efforts was prevention of a worsening strategic situation; the maximal objective was German support which might improve the prospects of success. Although the Germans became more willing to promise diplomatic and possible—though vague—military assistance in the spring of 1914, this support was not sufficient to make the Austro-Hungarians alter their strategy radically. Their attitude toward its implementation may, however, have altered since, like the Germans, they apparently became increasingly convinced that the chances of military success were diminishing. Thus, their strategy remained the same but their attitude toward it seems to have changed in the spring of 1914.[9]

This new view of their strategy was based on a political decision. Austro-Hungarian leaders assumed that the monarchy was threatened by the Balkans (particularly Serbia but also Rumania and perhaps Italy) and Russia. But they simultaneously perceived an opportunity to establish predominance at least in the western Balkans. Their strategy reflected this dualism and ambivalence: they planned campaigns against both northern and southern threats; both campaigns were justified in defensive and offensive terms and, if successful, promised both removal of a threat and expansion of influence. An alternate strategy which concentrated on either Russia or Serbia would not have been consistent with Austro-Hungarian preceptions of the political situation, i.e., the uncertainty of Russian support for Serbia and the offensive-defensive character of Austro-Hungarian policy. Renouncing plans for a campaign against Serbia would have implied the certainty of Russian support for Serbia, while renouncing the campaign against Russia would have implied the certainty of Russian nonsupport for Serbia. Since neither alternative was perceived in Vienna, it was logical to maintain both plans. Austro-Hungarian leaders might have altered their strategy if they had felt much stronger or weaker. If they had felt entirely confident of victory, they might have concentrated on one opponent without fearing the

other. If they had felt too weak to defeat either, they might have renounced an attack on either or even war altogether. Instead, they were
ambivalent: strong enough to defend their existence and even to plan an
offensive war which would give them Balkan predominance but weak
enough to feel they could not win a defensive war and to make their
strategic decisions contingent on the behavior of other powers. Thus,
like the Schlieffen plan, Austro-Hungarian strategy was ambivalent because it was based on an ambivalent policy. Austro-Hungarian policy
and strategy were not contradictory but consistent.[10]

French strategy changed most on the eve of war. Before 1911, it had
been basically defensive and, as such, conformed in general with French
policy. The major fact of French policy during the period from 1905 to
1911 was its resistance to German pressure during the two Moroccan
crises. French success in doing so had been due in large part to British
diplomatic support. Anglo-French diplomatic cooperation had been accompanied by military discussions which had—like diplomatic policy
—the basically defensive objective of resisting German attack. French
dependence on Britain during this period had been attributable in part
to Russian weakness and the consequent impotence of the Franco-
Russian alliance. This diplomatic fact had its military corollary: although a military agreement before a diplomatic alliance, the Franco-
Russian alliance was characterized during these years by little military
coordination. Hence, French diplomatic policy and military strategy before 1911 had been basically defensive and British-oriented.

The events of the years 1905–11 had, however, created impulses for a
basic change in French stategy. German pressures during the Moroccan
crises had caused a French desire for greater security, and the undepend-
ability of the Franco-Russian alliance as a diplomatic tool had demonstrated a weakness in French policy. The departure occurred first in personnel, where the offensive-minded Joffre and Messimy replaced more
defensive-minded colleagues as the determiners of French strategy. The
previous defensive strategy was transformed into the offensive Plan
XVII, which envisaged an attack at the German center while the Germans were concentrating on their advance through Belgium. This
change in strategy and simultaneous German increases seemed to require increases in the French army. Meanwhile, the French sought alterations in Russian strategy. With the bribe of financial assistance and the
promise of their own offensive, the French won Russian commitment to
a rapid offensive against Germany. At the same time, the French tried to
consolidate the previous cooperation with the British. The military
talks during the second Moroccan crisis had been more extensive than
during the first. An Anglo-French naval agreement extended coopera-

tion by allowing the French to concentrate their fleet in the Mediterranean in exchange for a British promise of protection against a German naval attack on the French channel coast. Although the British even promised consultation in time of war, the French were unable to get a firm commitment, and the military talks which had occurred during the second Moroccan crisis lapsed. In part because of Anglo-Belgian warnings and in part because it could only lead to a defensive stalemate, the French dropped the idea of meeting the German advance through Belgium. Accordingly French strategy became offensive and Russian-oriented after 1911.

The changes in French strategy after 1911 reflected the new French diplomatic policy. French leaders—above all, Poincaré—evidenced greater determination to assert French great-power status against German pressure, which in turn required revitalization of the alliance with Russia. The French government, therefore, promised more diplomatic support to Russia in order to receive more assistance from Russia against Germany. The military corollary of this Russian diplomatic backing was a rapid and large Russian attack against Germany. Such a Russian action was unlikely if France remained on the defensive and could be expected only if the French themselves attacked Germany. In short, the Russian offensive necessitated a French offensive. This French offensive at the German middle increased the risks for France by allowing the Germans easier passage through Belgium and thus augmenting the possibility of German encirclement. But this risk seemed more than offset by the prospect of massive Russian aid. In effect, the French assumed greater short-run vulnerability in order to gain long-run advantages. French diplomatic policy and military strategy toward Russia, however, contradicted French policy and strategy toward Britain. To insure Russian support, the French had to promise an offensive war; indeed, the French and Russian soldiers quite logically agreed to drop the distinction between defensive and aggressive wars. But, to insure British support, the French meanwhile had to maintain the distinction and make their policy and strategy look defensive. Although the French sought to retain this duality and thereby both British and Russian support, Russia had become more important. Consequently, French strategy had become more ambivalent. Seeking greater security, it assumed greater risks; to defend its great-power status, France promised an aggressive war. But in doing so, French strategy was merely reflecting the contradictions of French policy, and policy and strategy were consistent with one another.[11]

The emphasis, though not the essence, of Russian strategy altered on the eve of war. Before 1911 Russian strategists had resembled their Austro-Hungarian counterparts in envisaging two possible eventualities—

wars against Austria-Hungary alone or against an Austro-German alliance. This duality in Russian strategy reflected the ambivalence of Russian diplomatic policy. Like the Austro-Hungarians, Russian leaders would make their decision between these two options on the basis of German decision. Thus, Russian policy and strategy were consistent before 1911. But the experience of the pre-1911 decade produced pressures for change of policy and strategy, since both had proven unsuccessful. The Bosnian crisis had found Russia not only militarily unprepared (after the Russo-Japanese war and revolution) but also diplomatically isolated without French support and confronted by a united Austro-German alliance. Russian leaders decided to avoid such diplomatic defeats by a change of policy and strategy. This defensive consideration was probably reinforced by the opportunity presented in the form of Balkan events—defeat of the Ottoman Empire, emergence of strong Balkan states, and weakness of the Austro-Hungarian Empire. The simultaneous alteration in French policy and strategy facilitated a Russian reorientation.

These pressures caused changes in Russian strategy. Men determined to increase Russian military strength took office, and military preparations—financed in part by the French—were intensified. The old dualistic strategy remained in the sense that the possibilities of war with either Austria-Hungary alone or an Austro-German alliance both remained. French demands that Russia concentrate the majority of its forces on Germany were accepted in principle, and the Russians began construction of railroads in Poland which would facilitate more rapid concentration against Germany, accelerated mobilization plans, and thereby prepared a more genuine threat against Germany. In agreement with the French, they erased the distinction between offensive and defensive wars, thereby insuring the more speedy and certain entry of both into a war in which the other was involved. But Russian practice did not conform entirely with Russian promises. Rather than renounce their early offensive against Austria-Hungary so as to concentrate all available forces against Germany, the Russians planned to deploy large armies against both Austria-Hungary and Germany, while keeping in reserve considerable forces which could be employed against either enemy depending on developments. In short, the Russians maintained their dualistic strategy although they intensified preparations for a war against Germany.

These changes in Russian strategy corresponded with the adjustments in Russian policy. Dualistic Russian strategy reflected ambivalent Russian policy. Since Russian statesmen were still uncertain on the eve of war whether or not Germany would support Austria-Hungary, they would have been illogical to develop a monistic strategy. It would have been logical for Russian leaders to prepare for one eventuality—i.e., either against Austria-Hungary or against both Austria-Hungary and Germany—only if they had been certain about Germany's decision to support Austria-Hungary. Since not even the Germans were clear on this point, it is not surprising that the Russians were undecided. The Russians did, however, seek to increase the likelihood of a war against Austria-Hungary alone and to decrease the probability of German entry. Germany might be deterred by the threat of French involvement. If it were not deterred, the alliance with France would at least divert German forces from the Russian front. To insure French diplomatic and military support, the Russians therefore found it necessary to promise a rapid attack of Germany. In this sense, strategy and policy cooperated. The Russians sought similar objectives in negotiations with the British for a naval agreement. Such an agreement was regarded by neither side as a practical tool of war but rather as a diplomatic move in giving the appearance of greater Entente solidarity which might deter German support for Austria-Hungary. Like the Franco-Russian alliance, an Anglo-Russian naval agreement seemed to increase the prospect of a bilateral confrontation with Austria-Hungary which Russia preferred to a war against the Austro-German alliance. Hence, Russian strategy and policy were generally consistent.[12]

Like Russian strategy, British strategy remained essentially the same on the eve of war, although its emphasis changed. British military strategy before 1911 had assumed a Franco-German war in which the British would send an expeditionary force to aid the French left. British naval strategy envisaged the possibility of a great Anglo-German naval battle which required British retention of superiority in naval building and thus the naval race with Germany. British strategy was therefore French-oriented and defensive, with the emphasis on naval expansion. This strategy was appropriate in consideration of British policy which resisted German threats to the balance of power, most notably in supporting France during the first Moroccan crisis. The experience of the years 1905–11 produced some pressures for changes in British strategy. Renewed German threats to France in the second Moroccan crisis convinced the British that it would be useful to formalize consultation with the French in case of future German pressure on France. Talks between British and French staffs were accordingly revived and extended during the crisis, and the British even went so far as to make an agreement with the French on naval dispositions in case of war. But what the British did not do is as revealing as what they did. Unlike the continental powers, they did not commit themselves to a specific strategy in case of war, their promise to the French being only to consult on whether they would cooperate militarily. Even if they did cooperate militarily with the French, the British perceived the objective as basically defensive, i.e., resistance to the German advance. Furthermore, the staff conversations during the second Moroccan crisis were allowed to lapse after the crisis had passed. The Anglo-French naval agreement was specific, but its goal was also defensive, namely, to protect the northern French coast against a German landing. Preparations were made for a large naval battle with the Germans, but the occurrence of such a battle depended on a German decision to seek it, and the British could therefore not even insure implementation of an offensive strategy in the one area where they might have wanted to pursue it. The naval race which had dominated British thinking became less intense after 1912 because the Germans tacitly accepted British superiority and concentrated on military expansion. As already mentioned, the Anglo-Russian naval agreement pursued primarily diplomatic objectives and envisaged little practical naval cooperation. In short, British military and naval cooperation with the French was somewhat more formalized, and diplomatic cooperation with Russia was being considered, but the naval race had slowed and little change in strategy had occurred. British strategy remained defensive and French-oriented.

British strategy reflected British policy. The central British policy objective in Europe was to preserve the status quo and thus the balance of power between the continental alliances. The formalization of consultation and naval agreement with France, as well as negotiations over a naval agreement with Russia, served this end by resisting German pressure. But the refusal of the British to commit themselves unequivocally to a war against Germany served the same end by restraining the Franco-Russian alliance. Thus, there existed a certain duality in British strategy, as in the strategy of the other powers. Also, as in the case of the other powers, this duality was due to a fundamental ambivalence of British policy. British leaders were no more certain about the behavior of the continental powers than the continental powers were themselves. The British were not unanimous on whether the Austro-German or Franco-Russian alliance was the greater threat. British leaders might have committed themselves to an unconditional military-naval alliance with the French and Russians only if the British had decided that the Austro-German alliance was the only threat to the balance of power, or, conversely, against such an alliance only if they had been convinced that the Franco-Russian alliance was the main threat to the balance of power. Since British leaders were uncertain of the other powers' policies, it was logical for them to leave their strategy flexible and basically responsive to continental events. In this sense, British strategy and policy were consistent.[13]

The strategies of all the powers were generally consistent with their policies. The monism of German and French strategies reflected their unambiguous policies, namely, their perceptions of each other as the certain opponent. The dualism of Austro-Hungarian, Russian, and British strategies reflected their ambivalent policies—their uncertainty regarding opponents. Only French strategy changed fundamentally on the eve of war, because only French policy changed, i.e., in its reassertion of French great-power status. The strategies of the other powers altered in emphasis, detail, and articulation, but not in basic concept, because the other powers pursued fundamentally the same policies. A basic change did occur, however, in the attitudes of all the continental powers toward implementation of strategy. This change was due to a different perception of the general international situation, opponents' intentions, and the likelihood of war. It is indicated in their preparations for and perceptions of war.

PREPARATIONS FOR WAR: MEN, MATERIEL, MONEY

The most striking military fact on the eve of war was not change in strategy but increase in armaments. During the last years before the war, expenditures on arms rose by 37 percent throughout Europe. An understanding of the international situation necessitates an examination of this phenomenon.

German increases occurred in two stages during 1912 and 1913, followed by preparations for a third in 1914. The impulses for each were somewhat different. The 1912 increases were precipitated by the experiences of the second Moroccan crisis. They were motivated by a sense of frustration at failure and directed more at France and Britain than at Russia. The government's failure to produce a striking success which would satisfy an aroused public opinion caused severe criticism and thereby redounded to the advantage of those who advocated increases. Above all, this was Tirpitz, who commented during the crisis that it was a windfall for naval increases. In fact, the crisis had not only frustrated many Germans but also made them realize that German power was limited to the continent. Tirpitz argued that naval increases were necessary not only for the political reasons of prestige, world power, and equality with Britain, but also to force colonial concessions and even a promise of neutrality from Britain as envisaged by his risk theory. Tirpitz used all means at his disposal to win support for this view, including press propaganda and attacks on Bethmann, who resisted naval increases. Tirpitz's main object was to gain the kaiser's backing, and he was initially successful. Aroused by the excitement of the second Moroccan crisis, the kaiser spoke of Germany's place in the sun and regarded a stronger navy as the means of extracting colonial concessions from the British. Typically, the kaiser expressed defensive as well as offensive sentiments by favoring expansion, in the belief that France and Britain would attack Germany. Consequently, during the last stages of the crisis in the autumn of 1911, the kaiser seems to have favored naval increases.[14]

Around the beginning of 1912, he, however, swung over to increases of both the navy and the army. Meanwhile, the army was registering its demands for increases. These demands developed gradually. At first, the generals felt that the army was sufficiently large to insure German security, but during the autumn of 1911 sentiment among the soldiers shifted. Some made the essentially diplomatic argument that Anglo-French resistance during the second Moroccan crisis proved that German military superiority was no longer recognized by the Entente. Moltke asserted in December 1911 that all states except Germany were preparing for a war which was inevitable because it was the only solution to the existing political problems. Minister of War Heeringen argued that a weak German army would encourage, but a strong army would deter, enemy breach of the peace. The exponents of military expansion claimed that they were necessary to conduct a modern, mass war. But, since limited funds implied that expansion of one service would limit expansion of the other, the soldiers argued for military rather than naval expansion.[15]

Bethmann used this rivalry to limit naval expansion. The Moroccan crisis had placed him in a weak position to resist increases in general and Tirpitz's agitation in particular. The central question for him consequently became not whether, but what and how much, expansion. He opposed naval increases because of their effect on Britain, with which he was seeking to improve relations after the second Moroccan crisis. Both he and Tirpitz were anxious to win colonial concessions and neutrality in war from the British, but they differed over method. Tirpitz advocated threats, while Bethmann urged cooperation and was backed by Kiderlen and the Foreign Office, which also favored improved relations with Britain. Bethmann may have agreed to support army increases in exchange for the General Staff's help against Tirpitz. Although he succeeded in postponing naval increases until the second Moroccan crisis was concluded in November, Bethmann finally had to accept naval as well as military expansion at the beginning of January 1912. The army budget was presented to the Reichstag in February, the navy bill in March, and both were passed in May by large majorities and published as law in June. Thus, the impulses were a mixture of diplomatic pique, frustration, personal opportunism, service rivalries, and fears of other powers, particularly Britain and France.[16]

Although the increases of 1912 were extensive, they did not satisfy many German leaders. Again, as in the previous year, the decision to seek expansion was neither unanimous nor immediate among the generals. Many of the more conservative generals who controlled the ultimate decision initially resisted the suggestion, primarily on the practical ground that the army could not accommodate more recruits and on the social ground that further expansion would dilute the officer class. But during the autumn of 1912 they acceded. The explanation for this change of heart is not entirely satisfactory. New strategic considerations were probably not critical. Mounting pressure of unofficial military groups (like the Army League) and militant civilian publicists may have contributed. War in the Balkans and fear of war between the powers were probably important factors. The fact that the defeated Turkish army had been German-trained may have been a consideration. Preparations of the other powers may have played a role. Ludendorff's greater access to Moltke may have tipped the scales. In any case, the change seems to have been caused less by actual than anticipated events. Factors which had existed for years were suddenly reinterpreted in more desperate terms. The net result was confirmation of the belief that war must be prepared for. The victory for expansion was incomplete, since its main advocate, Ludendorff, alienated the conservatives sufficiently to be forced from office as Moltke's adviser in January 1913. Nonetheless, the bill on which Moltke, Heeringen, and Bethmann agreed in the same month constituted the largest single peacetime increase in German history.[17]

As usual, Bethmann's policy was an ambiguous compromise, a short-run success which assumed long-term risks. Again his main concern was not opposition to the increases, but minimization of their diplomatic implications. The magnitude of the expansion insured that their effects would be considerable. Bethmann recognized that publication of increases during the tensions created by the Balkan wars might jeopardize not only Anglo-German cooperation for a peaceful solution of the crisis but also his own efforts to neutralize Britain in a war. Consequently, he accepted the increases on condition that the Balkan crisis be resolved first and that no further demands be made for naval expansion. This condition made sense in terms of military preparations as well, since war had to be avoided in the period during which expansion would occur. The Germans may have had this concern in mind when they restrained the Austro-Hungarians in February and again in July 1913. As Moltke wrote Conrad in May 1913, diplomatic resolution of the Scutari crisis "was only a postponement but no solution. Thus the strengthening of the German army." The relationship of military and diplomatic policies were recognized when Bethmann commented to the kaiser in December 1912 that "all our future policy depends on the interdependence of these questions" and when Moltke wrote Conrad in February 1913 that "politics and strategy are closely intertwined."[18]

By the beginning of March 1913, Bethmann's political imperatives for expansion existed since tension caused by the first Balkan war had relaxed. In justifying its policy, the German government used contradictory arguments designed to excuse more than explain. It was rationalized at once as response to French and Russian increases, as an effort to dampen French chauvinism, and as necessary in case of war. The domestic political imperatives also had military and diplomatic implications. Since passage of the budget seemed to require a one-time tax and the expansion could probably not be repeated, Germany's military advantage would be temporary and maximal when the increases had been instituted but would lessen thereafter as its opponents responded. The bill eventually passed with considerable difficulty in July 1913, and new recruits were taken into the army by the autumn of 1913. Meanwhile, the Germans continued their naval building but did not keep pace with the British, and the kaiser refused a proposed expansion of naval personnel.[19]

The third phase of German increases began on the eve of war. As with the previous expansion, the impulses for this new stage are difficult to isolate. Despite the size of the 1913 bill, some Germans regarded it as insufficient. The Sanders episode during the autumn of 1913 and the press feud of the following winter increased Russo-German tensions. German leaders made statements on some occasions indicating that they did not regard France and Russia as serious threats in the near future, but in other instances they seem to have been genuinely worried by Franco-Russian expansion. Concern seems to have outweighed confidence increasingly during the spring. Bellicose articles in the Russian press during June reinforced the anxieties of German leaders. The impulses for new increases were, therefore, apparently mixed. Whatever the motives, first Moltke in May and then the kaiser in June urged further expansion whose objective was universal military conscription which would utilize all possible German manpower. As on the previous occasions, this pressure was resisted by conservatives like War Minister Falkenhayn, who argued that new increases were impractical until the army had adjusted to the last. The debate continued through the July crisis and was resolved only by the war. Meanwhile, Bethmann threatened the British that there would be renewed demands from the German public for greater naval building if Britain did not restrain Russia. It seems reasonable to predict that further expansion would probably have occurred had the war not intervened.[20]

The German government simultaneously considered economic and financial preparations for war. During and after the first Moroccan crisis, studies had been made of German food supplies in wartime which it had been decided would be sufficient. In 1909, some reforms had been made in the banking system in order to render it more capable of dealing with the problems of mobilization. The second Moroccan crisis, nonetheless, caused considerable financial dislocation, and criticism was leveled at the government for its insufficient preparations. Suggestions that a financial general staff should be established were rejected by the kaiser, who was "completely uninterested" in the question of German financial preparations, as well as by Interior Minister Clemens Delbrück and Treasury Secretary Kühn, who argued that it was both unnecessary and impractical for domestic political and diplomatic reasons. The outbreak of war in the Balkans in October 1912 caused new criticism and demands for preparations. Claims that Germany's food supply in war would be inadequate produced an interministerial commission in November 1912, which considered the problem regularly until the war, but Delbrück argued from the start that German food production would be adequate and no practical changes resulted. Criticism of German economic unpreparedness—primarily from financiers and heavy industrialists— resulted in the formation during December 1912 of a "Standing Commission for Mobilization Problems," whose mandate was broad (primarily the problem of food, but also including labor, raw materials, and transportation), yet the agrarians and Delbrück were opposed to it and the commission concluded that the German economy could not be organized for war in peacetime. Although the Balkan wars also caused a fall in the stock market and severe problems for the German banking system, Havenstein, head of the Imperial bank, argued that the German financial structure was strong enough to overcome the problems of mobilization. Most estimates of preparation and mobilization costs were far below the actual expenditures during World War I but nonetheless implied basic changes in financing methods, and the problem of paying for the conduct of a war was hardly considered at all. Consequently, no serious financial preparation was made except for an increase of reserves for the event of war. A slight intensification of pressures for economic measures may have occurred at the beginning of 1914. Moltke raised the question in January 1914 and urged the formation of a central commission but was again resisted by Delbrück, who argued for decentralization. The problem was considered in the Foreign Office in March 1914. Moltke emphasized the problem's importance again in May and finally succeeded in having convened an economic commission which actually established an agenda including labor, raw materials, transportation, and replacements for goods stopped by blockade. Delbrück, meanwhile, continued his resistance to extensive plans which he thought unnecessary in the short war predicted by the generals. Thus, in contrast to military preparations, little was done to prepare for the war economically.[21]

German military preparations were made in the context of preparations by the other powers. The Austro-Hungarians introduced increases in 1912, in late 1913, and early 1914, financed in part by loans from Berlin. To meet the demands of their new offensive strategy, the French, meanwhile, expanded their standing army by extending the length of military service from two to three years. The Three-Year Law was introduced by the government in March 1913, passed in August, implemented in November (when the new class of recruits was inducted), jeopardized by the Left's opposition during the spring of 1914, but rescued by the government in June. The Russians meanwhile made plans for large army and navy increases which were announced in June 1913, completed in October, presented to the Duma in November, supported by a French loan (agreed upon in December and the first payment received in February 1914), voted by the Duma in March 1914, signed by the tsar in April, became law in July, and were to be fulfilled by 1917. British increases during this period were slight.[22]

The new expenditures on arms altered relationships among the powers. The new budgets marked a sharp increase in total military spending for all the powers. Total expenditures on armies increased more rapidly than on navies but altered relative spending on armies and navies only slightly. Most of the increases were accounted for by Germany, Austria-Hungary, and Russia. As a result, the order of total expenditures among the powers altered, with Britain and Italy dropping, while Germany, Russia and Austria-Hungary rose. The relative total expenditures of the Austro-German and Franco-Russian-British alignments became more similar as a result but still favored the Franco-Russian-British group. The powers allocated their new funds quite differently, the Germans concentrating on the army, the Austro-Hungarians primarily on the army, the Russians splitting their funds, the French and British focusing on their navies. As a result, the Germans and Austro-Hungarians spent almost four times as much on their armies as their navies, the Russians and French twice as much on their armies as their navies, and the British almost twice as much on their navy as their army. Germany increased its spending most on the army in both absolute and relative terms, followed by Austria-Hungary and Russia. Consequently, the rank order of expenditures on armies altered, with Germany displacing Russia as the greatest spender and Austria-Hungary moving up from last to fourth and equal with Britain. The relative army budgets of the two alliances altered accordingly: whereas the Franco-Russian alliance alone outspent the Austro-German alliance on their armies in 1910, the Franco-Russian alliance was outspent by the Austro-German alliance and needed British army expenditures to offset Austro-German increases in 1914. In new expenditures on their navies, Austria-Hungary led in relative terms followed by Russia, while Russia led in absolute terms followed by Britain. As a result of these increases, the rank order of naval expenditures was altered as Russia rose rapidly from fourth to second behind Britain. Despite these shifts, the relative naval exenditures of the two alliances remained constant.[23]

These changes had revealing implications. The magnitude of increase in military spending constituted a quantum leap which marked a significant departure: whereas during the previous decade crises had remained largely diplomatic, now suddenly they were accompanied by radically increased military spending. The quality of this spending indicated policy priorities. In its concentration on army increases, the Austro-German alliance demonstrated its concern for a land war, whereas the Franco-Russian split of new increases implied that they were not preparing solely for such a war and the British were not preparing for it at all. The choice between army and naval spending also represented in general a choice between men and materiel. It may also imply a choice between short and long wars, although not necessarily. The emphasis in the programs of increased spending was universally on speed, both in the sense of speed of implementation and efficiency of mobilization (e.g., in Russian railroad building), and in general on improving offensive capability. What was not done was as revealing as what was. In emphasising their armies, the Austro-German alliance did not emphasise their navies, a notable reorientation particularly for the Germans, who had been competing with the British during the previous decade. Few economic preparations were made, largely because the short war envisaged by most seemed to make them superfluous. Although some—like Ludendorff—argued for a "nation in arms" which implied a social revolution, no such revolution occurred, the increases being fitted in all cases into the existing social and economic structure. With the possible exception of Germany's building of the Kiel canal and fortification of Heligoland, and perhaps the Anglo-French naval agreement regarding the French coast, defensive preparations were made by none of the powers.

It is easier to measure than to evaluate these events. To a certain extent, they probably reflected views of war, namely, that it was inevitable and must be prepared for. Alternatively, they may have affected attitudes in making war seem more inevitable. Hence, they may have been at once symptoms and causes of the prevailing mental state.[24] Like the military strategies of the powers, these increases reflected diplomatic policies. Austro-German expansion indicated their anxieties about the Franco-Russian alliance and hopes to exclude Britain. Franco-Russian spending implied not only concern for the European balance but also interest elsewhere, particularly of the Russians for the straits as implied in their massive naval building program. British concentration on the navy reflected their continuing relative disinterest in the continent and concentration on the empire. Considering their policy objectives, it would have been illogical for the powers to spend their funds in vastly different ways, except perhaps for the Russian naval expansion. Military spending, like military strategy, depended on diplomatic policy. But policy reflected perceptions of the international situation and war. Thus, the critical element for military as well as diplomatic considerations was the perception of war.

PERCEPTIONS AND PREDICTIONS: WHETHER, WHEN, WHAT, WHOM?

The perceptions and predictions of war by European leaders were ultimately the determinants of military plans and preparations. These views of war included various elements, namely, the questions as to whether, when, what, with, and against whom war would be fought.

German leaders expressed themselves frequently on the question of whether war would occur. The kaiser implied or stated specifically that war was inevitable in most—although not all—his statements, but his view of war was seen to be more ambivalent by others. Moltke consistently argued that war was inevitable, and Admiral Müller, Falkenhayn, and other soldiers apparently agreed. The statesmen were less certain: Bethmann was characteristically ambivalent, and Foreign Secretaries Kiderlen and Jagow, Ambassadors Lichnowsky, Pourtalès, and Tschirschky, and Bethmann's cousin, Dietrich Bethmann, all implied that it was possible but avoidable. Outsiders viewed German leaders contradictorily. Conrad and Francis Ferdinand thought German leaders regarded war as inevitable, while Berchtold felt that they did not.[25] Austro-Hungarian leaders likewise discussed the prospect of war repeatedly. Francis Joseph and Francis Ferdinand seem to have believed a general war avoidable, although Francis Ferdinand advocated war with Serbia, whereas Conrad regarded war as inevitable, and most Austro-Hungarian statesmen—with the possible exception of Tisza—expected war sooner or later.[26] Russian leaders planned for the possibility of war but seem to have regarded it as avoidable. French leaders were ambivalent. The soldiers saw war as possible, while civilian leaders like Poincaré regarded it as sometimes possible, sometimes inevitable, and Paleologue claimed it was inevitable—probably to frighten the government into maintaining the Three-Year Law. Those politicians who opposed the Three-Year Law presumably regarded war as avoidable. The French were perceived in different ways: by the Russians as believing war avoidable, by the Belgians as believing it unavoidable, and by the Germans as planning it. British leaders regarded war as possible but generally unlikely. Italian leaders were ambivalent. Belgian leaders probably felt war was avoidable, whereas at least one American leader saw it as avoidable only if the United States intervened.[27]

Attitudes toward the question of when war would occur were similarly mixed. The kaiser and Moltke were ambivalent: sometimes they expected war soon, other times late; sometimes they favored it immediately, sometimes they advocated postponement. Falkenhayn foresaw war later, but Ludendorff probably anticipated it soon. The admirals seem to have favored postponement in order to allow further preparations. Bethmann was again uncertain: war could occur at anytime but he probably did not expect it soon. Jagow does not seem to have expected it soon, although he may have regarded it as possible.[28] Austro-Hungarian leaders were likewise disagreed. Francis Joseph and Francis Ferdinand thought war could be avoided altogether, Berchtold and Tisza believed it might be postponed, whereas Conrad regarded it as imminent. The tsar may have reflected a consensus among Russian leaders in assuming that war was not imminent. French leaders may have expected war soon because of reported German statements, but their preparations implied that they did not. Some Italian generals favored war soon but were probably not representative of Italian leaders.[29]

Views varied on what war would be like. A racial war was predicted frequently by the kaiser and Moltke but less frequently by Bethmann, Jagow, Tschirschky, Waldersee, and others in and outside the government. A war threatening the existence of one or more powers was likewise foreseen more by the kaiser and Moltke than by Bethmann, Jagow, and others. Bethmann, Moltke, and the kaiser all spoke of a European war on some occasions and a world war on others; the kaiser, Tschirschky, and Waldersee mentioned a great war at other times. Moltke and the kaiser expected that the war would be a mass conflict. Despite these predictions of a large war, most German leaders implied or stated that a war would be short. They predicted the outcome infrequently and without excessive confidence. Among Austro-Hungarian leaders, Conrad spoke most frequently of war which he hoped would not be formulated as a racial struggle (since the Habsburg Empire was multiracial) but which he nonetheless expected would be a great war involving the existence of the Habsburg Empire.[30]

There was general agreement though not unanimity on the question of opponents. Most German leaders expected Germany to have to fight both France and Russia but on occasion emphasized one over the other. They discussed Britain most because its behavior in war was least certain. Some—particularly the kaiser, Bethmann, and Jagow—regarded initial British neutrality as a possibility, but others—particularly Moltke, Lichnowsky, Kiderlen, and even the kaiser on many occasions— regarded British entry as certain. Moltke and the kaiser sought to avoid fighting the Belgians by a combination of threats and bribes. They do not seem to have envisaged war with Switzerland, but the possibility of a future war with the United States was mentioned. German leaders may have hoped that an Austro-Serbian war would be localized, but most seem not to have expected it to be. Austro-Hungarian leaders generally hoped a war could be fought with Serbia alone but doubted the possibility and expected instead that Russia would support Serbia.[31] German leaders counted on the alliance with Austria-Hungary in general, although they doubted it on specific occasions—during the second Moroccan crisis and at the end of the second Balkan war. The larger question mark was Italy. Although they sought to extract promises from the Italians that they would fight on the Triple Alliance side, German and Austro-Hungarian leaders were uncertain of Italian behavior in war. They also occasionally hoped for alliances with Turkey, Rumania, Bulgaria, Albania, and even Japan and Sweden.[32]

The responses to these questions of whether, when, what, and against whom war would be fought conditioned the perceptions of German and other leaders toward the desirability of war, specifically of a preventive war. The question of preventive war applied at two points, namely, before and during the July crisis; the first is relevant here, while the second is discussed in chapter 8. Before the July crisis the issue was whether or not German (or other) leaders advocated and/or planned a preventive war. It seems fairly clear that many German and Austro-Hungarian leaders accepted the logic of a preventive war, that war was inevitable and should therefore be fought at the most advantageous (or least disadvantageous) moment. This supposition was reflected in statements that time was against the Austro-German alliance and that its enemies planned an aggressive war. The discussions among German and Austro-Hungarian leaders as to how war should most advantageously begin can be interpreted as a kind of planning for war. On occasion, some German and Austro-Hungarian leaders—most importantly, Moltke and Conrad—actually advocated preventive war; others—such as the kaiser— implied it; whereas others—such as Bethmann and Jagow—specifically rejected the proposition. The demands for preventive war together with German diplomatic, military, and domestic political policy can be conceived as a coordinated policy beginning in late 1912 and aiming at a preventive war in 1914. This assertion is, however, difficult to prove or disprove conclusively. The arguments of some German leaders—such as Moltke and the kaiser—for new arms increases in 1914 suggest that they were not planning war in 1914. It is perhaps more likely that a preventive war was becoming more compelling for German and Austro-Hungarian leaders during the spring of 1914, even though all did not make the conscious decision to seek it in the immediate future. There is no evidence that the Entente powers planned a preventive war either for 1914 or later. Nonetheless, all quite logically pursued what might be called preventive diplomacy in anticipating future events (particularly German diplomatic pressure or even military attack) which they sought to deter by diplomatic and military policies.[33]

The perception of a preventive war was affected by the attitudes prevailing among contemporary statesmen toward war. It was widely accepted that the threat of force was a prerequisite for successful diplomacy, and many leaders described a decision for war as proper under certain circumstances. Preparations for war were therefore regarded by many statesmen and soldiers as their duty.[34]

A certain inconsistency exists between this prevailing view of war and the logic of a preventive war on the one hand and the lack of either a consistent policy or specific decision to seek war on the other. German leaders in fact did not pursue the precise policy which was demanded by their assumptions. This contradiction may be best explained by a fundamental ambivalence among German leaders toward Germany's international position. They oscillated between feelings of anxiety and arrogance. This ambivalence is reflected by the advocates of a preventive war who implied—often in the same statement—short-term confidence in victory but long-term fear of defeat. Similar ambivalence was indicated by German leaders who perceived a necessary choice between absolute success and absolute failure. The objects of concern and confidence varied. During the second Moroccan crisis, German leaders expressed considerable fears but less confidence toward Britain, whereas they were more confident and less concerned about France. During 1913 and 1914 German leaders expressed increasing anxiety about France and particularly Russia. But these statements were offset by denials of concern and even some claims of great confidence. German leaders tended to dismiss the worries of Austro-Hungarian leaders but to fear for the Habsburg Empire's future within their own councils.[35] Some of these fluctuations can be explained by changing circumstances: the doubts about Britain during the second Moroccan crisis lessened because the crisis passed and was replaced thereafter by anxieties about France and Russia because of the Balkan wars and arms increases. Some of the disparities in the attitudes of German leaders can be attributed to political tactics: in order to restrain the Austro-Hungarians during the Balkan wars, German leaders minimized the Russian danger. But the variety of statements may also be due to a basic contradiction in German policy. German leaders were committed to maintain Germany's great-power status which seemed to imply an expansive policy, yet they were confronted with the resistance of the other powers. The resolution of this dilemma depended on an evaluation of German power. If it was sufficient to overcome resistance, an activist policy was justified, but, if it was not, a moderate or even defensive policy was logical. German leaders were, however, ambivalent about German power which seemed great enough to encourage ambitions but too weak to fulfill them—probably a valid evaluation.[36] This ambivalence was also in a certain sense appropriate to the general balance of power in Europe and was reinforced by the changes expected in the power relationships during the next few years. Hence ambivalence and uncertainty seem to have been the basic attitudes of German leaders.

The multiplicity of attitudes among German leaders is frequently interpreted in terms of factions usually described as war and peace parties, identified with soldiers and statesmen, respectively. This view has validity in the sense that the soldiers were in general more disposed toward war than the civilians. But, since all soldiers did not advocate war and those who advocated war were not all soldiers, the line between soldiers and statesmen is unclear. The more basic question is the issue of factions, i.e., whether war and peace parties existed. Such a breakdown implies two clearly distinguishable policies which would have caused fundamentally different consequences depending on which was pursued.[37] German leaders certainly had differences over policy which were perceived by some in terms of factions such as civilian-military but in fact obscured basic unanimity.[38] A consensus existed among German leaders on fundamental questions of German power and prospects: all were committed to maintaining German great-power status with an activist policy even at the risk of war and none advocated peace at the cost of German interests. All were agreed on the foundations of German policy (alliance with Austria-Hungary and enmity with the Franco-Russian alliance) and strategy (the Schlieffen plan, including the passage through Belgium).[39] The differences over immediate questions were perceived as fundamental and factional in part because of the respective roles of the military and civilian authorities: by definition, soldiers ponder and prepare for the possibility of war, while statesmen in general pursue policy objectives by peaceful means, and the soldiers quite naturally speak of war with less abhorrence than the civilians. The differences in their attitudes may have been exaggerated by contrasting styles:

soldiers tended to use more brutal, perhaps more candid and forthright, language than the statesmen, even though their views did not differ fundamentally. The factions interpretation also had the appeal of providing a scapegoat in allowing the blame for mistakes and even the war itself to be placed on militarists, chauvinists, and superpatriots. But the factions view has persisted, perhaps in part because it has a practical diplomatic function. As long as statesmen are determined to seek peace, it is necessary to assume that other governments are willing to do likewise. When other states nonetheless act belligerently, this behavior must be explained away as the result of pressures from a war party rather than the policy of the government. On the eve of war this procedure was frequently used by German leaders who perceived such war and peace parties in other countries, as others did in Germany.[40] When governments stopped making this distinction and attributed bellicosity to the governments of other powers, diplomacy became more difficult and peace threatened. This danger was accompanied and probably reinforced by a growing tendency of German and other statesmen to denigrate diplomacy during the winter and spring of 1914.[41]

The relationship between diplomatic and military policies can be perceived like the relationship between diplomatic policy and domestic politics as causal, complementary, congruent, or complex. The causal interpretation implies a basic difference and even conflict between military and diplomatic policies. This conflict is usually presented in terms of factions, i.e., soldiers versus statesmen or war and peace parties. The causal relationship can be seen as either consistent or alternating. Military policy is frequently perceived as consistently determining diplomatic policy, whereas diplomacy is infrequently perceived as consistently determining military policy. Sometimes military and diplomatic policy are seen as affecting each other alternatingly: first military policy as the determinant, then diplomatic policy. German foreign policy is then perceived as a conflict with strategy which the military ultimately won. The complementary interpretation assumes a distinction but not conflict between military and diplomatic policies which are merely different areas of activity, set limits for each other, and operate within their respective spheres more or less autonomously. Accordingly German diplomatic policy before the war can be understood more or less without consideration for military policy except in the broadest sense. The interpretation of congruity assumes that strategy and diplomacy are merely different applications of the same general policy. Rather than conflicting, they are agreed on basic assumptions, and the distinctions between soldier and statesmen or war and peace parties are regarded as relatively insignificant personality conflicts or bickering over authority. In this sense German diplomacy is seen as part of a general policy in which strategy is an essential and basically harmonious element. The interpretation of complexity assumes that the relationship between military and diplomatic is indefinable because the two activities are inseparable and can only be described in general terms.

There is evidence to support all of these interpretations. Paradoxically, the two most popular are probably the two most contradictory, namely, causality and complexity. The most appealing to the present writer is, however, congruity. Conflicts emerged over details of tactics and timing but did not involve basic policy changes which would have altered the course of German international behavior. German diplomatic and military policies on the eve of war were based on the same assumptions about the international situation and German aspirations. Indeed, given the situation and assumptions, these policies were virtually imposed on German leaders.

THE PREWAR PARADOX: CALM OR CATACLYSM?

An analysis of the relationship between diplomatic, military, and domestic policies may suggest an insight into the international situation on the eve of war. There exists what might be called a prewar paradox. Relations between the powers were perceived in radically different ways. Nicolson, the permanent undersecretary of the British Foreign Office, wrote Goschen, the British ambassador in Berlin, in mid-May 1914 that "there is very little of interest taking place at this moment in Europe and, were it not for the troubles in Mexico, we should be in comparative calm here." In fact he went on to describe two exceptions—Persia and Ireland—which caused "great anxiety and crisis in this country." But Europe he perceived as calm. Ten days later, Colonel House, President Wilson's adviser, wrote Wilson that "the situation is extra-ordinary. It is militarism run stark mad. Unless someone acting for you can bring about a different understanding, there is some day to be an awful cataclysm."[42] These contradictory perceptions demand an explanation.

Historical sense can be made of this paradox by rejecting one of its elements. War can be seen as the result of prewar attitudes by choosing from the mass of contradictory evidence that sample which resembles war and by rejecting that part which looks unlike it. The difficulty with this approach is that statements about the imminence of war can be found in all periods. To establish conclusively that attitudes toward war changed on the eve of war, it is necessary to demonstrate a change in quality and/or quantity which is difficult. This difficulty does not prove that such a change did not occur since it is quite conceivable that it did. But even if such a change can be demonstrated, it need not have caused war. The search for predictions of war on the eve of the conflict assumes that there is a connection between what happens and what men—particularly statesmen and soldiers—expect to happen. Such predictions can be shown to have caused war only if they were acted upon, i.e., only if they were in fact decisions for war. No such decision can, however, be documented. Ultimately, this method demonstrates only what is already known, namely, that statements about war were made and that war broke out in August 1914. Its circular logic is illustrated by Fischer's comment: "the feeling that a great European conflagration in the foreseeable future would be unavoidable had entered ever more into the general consciousness of Europe, despite all apparent calm."[43] The statement may be true but cannot be demonstrated. Indeed, it rejects what is demonstrable, the "apparent calm," in favor of what is not, the "general consciousness of Europe." Thus, it falls into the tautological trap of assuming what it asserts.

Conversely, war can be seen as a departure from prewar attitudes if one chooses from the mass of contradictory evidence that which resembles peace, while rejecting that part which looks like war. The problem with this approach is the same as the previous: that statements about peace can be found in all periods. It is difficult to demonstrate that such statements increased and/or that bellicose remarks did not increase on the eve of war. In this view, governments and peoples were no more bellicose than they had been previously. To reverse Fischer's proposition, Europe was characterized by calm, despite all talk of a great conflagration. War was thus a departure from, not a result of, the prevailing attitudes. This may be true but it is difficult to demonstrate. Like the previous interpretation, this approach ultimately falls into the tautological trap of proving what it assumes, namely, that the war was caused by chance events beyond the control of governments.

Better sense can perhaps be made of the prewar paradox by accepting it. Paradox may indeed have been characteristic of the prewar mood, as desperation mixed with determination, anxiety with aggressiveness, optimism with pessimism, activism with apathy, rigidity with fluidity, preparation with procrastination. In short, contradiction rather than consistency is the striking feature. This situation caused an uncertainty about the future which was conducive to gambling, either to gain the best or avoid the worst. At the same time, it produced a contradictory determination to preserve the status quo. Confusion rather than either consistent concern or confidence seems to have been the prevailing spirit in 1914.

This uncertainty can be related to the fundamental congruity between the views of soldiers and statesmen. It tended to impose the same basic assumptions upon them, however they would differ over tactics and timing. It also caused leaders of all countries to commit themselves to mutually incompatible policies. These policies could peacefully coexist as long as they were not consistently pursued. No government committed itself consciously to seeking war. But, if these policies confronted one another, either one would have to be disavowed or war would result. The European situation in 1914 virtually insured that they would confront each other and that these policies would not be disavowed.

NOTES

1   Gasser, "Entschluss," pp. 175–84. For a general consideration of prewar military planning, see: Paul R. Kennedy, ed. *The War Plans of the Great Powers* (London, 1979).

2   For German increases, see pp. 135–40 above.

3   Conrad, *Dienstzeit*, 3:87, 145–55, 275, 294, 435, 467, 478, 488, 495, 501–3, 596–612, 669, 754; Foerster, "Generalstabes," pp. 837–42, 874–78; *GP*, 39:15713.

4   *OU*, 7:8934.

5   Beyens, *L'Allemagne*, pp. 24–26 and *Années*, 2:38–39.

6   For German efforts to separate Britain from its allies, see chapter 3. For discussions among Moltke, Bethmann, and Jagow over whether the passage through Belgium was necessary, see: Fischer, *Krieg*, pp. 240, 566–67; Müller, *Kaiser*, p. 126; Ritter, *Staatskunst*, 2:268–72.

7   For Moltke's attitude toward the timing of war, see note 29 below.

8   See note 3 above.

9   Ibid.

10 For Austro-Hungarian diplomatic policy, see chapter 4 this volume.

11 Joffre, *Memoirs*, 1:11, 23, 37–44, 49, 56–58, 66, 83; Tuchman, *Guns*, pp. 34–37, 42–43, 57–58; Taylor, *Struggle*, p. 488; *Weltkrieg*, 1:85; Ritter, *Staatskunst*, 2:107–13.

12 Ibid.

13 Samuel R. Williamson, *The Politics of Grand Strategy: Britain and France Prepare for War, 1904–1914* (Cambridge, Mass., 1969), passim; Zara S. Steiner, *Britain and the Outbreak of the First World War* (London, 1977), passim.

14 Wernecke, *Wille*, pp. 144–47; Tirpitz, *Aufbau*, p. 200; Hubatsch, *Ära*, p. 91; Müller, *Kaiser*, pp. 89–92; *Kriegsrüstung*, 1:126.

15 Müller, *Kaiser*, p. 105; *Kriegsrüstung*, 1:126–35, 138; Fischer, *Krieg*, pp. 172–79.

16 Tirpitz, *Aufbau*, p. 209; Müller, *Kaiser*, pp. 90–92, 105, 107; Wernecke, *Wille*, pp. 151, 167–68; *Kriegsrüstung*, 1:138, 142–46, 150–51, 472, 491, 497, 503.

17 Fischer, *Krieg*, pp. 159–64, 235, 251, 272–76; Fischer, *Weltmacht*, p. 38; *Kriegsrüstung*, 1:146, 162, 188, 311; Ritter, *Staatskunst*, 2:276–79; *Weltkrieg*, 2:11; *GP*, 34:346–48; *GP*, 39:9–11; Strandmann, *Erforderlichkeit*, p. 12; Geiss, *Erforderlichkeit*, p. 55; Müller, *Kaiser*, p. 126; Conrad, *Dienstzeit*, 2:144.

18 *GP*, 39:9–11, 123, 177–78; Conrad, *Dienstzeit*, 2:144–47, 328.

19 *GP*, 39:70, 74–99, 177–78; *Weltkrieg*, 1:14; Barnes, *Genesis*, pp. 65–66; Fischer, *Griff*, pp. 44–45; Fischer, "Weltpolitik," pp. 330, 334; Ritter, *Staatskunst*, 2:268; Strandmann, *Erforderlichkeit*, p. 14; Bethmann, *Betrachtungen*, 1:87, 90–91; Taylor, *Struggle*, p. 496.

20 For evidence that German leaders were not seriously concerned about France and Russia, see: *GP*, 39:15844, 505–6; Conrad, *Dienstzeit*, 3:668–73; Tirpitz, *Erinnerungen*, p. 195. For evidence that German leaders were concerned, see: *GP*, 39:533–39, 564–65, 587, 628–30; Schäfer, "Präventivkrieg," p. 549; *BD*, 10:802–4, part 2; House, *Papers*, 1:278; Fischer, *Griff*, pp. 57–58; Bethmann, *Betrachtungen*, 1:93, 99; *Kriegsrüstung*, 1:206–10.

21 *Kriegsrüstung*, 1:197–244, 271–84, 331–78, 400–412, 476; Fischer, *Krieg*, pp. 280–88; Müller, *Kaiser*, p. 106; Burchardt, *Friedenswirtschaft*, p. 248; Schröter, *Krieg*, p. 47.

22 Joffre, *Memoirs*, 1:63; *Weltkrieg*, 1:14; *GP*, 39:256–58, 260–74, 582, 587; Fischer, *Griff*, pp. 57–58; Fischer, *Krieg*, pp. 621–22; Fay, *Origins*, 1:538–41; *Kriegsrüstung*, 1:202; Suchomlinow, *Erinnerungen*, p. 242.

23 European arms expenditures increased by 43 percent between 1900 and 1910. They increased by 37 percent between 1910 and 1914. If this rate of increase is prorated for ten years, it is equivalent to an increase of 92.6 percent. Between 1910 and 1914 expenditures on armies rose by 41.5 percent, on navies by 34 percent. But the ratio of total army to navy expenditures changed only slightly (1.98 to 2.1). The army expenditures of Germany, Austria-Hungary, and Russia constituted 84 percent of total army expenditures between 1910 and 1914. In 1910, the order of total defense spending was Britain (23.4 percent), Germany (22.1 percent), Russia (21 percent), France (18.2 percent), Italy (8.3 percent), and Austria-Hungary (6 percent); in 1914, the order had become Germany (28.7 percent), Russia (22.1 percent), Britain (19.3 percent), France (14.4 percent), Austria-Hungary (9.2 percent), and Italy (7.1 percent). In 1910, the Austro-German alliance spent a total of 28.1 percent of total European expenditures, the Franco-Russian-British group spent 63.5 percent; in 1914, the Austro-Germans spent 37.8 percent, the Franco-Russian-British spent 55.8 percent. The Germans spent almost 100 percent of their new funds on the army, the Austro-Hungarians 73.7 percent, the Russians 46 percent, the French 36 percent, and the British 20.5 percent. Between 1910 and 1914, the ratio of army to navy expenditures changed in Germany from 2 to 3.94, in Austria-Hungary from 5.2 to 3.76, in Russia from 5.7 to 2.8, in France from 2.5 to 2.2, in Britain from 0.78 to 0.6. The Germans increased their spending between 1910 and 1914 on the army by 116.5 percent, the Austro-Hungarians by 96 percent, the Russians by 21.3 percent, while the French, British, and Italians left theirs almost constant. In 1910, the rank order of spending on armies was Russia (28.1 percent of European total), Germany (21.5 percent), France (19.8 percent), Britain (14.5 percent), Italy (8.6 percent), and Austria-Hungary (7.7 percent); by 1914, it was Germany (32 percent), Russia (24.1 percent), France (14.7 percent), Britain (10.9 percent), Austria-Hungary (10 percent), and Italy (6.8 percent). In 1910, the Austro-German alliance spent 29.2 percent of total European expenditures on armies, the Franco-Russian 47.9 percent, the Franco-Russian-British group 62.4 percent; in 1914, the Austro-German alliance spent 42 percent, the Franco-Russian alliance 38.8 percent and the Franco-Russian-British group spent 49.7 percent. In relative increased spending on navies between 1910 and 1914, Austria-Hungary was highest (172 percent increase), followed by Russia (150 percent), France (21.6 percent), Italy (19.5 percent), Britain (17.3 percent), and Germany (8.7 percent). In absolute terms, Russia led (14.2 million pounds), followed by Britain (7), Austria-Hungary (4.8), France (3.2), Germany (1.8), and Italy (1.6). Russia's increased naval spending comprised 43 percent of total increased naval spending. In 1910, the order of expenditures on navies was Britain (42.2 percent of total naval spending), Germany (21.4 percent), France (15.4 percent), Russia (9.7 percent), Italy (8.5 percent), Austria-Hungary (2.9 percent); in 1914, it was Britain (36.9 percent), Russia (18.5 percent), Germany (17.4 percent), France (14 percent), Italy (7.6 percent), and Austria-Hungary (5.9 percent). In 1910, the Austro-German alliance spent 24.3 percent of total naval expenditures, the Franco-Russian-British group 67.3 percent; in 1914 the Austro-German alliance spent 23.3 percent, the Franco-Russian-British group spent 69.4 percent. All calculations are based on statistics found in Taylor, *Struggle*, pp. xxvii–xxviii.

24 For an example of military increases perceived as a symptom of the assumption that war was inevitable, see Moltke's remark to Conrad (Conrad, *Dienstzeit*, 3:328). As an example of arms seen as encouraging the view that war was inevitable, see Berchtold's remark (*OU*, 7:395–403).

25 The kaiser frequently stated or implied that he thought war was inevitable: *GP*, 39:15612, 15613, 9–11; Fischer, "Weltpolitik," p. 311; Fischer, *Krieg*, p. 239; *Kriegsrüstung*, 1:127; *GP*, 34:811, part 2; *OU*, 7:8934; Conrad, *Dienstzeit*, 3:467; Beyens, *L'Allemagne*, p. 24; *GP*, 39:15861, 587; Fischer, *Griff*, pp. 57–58; House, *Papers*, 1:261–62. He implied infrequently that it was not necessarily unavoidable (*GP*, 35:115–16). Most observers believed the kaiser was not inclined to war: Jagow (Zechlin, "Motive," pp. 91–95), Tschirschky (Conrad, *Dienstzeit*, 3:597), and Kageneck (Conrad, *Dienstzeit*, 3:275, 294, 596). Bethmann sought to frighten the British with the kaiser's bellicosity (*GP*, 39:15883). Moltke consistently spoke of the war as inevitable: *Kriegsrüstung*, 1:126–35; Müller, *Kaiser*, p. 124; Conrad, *Dienstzeit*, 2:144–47; Conrad, *Dienstzeit*, 3:609–12, 668–73; Beyens, *L'Allemagne*, pp. 24–26; Zechlin, "Motive," pp. 91–95; *Kriegsrüstung*, 1:206–7, 349; Fischer, *Griff*, p. 59. Infrequently Moltke implied that war was not inevitable: *GP*, 34:12793, part 1; *GP*, 39:332–36, 572–77. Other German generals seem to have agreed with him: *Kriegsrüstung*, 1:132–35; Conrad, *Dienstzeit*, 3:275, 294; Craig, *Politics*, p. 291. Falkenhayn may have been an exception (*Kriegsrüstung*, 1:207–10). Kiderlen risked war but did not seem to regard it as inevitable (Erdmann, "Beurteilung," p. 534). Bethmann generally implied or stated that it was not inevitable: Wernecke, *Wille*, p. 194; RT, 268:7708; Hantsch, *Berchtold*, 1:362; *GP*, 34:12763; Stenkewitz, *Bajonette*, p. 109; Fischer, *Krieg*, p. 261; Strandmann, *Erforderlichkeit*, pp. 35–36; Tirpitz, *Erinnerungen*, p. 195; *Bayerische Dokumente*, no. 1. On other occasions Bethmann granted the possibility and even the likelihood of war: Brandenburg, *Bismarck*, p. 542; RT, 268:7708; Müller, *Kaiser*, p. 126; Fischer, "Weltpolitik," p. 330; Fischer, *Griff*, p. 45; Zmarzlik, *Bethmann*, pp. 80–81; RT, 289:4512; Theodor Heuss, *Friedrich Naumann, der Mann, das Werk, die Zeit* (Stuttgart and Berlin, 1937), p. 512; *GP*, 39:15883; Naumann, *Profile*, p. 58. Tirpitz may have thought war inevitable but was unclear: Tirpitz, *Erinnerungen*, p. 195; Müller, *Kaiser*, pp. 124–25. Müller regarded war as inevitable (*Kaiser*, pp. 92, 124). Lichnowsky did not: *GP*, 34:12748, part 1; *GP*, 39:630–33. Tschirschky may have disagreed with Lichnowsky: *GP*, 34:12797, part 1; Conrad, *Dienstzeit*, 3:597. Portalès does not seem to have regarded war as inevitable (*GP*, 39:15844). Dietrich Bethmann Hollweg implied that war was necessary to preserve Germany's great-power status (Redlich, *Tagebuch*, 1:221). Conrad believed the Germans saw war as inevitable (*Dienstzeit*, 3:87), but Berchtold disagreed: (Hantsch, *Berchtold*, 1:362; *OU*, 8:979).

26 Francis Joseph may have believed war avoidable (Fischer, *Krieg*, p. 602). Francis Ferdinand may have believed a war with Serbia necessary (Hantsch, *Berchtold*, 1:362), but he seems to have seen war with Russia as avoidable: Conrad, *Dienstzeit*, 3:155; Fischer, *Krieg*, p. 544; Redlich, *Tagebuch*, 1:221, 226; *GP*, 39:15736. Conrad consistently regarded war as inevitable: *OU*, 7:397–403; Conrad, *Dienstzeit*, 3:597–98, 604, 615–16, 627–28. Other soldiers seem to have regarded war as highly likely: Fischer, *Krieg*, p. 599; *OU*, 7:395–403. Berchtold implied that it was (*OU*, 7:395–403). Tisza felt that it was highly possible but avoidable if the correct policy were pursued (*OU*, 7:9482).

27 Russian leaders thought war might be avoided (Fay, *Origins*, 1:532–35, 538–41). Sazonov discussed the possibility of war frequently in the spring of 1914 but does not seem to have regarded it as inevitable: *OU*, 8:168–69; Taylor, *Struggle*, p. 511; *BD*, 10:777–79, part 2; *GP*, 37:593; *Schriftwechsel Iswolskis*, 4:1338. The French soldiers seem to have seen war as avoidable (*Schriftwechsel Iswolskis*, 2:567). Poincaré described it as possible in January 1913 (*Schriftwechsel Iswolskis*, 3:711) but inevitable in the spring of 1914 (*GP*, 39:573). Paleologue claimed it was inevitable in June 1914 (Michon, *Alliance*, pp. 272–74). A Russian leader saw the French as antiwar in November 1913 (*Schriftwechsel Iswolskis*, 2:1169), whereas a Belgian observer thought the French people expected war in the spring of 1914 (Fischer, *Krieg*, p. 624). Among British leaders, Crowe and Nicolson thought Germany might provoke war in 1911 (*BD*, 7:269, 607), but Nicolson, Grey, Goschen, and others were less concerned about war by the spring of 1914: *BD*, 10:745–46, 777–79, 786–87, 801–4, part 2; *GP*, 39:630–33; Michon, *Alliance*, pp. 272–74. Italian General Pollio expected war: Foerster, *Generalstabes*, p. 877; Fischer, *Krieg*, p. 583. The Belgians regarded war as possible but not inevitable: Beyens, *L'Allemagne*, pp. 24–26; *GP*, 39:587–88; *BD*, 10:802–4, part 2. Co-

lonel House regarded war as likely unless Wilson intervened (House, *Papers*, 1:255, 264, 267).

28 The kaiser sometimes expected war soon: Müller, *Kaiser*, p. 124; *OU*, 5:5604; Beyens, *L'Allemagne*, pp. 24–26; Conrad, *Dienstzeit*, 4:36–39; *GP*, 39:587; *GP*, 36:811; House, *Papers*, 1:261–62; Fischer, *Griff*, pp. 57–58. At other times he seems to have expected it later: *GP*, 34:12865, 12881, part 1; *OU*, 5:5923, 5947, 5958; Beyens, *L'Allemagne*, pp. 24–26; *GP*, 39:587. At still other times, he does not seem to have been sure (*GP*, 34:811, part 2). Moltke too expected it soon: Müller, *Kaiser*, p. 124, Fischer, *Krieg*, pp. 233–35, 573; Beyens, *L'Allemagne*, pp. 24–26; Conrad, *Dienstzeit*, 3:604; Zechlin, "Motive," pp. 91–95; Schäfer, "Präventivkrieg," pp. 549–50. At other times he implies that war is not imminent: Baernreither, *Weltbrand*, p. 195; *GP*, 34:12793, part 2; Conrad, *Dienstzeit*, 3:30, 145–46, 328, 609–12; Baernreither, *Weltbrand*, p. 298. Sometimes he seemed uncertain: Conrad, *Dienstzeit*, 3:144–46; *Kriegsrüstung*, 1:349. Tirpitz urged postponement: Tirpitz, *Aufbau*, p. 203; Fischer, *Krieg*, p. 234. Müller seems to have agreed: Müller, *Kaiser*, p. 92; Fischer, *Krieg*, pp. 233–34. But Ludendorff seems to have favored war soon (Fischer, *Krieg*, p. 246). Prussian Minister of War Heeringen favored postponement (Fischer, *Krieg*, p. 235). His successor, Falkenhayn, did likewise (*GP*, 36:587). Bethmann infrequently foresaw war soon: *GP*, 39:628–30; *BD*, 10:802–4, part 2. Generally, he expected it later: *GP*, 39:12818, part 1; Hantsch, *Berchtold*, 1:388; *RT*, 289:4512. At other times he was uncertain (Naumann, *Profile*, p. 58). Tschirschky implied that war was imminent (Conrad, *Dienstzeit*, 3:597). Jagow sometimes implied it was imminent: Schulthess, *Geschichtskalender*, pp. 281–84; *BD*, 10:802–4, part 2. At other times he implied or said it might come later: Schulthess, *Geschichtskalender*, pp. 281–84; Zechlin, "Motive," pp. 91–95; he left for a protracted honeymoon in June 1914 which suggests that he did not regard war as imminent.

29 Conrad generally implied that war was imminent (Conrad, *Dienstzeit*, 3:147–48, 596–97, 604). Tisza hoped to postpone or even deter war (*OU*, 7:9482). Berchtold agreed with Tisza (*OU*, 7:397–403). Redlich expected it soon (Redlich, *Tagebuch*, 1:221). Italian General Pollio predicted it soon (Foerster, "Generalstabes," pp. 877–78).

30 A racial war was predicted by most German leaders. The kaiser: *GP*, 34:811, part 2; *GP*, 39:15613; Fischer, *Griff*, p. 41; Fischer, *Krieg*, pp. 236–37; Huldermann, *Ballin*, p. 272; *OU*, 7:8934. Moltke: Conrad, *Dienstzeit*, 3:145; *GP*, 34:12824, part 1. Bethmann: *RT*, 289:4512. Jagow: Fischer, *Krieg*, p. 298. Tschirschky: Hantsch, *Berchtold*, 1:420. Waldersee: Conrad, *Dienstzeit*, 3:78. Eisendecher: Fischer, *Krieg*, p. 238. Most spoke of a war of existence, including the kaiser: *GP*, 39:15613; Fischer, *Griff*, p. 41; Fischer, *Krieg*, pp. 237, 316–17; Huldermann, *Ballin*, p. 272; Moltke: Conrad, *Dienstzeit*, 3:144–45, 669–70; Bethmann: *RT*, 289:4512; Jagow: Paul Herre, *Weltgeschichte der neuesten Zeit 1890–1925* (Berlin, 1925), 1:574. Many also spoke of a European war. Moltke: Conrad, *Dienstzeit*, 3:144–45; Beyens, *L'Allemagne*, pp. 24–26. The kaiser: Fischer, *Griff*, pp. 41, 42. They also discussed a world war. The kaiser: *GP*, 34:760, 783, part 2. Moltke: Conrad, *Dienstzeit*, 3:144–46, 151–52. Bethmann: *RT*, 289:4512. Several mentioned a great war. The kaiser: Fischer, *Griff*, p. 41; Beyens, *L'Allemagne*, pp. 24–25. Tschirschky: *GP*, 34:12797, part 1. Waldersee: Conrad, *Dienstzeit*, 3:87–88. A mass war was also postulated by some. The kaiser: *OU*, 7:8934. Moltke: Conrad, *Dienstzeit*, 3:144–46. They generally expected the war to be short. Moltke: Fischer, *Krieg*, p. 176; Conrad, *Dienstzeit*, 3:144–45; *Kriegsrüstung*, pp. 287–88. Delbrück: Fischer, *Krieg*, pp. 288, 640. A few expected the war to be long (Fischer, *Krieg*, p. 281). Several implied that the war would be successful. The kaiser: Beyens, *L'Allemagne*, pp. 24–25. Moltke: Beyens, *L'Allemagne*, pp. 24–25; Zechlin, "Motive," pp. 91–95. Bethmann implied that it might not be successful (*RT*, 289:4512). Conrad rejected the racial formulation suggested by his German counterparts but described the war as great and involving Austro-Hungarian existence (Conrad, *Dienstzeit*, 3:87–88, 245, 575–76, 596–97).

31 German leaders generally expected to fight both France and Russia. All statements envisaging a racial war with Slavs and Gauls implied such a war (see note 30 above). The kaiser expected a war with the Franco-Russian alliance: *GP*, 39:15613; Fischer, *Griff*, pp. 57–58. Moltke: Fischer, *Krieg*, p. 176; *Kriegsrüstung*, pp. 155–56; Schäfer, "Präventivkrieg," pp. 549–50. Bethmann: *GP*, 28:10325; *GP*, 34:12763, part 1; *GP*, 39:638–40; *RT*, 289:4512. On other occasions German leaders implied that Russia

might fight alone. The kaiser: *GP*, 34:811, part 2; *OU*, 7:8934; Hantsch, *Berchtold*, 1:506–7. Moltke: Conrad, *Dienstzeit*, 3:144–45. Kageneck: Conrad, *Dienstzeit*, 3:275, 294. Bethmann: Egmont Zechlin, "Deutschland zwischen Kabinettskrieg und Wirtschaftskrieg," *HZ*, 199:400; RT, 289:4512; Erdmann, "Beurteilung," p. 563. Bethmann implied that Russia might not enter on at least one occasion (Müller, *Kaiser*, p. 107). Jagow: Fischer, *Krieg*, p. 298. Jagow implied on at least one occasion that Germany and Russia might not fight (Schulthess, *Geschichtskalender*, pp. 281–84). German leaders infrequently expected to fight France without Russia. The kaiser: *Kriegsrüstung*, p. 126; *GP*, 33:12405; Beyens, *L'Allemagne*, pp. 24–25. Moltke: Beyens, *L'Allemagne*, pp. 24–25; Conrad, *Dienstzeit*, 3:609–12. Britain received the most attention from German leaders. Some thought there was a possibility that Britain would remain neutral, at least at first. Bülow: *GP*, 28:10241. Bethmann: *GP*, 28:10325; *GP*, 39:15560, 15883; RT, 268:7708, 8348; RT, 289:4512: Fischer, *Krieg*, p. 238; Conrad, *Dienstzeit*, 3:669–70. The kaiser: *GP*, 33:12405; Müller, *Kaiser*, p. 124; Fischer, *Griff*, pp. 57–58. Moltke: Beyens, *L'Allemagne*, pp. 24–25 (probably doubted British neutrality). Jagow: *GP*, 34:12982, part 2; *GP*, 37:102–5, 108–11; Fischer, *Krieg*, pp. 298, 561–62; *BD*, 10:802–4, part 1. Eisendecher: Fischer, *Krieg*, p. 237. Tschirschky: *GP*, 34:13087, part 2. Kiderlen: *GP*, 29:318–19; Müller, *Kaiser*, p. 106. But at other times German leaders expected Britain to be an enemy. Moltke: Fischer, *Krieg*, p. 176; *Kriegsrüstung*, pp. 156–58; Conrad, *Dienstzeit*, 3:154–55, 669–70. The kaiser: Wernecke, *Wille*, p. 54; *Kriegsrüstung*, p. 126; Müller, *Kaiser*, p. 106; *GP*, 39:15612; Fischer, *Krieg*, 236–37. Lichnowsky: *GP*, 39:15612; *GP*, 34:12561, 12707, part 1; *GP*, 37:101–5; *GP*, 39:15612. Kiderlen: Müller, *Kaiser*, p. 87. Müller, Bethmann, Holzendorff, and Heeringen: Müller, *Kaiser*, pp. 90–92. Some German leaders mentioned the possibility of war with the United States. Eisendecher: Fischer, *Krieg*, p. 238. Moltke and the kaiser sought to avoid war with Belgium (Beyens, *L'Allemagne*, pp. 24–25). The kaiser expected Germany would not have to fight Switzerland (*Julikrise*, 2:622). Several leaders hoped on occasion for a local Austro-Serbian war. The kaiser: Müller, *Kaiser*, pp. 124–25; Fischer, *Krieg*, p. 233. The kaiser doubted it on other occasions: *GP*, 35:13475; Fischer, *Griff*, pp. 57–58. Bethmann doubted the possibility (Fischer, *Krieg*, p. 306). Jagow hoped to localize such a war (Fischer, *Krieg*, p. 298). Waldersee doubted such a war could be localized (Conrad, *Dienstzeit*, 3:87–88). Conrad hoped to localize a conflict with Serbia (Conrad, *Dienstzeit*, 3:87–88), but he doubted it could be (*Dienstzeit*, 3:596). Francis Ferdinand was ambivalent on the possibility too: Fischer, *Krieg*, p. 609; Hantsch, *Berchtold*, 1:362. Francis Ferdinand opposed a war with Russia: Conrad, *Dienstzeit*, 3:155; Redlich, *Tagebuch*, 1:221–22. Francis Joseph seems to have agreed with Francis Ferdinand (Fischer, *Krieg*, p. 602). Berchtold seems to have expected war with Russia: *GP*, 35:13410; Conrad, *Dienstzeit*, 3:353.

32 German leaders frequently discussed the problem of allies in war. Most expected Austro-Hungarian support, but there were some doubts during the Moroccan crisis. Tschirschky: Fischer, *Krieg*, p. 134. Bethmann: Brandenburg, *Bismarck*, p. 542. Tirpitz: Tirpitz, *Aufbau*, p. 203. Bülow: Rathenau, *Tagebuch*, p. 172. These doubts persisted. Jagow: Fischer, *Krieg*, p. 607; *BD*, 10:802–4, part 2. German leaders were more concerned and uncertain about Italy. Moltke: Foerster, *Generalstabes*, pp. 837–42, 874–78; *Kriegsrüstung*, pp. 156–58. Tschirschky: Hantsch, *Berchtold*, 1:420; Conrad, *Dienstzeit*, 3:495; *GP*, 39:15713. Waldersee: Foerster, *Generalstabes*, p. 878. Conrad was also dubious (Conrad, *Dienstzeit*, 3:495). This uncertainty was understandable since the Italians made contradictory statements: Fischer, *Krieg*, p. 305; Foerster, *Generalstabes*, pp. 877–78. German and Austro-Hungarian leaders hoped to win other allies. The kaiser and Conrad hoped to win over Turkey. William: Müller, *Kaiser*, pp. 124–25. Conrad: Conrad, *Dienstzeit*, 3:754–55. The kaiser and Moltke hoped for Rumania. Kaiser: Müller, *Kaiser*, pp. 124–25. Moltke: *Kriegsrüstung*, pp. 155–58. But Conrad was dubious (Conrad, *Dienstzeit*, 3:754–55). The kaiser thought Bulgaria and Japan might be possible allies on infrequent occasions (Müller, *Kaiser*, pp. 124–25). Conrad expected Bulgaria and Albania and hoped for Sweden (Conrad, *Dienstzeit*, 3:754–55).

33 German, Austro-Hungarian, and Italian leaders were generally in agreement that time disfavored them and that a war might be won soon but not later. Moltke: Müller, *Kaiser*, pp. 124–25; Conrad, *Dienstzeit*, 3:209–12, 669–70; Schäfer, "Präventivkrieg," pp. 849–50. Pollio: Foerster, *Generalstabes*, pp. 877–78. Conrad: Conrad, *Dienstzeit*, 3:604–5. They agreed that the Entente powers were increasing their arms in order to attack the Triple Alliance. Moltke: *GP*, 39:15839; Conrad, *Dienstzeit*, 3:669–70;

Schäfer, "Präventivkrieg," pp. 549–50. The kaiser: *GP*, 39:15844. Russian reports of German leaders: *IB*, 1:434. Pourtalès disagreed (*GP*, 39:15844). Conrad agreed with Moltke and the kaiser (Conrad, *Dienstzeit*, 3:626, 597–98, 604–6). So did Pollio (Foerster, *Generalstabes*, pp. 877–88). German and Austro-Hungarian leaders infrequently advocated a preventive war, however. Moltke: Müller, *Kaiser*, pp. 124–25; Zechlin, "Motive," pp. 91–95. Other soldiers: *Bayr. Dok.*, 3:113–15. The kaiser: Müller, *Kaiser*, pp. 124–25; *GP*, 36:811; *GP*, 39:15736. The kaiser was seen by others, however, as opposed to war (Redlich, *Tagebuch*, 1:226). Bethmann generally opposed a preventive war quite explicitly: RT, 268:7708; Hantsch, *Berchtold*, 1:362; Fischer, *Krieg*, p. 380; Strandmann, *Erforderlichkeit*, pp. 32–33; *Bayr. Dok.*, 3:1. He may have accepted the logic nonetheless: Müller, *Kaiser*, pp. 126–27; Heuss, *Naumann*, p. 512. Jagow opposed Moltke's suggestion of a preventive war (Zechlin, "Motive," pp. 91–95), but he later implied that Moltke had been correct. Tirpitz favored postponement of war (Fischer, *Krieg*, pp. 234–35). Lichnowsky opposed war (*GP*, 34:12748, part 1). Conrad had advocated it frequently, most recently, in March 1914: *GP*, 39:565–66; Conrad, *Dienstzeit*, 3:597–98, 604, 615–16, 626–28. Francis Ferdinand opposed it: Conrad, *Dienstzeit*, 3:597–98; Jux, *Kriegsschrecken*, p. 36. Czernin may have been sympathetic to it (Conrad, *Dienstzeit*, 3:782). Other Austro-Hungarian leaders may have been as well (*OU*, 7:397–403). Pollio favored it (Foerster, *Generalstabes*, p. 877). Discussions among German and Austro-Hungarian leaders as to how war should most favorably begin implied sympathy for a preventive war. The kaiser: *OU*, 5:5604. Moltke: Conrad, *Dienstzeit*, 3:144–45, 609–12. Bethmann: Brandenburg, *Bismarck*, p. 542. Tschirschky: *GP*, 34:13087, part 2; Hantsch, *Berchtold*, 1:420; Conrad, *Dienstzeit*, 3:597; Fischer, *Krieg*, p. 298. Conrad: Conrad, *Dienstzeit*, 3:597. For the thesis that German policy constituted a consistent effort to prepare for a preventive war, see: Fischer, *Krieg*, pp. 231–41, 244, 289–323, 563–65, 573, 577–86, 609–11, 627, 633; Gasser, "Entschluss," pp. 175–76. Entente statesmen sought to anticipate German moves. Crowe and Nicolson: *BD*, 7:269, 607. Sazonov: Taylor, *Mastery*, p. 511.

34   Most German leaders regarded the threat of force as a necessary part of successful diplomacy. The kaiser: *GP*, 24:8226. Moltke: Moltke, *Erinnerungen*, p. 362. Bethmann: RT, 268:7708; Strandmann, *Erforderlichkeit*, pp. 35–36. Kiderlen: Erdmann, "Beurteilung," p. 534; Jäckh, *Kiderlen*, 2:123–24. They also recognized that war was the only acceptable option under certain conditions. Bethmann: RT, 268:7708; Strandmann, *Erforderlichkeit*, pp. 35–36. Jagow: Zechlin, "Motive," pp. 91–95. Moltke: Schäfer, "Präventivkrieg," p. 546. This is the basic thesis of Lloyd George's Mansion House speech (Lloyd George, *Memoirs*, 1:26). German leaders therefore concluded that it was their duty to prepare for war. Moltke: Conrad, *Dienstzeit*, 3:144–45; Schäfer, "Präventivkrieg," pp. 549–50.

35   German leaders expressed their anxiety-arrogance ambivalence in various ways. The discussions over a preventive war implied it (see note 33 above). They frequently perceived a necessary choice between victory and defeat. Kiderlen: Jäckh, *Kiderlen*, 2:128–29; Wernecke, *Wille*, p. 54; *GP*, 29:10572. Bethmann: Redlich, *Tagebuch*, 1:221. Sometimes they expressed anxiety and arrogance in the same statement. Moltke: *Kriegsrüstung*, pp. 155–56. Stern suggests this perception of Bethmann (Stern, "Bethmann," pp. 257–58). German leaders expressed anxiety toward Russia on frequent occasions. Moltke: *GP*, 39:533–39, 564–65; Zechlin, "Motive," pp. 91–95; Schäfer, "Präventivkrieg," pp. 549–50; Conrad, *Dienstzeit*, 3:668–73; *Kriegsrüstung*, pp. 206–10, 349. Waldersee: Foerster, *Generalstabes*, pp. 878–79. The kaiser: *OU*, 7:8934; Hantsch, *Berchtold*, 1:506; Conrad, *Dienstzeit*, 3:597–98; Fischer, *Griff*, pp. 57–58; Egmont Zechlin, "Probleme des Kriegs Kalküls und Kriegsbeendigung im Ersten Weltkrieg," *GWU*, September, 1963, pp. 70–71; *GP*, 36:811; *GP*, 39:587; House, *Papers*, 1:261–62. Jagow: Schulthess, *Geschichtskalender*, pp. 281–84; *BD*, 10:802–5, part 2; Grey, *Years*, 1:274–75. Bethmann: *GP*, 39:15883; Zechlin, "Kabinettskrieg," p. 400; Erdmann, "Beurteilung," p. 563. On almost as many occasions, they denied fear of Russia. Moltke: Conrad, *Dienstzeit*, 3:609–12, 668–73; *GP*, 39:333–36, 572–77. The kaiser: *OU*, 7:8934; Hantsch, *Berchtold*, 1:506–7; *GP*, 39:15715. Bethmann: Tirpitz, *Erinnerungen*, p. 195. Jagow: *GP*, 39:505–6; Zechlin, "Motive," pp. 91–95; this was reinforced by his departure for a protracted honeymoon in June 1914. Pourtalès: *GP*, 39:579–82. Lichnowsky: *GP*, 39:630–33. Falkenhayn: *Kriegsrüstung*, pp. 207–10. Infrequently they were confident or even arrogant about Russia. Moltke: Fischer, *Griff*, p. 59. They expressed anxiety about France frequently. Moltke: Conrad, *Dienstzeit*, 3:609–12; Schäfer, "Präventivkrieg," pp. 549–50; Zechlin, "Motive," pp. 91–95. The

kaiser: *Kriegsrüstung*, p. 126; Fischer, *Griff*, pp. 57–58; *GP*, 39:587. Jagow: *BD*, 10:802–5, part 2; Grey, *Years*, 1:274–75. Bethmann: *GP*, 39:15883. On other occasions, they denied anxiety toward France. Moltke, Jagow, Zimmermann, and Koerner (Foreign Office official): Baernreither, *Weltbrand*, pp. 302–8. Moltke: Conrad, *Dienstzeit*, 3:609–12. On still other occasions, they demonstrated arrogance or confidence toward France. Kiderlen: Erdmann, "Beurteilung," p. 534; Wernecke, *Wille*, pp. 54–55, 102; *GP*, 29:10549, 10572; Jäckh, *Kiderlen*, 2:122. Moltke: Beyens, *L'Allemagne*, p. 24; Foerster, *Generalstabes*, p. 877; Conrad, *Dienstzeit*, 3:609–12. The kaiser: Beyens, *L'Allemagne*, pp. 24–25. Bethmann: RT, 268:7708–9. On other occasions, Moltke indicated that he was not confident: Conrad, *Dienstzeit*, 3:668–73; Zechlin, "Motive," pp. 91–95. German leaders frequently demonstrated concern in regard to Austria-Hungary. Kiderlen: Müller, *Kaiser*, p. 871. Bülow: Rathenau, *Tagebuch*, p. 172. Tirpitz: Tirpitz, *Aufbau*, pp. 203–4. Bethmann: Brandenburg, *Bismarck*, p. 542; Fischer, *Krieg*, p. 261. Moltke: Schäfer, "Präventivkrieg," pp. 546–47. Tschirschky: *GP*, 39:15734. Zimmermann: *GP*, 36:14161. Jagow: Fischer, *Krieg*, p. 607. Infrequently they were confident or even arrogant toward Austria-Hungary. Zimmermann: *OU*, 7:8938. Bethmann: *GP*, 38:15549. They likewise demonstrated anxiety toward Britain. The kaiser: *Kriegsrüstung*, p. 126. Sometimes they explicitly denied anxiety toward Britain. Kiderlen: Müller, *Kaiser*, p. 106. Moltke: Fischer, *Krieg*, p. 567. On occasion, they were arrogant toward Britain. The kaiser: *GP*, 39:15613.

36 In 1914 the division of power was 44.4 percent for the Austro-German alliance and 55.6 percent for the Anglo-French-Russian group.

37 For the argument that war and peace parties existed, see: Craig, *Politics*, pp. 255–57, 286–95 (war party = soldiers and peace party = civilians); Fischer, *Krieg*, pp. 246 (Austro-Hungarian peace and war parties) and 381 (German peace and war parties); Jarausch, "Illusion," pp. 70–74 (German and Russian); Brandenburg, *Bismarck*, p. 443 (Russian); Albertini, *Origins*, 3:410 (British). For various attitudes on war, see notes 25, 28, and 30 above. Among the soldiers and sailors who were unenthusiastic about war or who wanted to postpone it were Falkenhayn, Heeringen, Müller, and Tirpitz. Among the civilians who favored or risked war were Kiderlen, the kaiser, Tschirschky, Dietrich Bethmann, Jagow (in retrospect) and some conservatives and Pan Germans.

38 Contemporaries perceived war and peace parties. Conrad: Conrad, *Dienstzeit*, 3:275, 294, 596–97; Redlich, *Tagebuch*, 1:226. Tschirschky: Conrad, *Dienstzeit*, p. 597. The kaiser: *GP*, 39:15844.

39 German leaders agreed on the necessity of violating Belgian neutrality: Müller, *Kaiser*, p. 126; Fischer, *Krieg*, p. 567.

40 German leaders were particularly inclined to perceive Russia in these terms. Jagow: Fischer, *Krieg*, p. 298; Schulthess, *Geschichtskalender*, pp. 281–84; *BD*, 10:802–5, part 2. Bethmann: *GP*, 39:628–30. Pourtalès: *GP*, 39:15844. The kaiser rejected this view (*GP*, 39:15844). Austro-Hungarian leaders perceived Russia in these terms on at least one occasion (*OU*, 5:5698).

41 German leaders denigrated or doubted the efficacy of diplomacy on frequent occasions. The kaiser: *GP*, 34:12677, part 1. Bethmann: *GP*, 39:628–33. Jagow: *GP*, 36:490; *BD*, 10:802–4, part 2. Leaders of the other powers expressed similar views. Grey: *IB*, 1:144; *GP*, 38:183–84. The tsar: *BD*, 10:780–82, part 2. Sazonov: *GP*, 36:507–8. Berchtold: *GP*, 38:183–84; *GP*, 36:507–8.

42 *BD*, 10:745–46, part 2; House, *Papers*, 1:255, 264, 267.

43 Fischer, *Griff*, p. 59.

VII / POWER VERSUS PEACE:

The Diplomacy of the July Crisis
(28 June–4 August 1914)

RESPONSIBILITY, CHANCE, LIMITED CHOICE, AND MULTIPLE EXPLANATION: THE DEBATE OVER THE JULY CRISIS

The discussion of the outbreak of World War I was a classic historical debate. It raised most historical questions and a number of historians made their reputations debating it. Not only popular and professional historians, but also politicians, journalists, and the educated public became involved in what was probably the most burning historical question for the interwar generation. Although as a consequence it produced a vast quantity of original documents and secondary literature, the great effort resulted in little agreement. This paradox seemed to make nonsense of history: the more historians knew, the less they agreed. The debate seemed to demonstrate that history is nothing more than national propaganda, subjective prejudice, or intellectual exercise. This conclusion was partially justified since many participants sought immediate political objectives rather than historical objectivity. Indeed, precisely the political implications of the debate which attracted public attention virtually insured against objectivity and, in this sense, the debate tells us more about the interwar than prewar period. To the extent that participants genuinely sought to explain, however, their disagreement was due largely to questions of interpretation since the facts could be generally agreed upon after the publication of the official documents. The debate is therefore understandable only if these interpretations are isolated.

The July crisis can be understood in terms of the four basic interpretations of responsibility, chance, limited choice, and multiple explanation. The most commonly argued interpretation and starting point for the interwar debate was responsibility. During the war, each government had naturally sought to mobilize popular support with assertions that the enemy was responsible for the war. After the war there was an understandable psychological and political compulsion to believe that someone else had been responsible and the Versailles treaty established the concept of responsibility so firmly as the framework of debate that it was seldom questioned at first. The concept was applied in varied and frequently contradictory ways. Some argued that all governments were responsible to some degree and that this responsibility could be ranked, whereas others asserted that only some governments were responsible. Still others blamed specific groups within governments or societies such as the military, vengeful politicians, foreign ministries, conservatives, industrialists, or other interest groups. The concept of responsibility was also interpreted in different ways. Some perceived conscious decisions to seek war, i.e., responsibility of commission. More found conscious decisions to risk although not to seek war, i.e., a lessened responsibility of commission. Probably even more saw unconscious willingness to risk and conscious desire to avoid war, i.e., responsibility of omission: statesmen were responsible because they had been irresponsible. Thus, responsibility of commission depended on motives, while responsibility of omission depended on consequences.

The concept of chance competed with responsibility increasingly as the interwar years passed. Like responsibility, this interpretation had immediate political implications in seeming to facilitate international reconciliation by justifying dismantlement of the Versailles treaty. Its appeal since World War II is the implied warning against precipitating World War III by mistake. It rejected responsibility of commission: since no one had wanted war, no one was responsible. It also rejected responsibility of omission because irresponsibility precluded responsibility. Instead incompetence, weakness, stupidity, miscalculation of risks, and unforeseen events were seen as the real causes of war. Some argued a lack-of-great-man theory: if a great statesman like Bismarck had existed, the war might have been prevented. Many regarded nondiplomatic factors such as the assassination and military timetables as critical. A few believed a crisis mentality paralyzed statesmen. Still others were even less specific and blamed "fate" in the sense of bad luck.

The concept of statesmen's limited choice was specifically advocated by few participants in the debate but was implied by all those who asserted that the old diplomatic system had caused the war. Like responsibility and chance, limited choice had fundamental political implications, above all, that war might recur unless that system were changed. This interpretation, however, implied a rejection of responsibility and chance and suggested instead that the cause lay in long-term factors such as the alliance system, militarism, nationalism, economic competition and imperialism, anachronistic diplomacy, domestic political problems, the press and public opinion, a pervasive sense of doom, and/or "fate" in the sense of destiny. Some or all of these forces limited so severely the options open to statesmen that war was a virtual certainty once the crisis began.

The concept of multiple explanation became increasingly popular as mounting evidence made the July crisis seem more complex and therefore less susceptible to any single theory. Like the other interpretations, it had fundamental political implications that, if the outbreak of war could not be easily explained, it would be difficult to adjust the system in order to avoid its recurrence. Multiple explanation rejected the assumption basic to the other interpretations that they could be isolated and assumed instead that some combination was necessary. Thus all interpretations which perceived *both* long-term (limited choice) and short-term (responsibility and chance) causes can be gathered under the general rubric of multiple explanation.

Limited choice seems to be the most satisfactory explanation. Once the crisis began, the choices perceived by European statesmen proved so narrow that war was highly likely. The fact that other hypothetical choices can be suggested in retrospect does not in itself diminish the usefulness of this interpretation. Instead, the issue is whether the statesmen of 1914 could be expected to perceive alternatives which might have avoided war. The perceptions of these statesmen were seriously affected by their "unspoken assumptions" about the great powers and great-power statesmen.[1] All great-power statesmen assumed that it was their duty to protect and expand the power of their states by diplomacy if possible and by war if necessary. When confronted with the choice between a peace which they perceived as detrimental to their state's interests and an advantageous or less disadvantageous war, it was their duty to opt for war. The central problem in understanding the July crisis therefore becomes one of analyzing the choices with which the statesmen of 1914 were confronted and of deciding whether they could reasonably be expected to make different choices within the existing conditions.

ERUPTION NOT CREATION: FROM ASSASSINATION TO ULTIMATUM (28 JUNE–23 JULY)

Crises can be perceived in two opposite ways. It can be argued that diplomatic crises are the responsibility of governments, since only governments can designate certain events as crises. In this view, events are assumed to have presented governments with valid alternatives and not to have forced decisions. Accordingly the fact that the July crisis occurred and then eventuated in war is attributed primarily to governmental decisions and only secondarily to events. Conversely it can be argued that diplomatic crises are the result of events which force governmental decisions and leave little room for choice. In this view, the July crisis is attributed primarily to events and secondarily to governmental decisions. The choice between these two assumptions determines whether the July crisis is perceived as a diplomatic creation or an unavoidable eruption. The crisis is best understood as an eruption since diplomatic decisions were more result than cause of events.

The assassination of Francis Ferdinand on 28 June 1914 inaugurated what the kaiser had presciently predicted would be "the third chapter of the Balkan war in which we shall all become involved.''[2] The assassination forced Austria-Hungary and Serbia to confront one another directly for the first time. The Austro-Serbian crises of the previous eighteen months had proven false beginnings for several reasons. Vienna had not yet become entirely convinced that its existence depended on crushing Serbia. Serbian nationalism had touched the monarchy only indirectly in Albania and the Balkans in general. The previous crises had remained under the control of the two governments. But subsequent events culminating in the assassination had altered the situation. Vienna had become increasingly desperate because of general Balkan developments.[3] The assassination seemed to prove not only that Serbian nationalism was a direct threat to the monarchy but also that relations between the two countries could not be controlled by their governments. In short, the situation had become both more desperate and less containable.

The motives of the assassins and secret Serbian national societies were probably complex. They may have feared that Austria-Hungary would preserve Albania, establish an anti-Serbian Balkan league, or even resolve the South Slav problem within the monarchy. Conversely they may have been more anxious to activate the moderates in their own government than to anticipate the militants in Vienna. It is equally possible that their thinking was vague but dominated by the anarchist conviction that violence of any kind would serve the cause of Serbian nationalism in some unforeseeable way. But the very nature of such secret organizations makes it unlikely that their motives will ever be known precisely.[4] In the last resort, their motives are less important than their actions which forced Belgrade and Vienna to confront their irreconcilable objectives.

The ultimate objectives more than the conscious policies of Belgrade and Vienna made a conflict between them virtually unavoidable. Vienna sought unsuccessfully to prove official complicity. Such involvement was unlikely since the assassination faced Belgrade with the awkward choice between making amends and appearing aggressive. But it was equally improbable that the Serbian government could have prevented the assassination since the societies symbolized the national movement and were immensely difficult to control, considerations which discouraged the Serbian government from moving against the societies even after the assassination.[5] The Serbian government therefore contributed in a negative way to the crisis by not preventing the assassination but did not believe it could have done otherwise. The same may be said of the Austro-Hungarian government. It played a part in the assassination in the sense that Francis Ferdinand presented himself in Sarajevo as a target for assassination. But the preservation of the monarchy depended in part on its ability to demonstrate Habsburg authority in areas where it was jeopardized by Serbian nationalism.[6] In short both Vienna and Belgrade had done what seemed necessary. But what would preserve Austria-Hungary as a great power would provoke Serbian nationalism, whereas what would satisfy Serbian nationalism would threaten Austria-Hungary as a great power. Hence coexistence seemed virtually impossible and conflict almost inevitable.[7]

The assassination forced Vienna to make a fundamental choice. Hypothetically it had the options of reform, renunciation, and reprisal.[8] Vienna might have sought to nullify the threat of Serbian nationalism by pacifying the South Slavs inside the monarchy with domestic reform. But reform was probably not a practical means of preserving the monarchy since the ruling minorities—particularly the Magyars—would probably have seceded rather than renounce their privileges.[9] Alternatively Vienna might have tried to preserve the existence of the monarchy by renouncing its great-power status and becoming a mandate of the other great powers. But this decision was never seriously contemplated since Austria-Hungary, like any state, would consider becoming a mandate only when it had already ceased to be a power and the only alternative was dissolution. Consequently, the only perceived option was to remove the threat of Serbian nationalism by reprisal.

Such logic seemed to confirm a program which had already been devised in Vienna before the assassination provided the pretext for its implementation. This program reiterated more strongly than ever before the Viennese argument for establishing a Balkan league under Austro-Hungarian control and at Serbian expense by the conclusion of an alliance with Bulgaria and the improvement of relations with Rumania and Greece.[10] The syndrome of anxiety and arrogance which had become increasingly characteristic of Austro-Hungarian thinking was expressed in the polarization of alternatives: either the monarchy would be preserved by its reconstruction and domination of the Balkans or it would collapse.[11] Austro-Hungarian leaders argued for implementation of the program with circular logic. It would succeed if Russia renounced the Balkans which might occur if Russia were not yet prepared to risk war or if Russian support for Serbia could be made to appear aggressive. The program would fail if Russia refused to renounce the Balkans, thereby demonstrating that it was already determined to destroy Austria-Hungary.[12] Since Austro-Hungarian chances for survival would diminish with time, an immediate confrontation with Russia was preferable to postponement.[13] Therefore either eventuality argued for immediate implementation of the Austro-Hungarian program.

Austro-Hungarian policy is generally condemned, but this criticism is misleading. Berchtold is almost universally stigmatized for seeking to preserve a doomed empire at the risk of a European war.[14] Although espoused by pacifists and apologists for the other powers, this criticism could have little relevance for Austro-Hungarian statesmen. It was their duty to preserve Austria-Hungary, not peace. Since they perceived that Austria-Hungary was doomed unless war was risked, it was their responsibility to do so. In being directed at Berchtold personally, this criticism implies that other Austro-Hungarian statesmen might have acted differently. Although hypothetically possible, this is unlikely; indeed it is more likely that Berchtold postponed rather than precipitated the use of force.[15] Most leading Austro-Hungarian statesmen regarded war with Serbia as necessary even though they recognized that it would probably cause a European war.[16] After initial opposition to the use of force, even Tisza concluded that "we could not do otherwise."[17] Consequently, if Berchtold is criticized, his Austro-Hungarian colleagues must share the responsibility for risking war to preserve their state. But all great-power statesmen did the same and must therefore be condemned. In fact, if in contrast to Austria-Hungary the other powers were viable in peace but vulnerable in war, their statesmen must be criticized even more than the statesmen in Vienna. Thus, it is inconsistent to criticize Austro-Hungarian policy because it risked war if the European system presupposed that a great power would defend its existence by doing so. In this sense Austro-Hungarian policy was determined by circumstances.[18]

Since Austro-Hungarian domination over Serbia seemed to require Russian renunciation of Serbia which apparently necessitated German support for Austria-Hungary, Austro-Hungarian domination over Serbia seemed to depend on German backing. The Austro-Hungarian request for support confronted German leaders with the three hypothetical choices of refusal, restraint, and response.[19] German policy on the eve of war had fluctuated between these three courses and can be explained in large measure as an effort to maintain both peace and the alliance with Austria-Hungary. But the Austro-Hungarian request for support necessitated a German choice between maintaining the alliance and peace. If Germany refused or restrained Vienna in order to preserve peace, it risked Austro-Hungarian dissolution or defection to the Entente and thus the destruction of the alliance.[20] Conversely, if it supported Vienna to preserve the alliance, it risked war.[21] In fact the alliance was jeopardized over the long run even if Berlin supported Vienna's efforts to resolve the dispute with Serbia. The alliance assumed Austro-Hungarian dependence on Germany in the Balkans, particularly in the Austro-Serbian problem; but, if this problem were resolved as implied by Vienna's request for support, Austria-Hungary would need Germany less and probably pursue a more independent policy.[22] Likewise, if

Germany no longer supported Austria-Hungary in the Serbian question, Berlin might seek better relations with Russia which might affect the Franco-Russian alliance.[23] As a consequence the Austro-Serbian dispute was one of the foundation stones not only of the Austro-German alliance but of the whole alliance system. The Germans were therefore faced with an awkward choice between two evils: on the one hand, rapid Austro-Hungarian dissolution or defection if they refused or restrained Vienna; on the other, subsequent Austro-Hungarian defection if they supported Vienna.

Berlin's response was determined by its evaluation of the alliance. German great-power status depended in part on Austria-Hungary as a diversion for Russia if war occurred.[24] If war were not perceived as imminent, Germany could refuse or restrain Austria-Hungary in order to preserve peace and seek an alternative to the alliance.[25] Indeed, some German diplomats favored the latter course early in the July crisis.[26] But, if war were perceived as inevitable or even imminent, Germany could not risk the alliance. In the spring of 1914 war seemed increasingly imminent to German leaders, primarily because of Franco-Russian military preparations.[27] At the same time the likelihood of Austro-Hungarian diversion from the Russian front or even dissolution appeared to increase because of problems with Rumania and Italy.[28] The assassination seems to have persuaded German leaders not only that an Austro-Serbian *modus vivendi* was impractical but also that the Serbian threat to Austria-Hungary would increase.[29] In short the prospect of Austro-Hungarian dependability decreased as the prospect of war increased. Restraining Vienna would only postpone war until a less advantageous juncture when Austria-Hungary would be weaker and the Franco-Russian alliance stronger.[30] Thus, German leaders decided that it was necessary to support Vienna.[31]

German support for Vienna implied the eventualities of a German diplomatic victory or immediate war. German leaders hoped several considerations would render a diplomatic victory possible. Russia might not support Serbia, either because Russian military preparations were incomplete or because the tsar might refuse to condone regicide.[32] Even if Russia wanted to support Serbia, France might restrain Russia or at least refuse to support it.[33] Britain might hold back the Franco-Russian alliance or at least not back it.[34] Such eventualities would constitute a German diplomatic victory by allowing Germany to preserve Austria-Hungary and thus the alliance.[35] They might even shatter the enemy alliance.[36] German leaders, however, recognized and assumed the risk of war. They were aware from the beginning of the crisis that Austria-Hungary planned to attack Serbia, that Russia was unlikely to sacrifice Serbia, that France would probably support Russia, and that Britain might join France.[37] Berlin anticipated this eventuality with circular logic like that used in Vienna: war was inevitable by 1917 but preferable in 1914 because Austria-Hungary was stronger and Franco-Russian preparations incomplete.[38] Furthermore, British intervention seemed less certain in 1914 than in 1917 if the Anglo-Russian naval negotiations during the spring of 1914 were an accurate indication.[39] In short either eventuality which might follow from supporting Vienna seemed preferable to the alternative.

German leaders made their decision to support Vienna with even less serious consultation or dissent than their counterparts in Vienna.[40] This has usually been interpreted as proof either of German stupidity or aggressiveness.[41] But it can also be viewed as an indication that German leaders perceived no alternative.[42] Their options seemed to have polarized: on the one hand, restraint of Austria-Hungary appeared to imply dissolution of Austria-Hungary, thus weakening of the Austro-German alliance, thus a threat to German great-power status; on the other, support of Austria-Hungary seemed to imply revival of Austria-Hungary, thus strengthening of the Austro-German alliance, thus preservation or even extension of German great-power status. Like their Austro-Hungarian counterparts, German leaders were motivated by both anxiety and arrogance.[43] This mentality almost insured that they would perceive no alternative compatible with their view of German interests. Indeed, granted their assumptions about German interests and the existing situation, there was none. It would therefore have been both illogical and irresponsible for them to jeopardize German power in order to preserve peace. In this sense their decision was determined by circumstances.

Between its assurance of support to Vienna (on 5 July) and the presentation of the Austro-Hungarian ultimatum to Serbia (on 23 July), Berlin sought to create conditions conducive to diplomatic or—failing that—military success by supporting Austria-Hungary and confronting Russia with a diplomatic defeat. If Russia were forced to accept diplomatic defeat, the Franco-Russian alliance might be threatened and its ability to conduct war in 1917 jeopardized. Alternatively, if Russia refused to accept diplomatic defeat and opted instead for war, it might improve the chances for German military success in 1914 by alienating Britain and thus forcing the Franco-Russian alliance to fight without British assistance.[44] Consequently, far from moderating Austro-Hungarian policy toward Serbia, Berlin urged Vienna to present Europe with a *fait accompli*.[45] By doing so Vienna would not only confront Russia with a diplomatic defeat but would also deter mediatory proposals which could preclude both Austro-Hungarian revival and an Austro-German diplomatic victory.[46] Meanwhile, Berlin pursued these objectives with its own policy of localization based on the claim that the Serbian question was a strictly Austro-Hungarian (i.e., local) rather than European problem.[47] To buttress this assertion and avoid alarming the Franco-Russian alliance into warning Austria-Hungary or Britain into proposing mediation, Berlin claimed ignorance of Austro-Hungarian intentions and assumed an air of studied calm.[48] But Berlin also stated clearly that the alternative to localization was war in order to deter Franco-Russian resistance or, if it occurred, to make such resistance look like aggression and thus alienate Britain.[49] Accordingly Germany pursued a dual policy of encouragement in Vienna and localization elsewhere.

Vienna moved slowly, however. Although Austro-Hungarian leaders were agreed on the aim of destroying Serbian independence, they were not agreed on the means.[50] Since other powers—particularly Russia— were unlikely to perceive the assassination as sufficient justification for destroying Serbian independence, Tisza persuaded his colleagues to present Serbia with an ultimatum designed to justify crushing Serbia by making Serbia assume the onus of provocation.[51] This procedure trapped Vienna in a vicious cycle, however. Serbia would perhaps justify its own destruction as far as the other powers were concerned only if it rejected an Austro-Hungarian ultimatum.[52] Vienna could insure rejection only by posing unacceptable terms (which it sought to do).[53] Austro-Hungarian reprisal would not seem justified, however, by rejection of unacceptable conditions but only of acceptable terms. In short Austro-Hungarian success required that Serbia commit suicide to justify its murder by Austria-Hungary.[54] Vienna's ultimatum policy was, however, not only unlikely to succeed but also involved risks for Vienna. If Serbia accepted the ultimatum, Austria-Hungary would have to choose between its own ultimatum and war. If Vienna abided by the ultimatum, it imposed conditions on itself as much as on Serbia. Conversely, if Vienna attacked despite Serbian acceptance, it would appear even more aggressive than if it had invaded Serbia without the ultimatum. Thus, although Berlin repeatedly urged haste to insure success, Vienna's delay in formulating the ultimatum probably made success neither more nor less likely.[55] In the final analysis, Austro-Hungarian policy could not escape its contradictions.

The assassination confronted Russian leaders with fundamental issues. Like Berlin when asked for support by Vienna, St. Petersburg had the three hypothetical choices of renouncing, reassuring, and restraining Serbia. It was theoretically possible that Russia would renounce Serbia. But preservation of Russian great-power status assumed the protection of its interests. Russian interests included its influence in the

Balkans which depended in turn on Russian patronage of Serbia, thus Serbian dependence on Russia, thus Austro-Serbian tension, thus Russian support of Serbia.[56] Consequently, since Russian great-power status appeared to require Russian support of Serbia, renouncing Serbia was not a viable option. Alternatively, it was hypothetically possible that Russia reassure Serbia of its unqualified support, as Berlin had done in Vienna. But Russian protection of Serbia against Austria-Hungary depended in turn on deterring German support for Austria-Hungary, thus on winning French support, thus perhaps on British support, thus on not alienating Britain by appearing provocative because of unqualified support to Serbia.[57] Consequently unqualified Russian support for Serbia was not practical. Since only restrained support remained, Russia urged Serbia to accept all Austro-Hungarian demands compatible with its independence.[58] This sole recourse in fact served Russian interests by perpetuating Austro-Serbian tension which was a precondition of Russian great-power status. Nonetheless Russian policy was determined by circumstances in the sense that Russian leaders perceived no viable alternative.

French leaders had the analogous hypothetical choice between refusing, reassuring, and restraining Russia. It was theoretically possible for them to refuse or restrain Russia. But French great-power status necessitated the alliance with Russia which assumed Russian dependence on France, thus Russo-German tension, thus Austro-Serbian tension, thus Russian support of Serbia. Hence French refusal or restraint of Russia were not valid options and Paris had to reassure St. Petersburg of its unqualified support, as Berlin had done in Vienna.[59] Hypothetically, France could have done the same with Serbia, but the consideration of Britain's reaction precluded such an option for France as it did for Russia, and France instead endorsed Russian restraint of Serbia.[60] As in the case of Russia, this sole recourse in fact served French interests by perpetuating Austro-Serbian tension which was a precondition of French great-power status. Nonetheless French policy was determined by circumstances in the sense that no viable alternative was perceived by French leaders. In short, all the continental powers had commited themselves to policies which were dictated by events.

Only Britain remained uncommitted. Unlike the continental powers, Britain had not yet been forced to make the choice between refusal, reassurance, and restraint. On the contrary, British interests seemed best served by avoiding this choice as long as possible. British great-power status depended on preserving both its colonial hegemony and the continental balance of power. Both purposes were suited by the existing alliance system. The Austro-German alliance served to perpetuate British colonial hegemony by tying down the Franco-Russian alliance in Europe, while the Franco-Russian alliance helped to preserve the European balance by checking Germany.[61] It was therefore logical that Britain should endeavor to maintain the status quo by preserving peace.[62] But it was also to be expected that the continental powers should seek to exploit for their own purposes this British interest in maintaining the status quo. Berlin hoped it could induce London to second the German policy of localization.[63] The British reply that localization could not succeed if it implied destruction of Serbian independence was both realistic and reflected British interests. Localization in the German sense either would resolve the Serbian problem, which was a precondition for the existing alliance system, or it would precipitate a European war.[64] Meanwhile Paris and St. Petersburg hoped British interest in maintaining the status quo would induce London to restrain Berlin and Vienna.[65] The British refused on the ground that it would thereby jeopardize the possibility of mediation.[66] Instead the British urged a compromise which would preserve the Austro-Serbian problem and avoid the extremes of complete resolution or war but their suggestion failed to elicit response.[67] In fact a compromise was impossible since resolution of the Austro-Serbian problem would threaten Russian great-power status and thus the Franco-Russian alliance but nonresolution would threaten Austro-Hungarian great-power status and thus the Austro-German alliance. Consequently, it seemed to London that peace and the status quo might best be preserved by British inaction since the continental powers might remain cautious as long as Britain was uncommitted. Thus, rather than forcing a British commitment, circumstances prevented British involvement.[68] But the logic worked both ways. If Britain could discourage the eruption of an Austro-Serbian crisis by not choosing sides, it could also avoid engagement only as long as the crisis did not erupt. A crisis was, however, implicit in the decisions already taken by the continental governments and would become explicit if all abided by these decisions.

WAR PROVES NECESSARY: FROM ULTIMATUM TO DECLARATION (23 JULY–4 AUGUST)

The first Austro-Serbian stage of the crisis reached its climax and the actual European crisis began with the delivery of the Austro-Hungary ultimatum to Serbia on 23 July.[69] The ultimatum implied that Vienna sought a diplomatic humiliation under threat of military operations which would be forgone if the ultimatum were accepted.[70] It confronted the Serbian government with three hypothetical choices. Serbia could reject the ultimatum out of hand and thereby risk having to stand alone against Austria-Hungary. Or it could submit completely and thereby renounce its political independence to Austria-Hungary. Or it could win Russo-French support by accepting Russo-French advice to navigate between these extremes and accept a diplomatic humiliation but preserve its independence. Although the Serbian government may have considered the extreme alternatives, it eventually opted for the middle road.[71] In fact, this was the best of all possible worlds for Serbia since it would either force Austria-Hungary to recognize Serbia's right to exist if Austria-Hungary accepted, or it would force Russia to defend Serbia if Austria-Hungary refused. The Entente powers and even the kaiser reacted with relief to the Serbian reply since it seemed to facilitate a solution least unsatisfactory to the powers, i.e., at Serbian expense but without jeopardizing the balance of power.[72] Thus, as the crisis was about to explode, it seemed most likely to be defused.

The Serbian answer hypothetically placed Vienna before awkward alternatives. The Serbs had refused to commit suicide by accepting the ultimatum unqualifiedly or to justify murder by rejecting the ultimatum. Vienna could now accept the Serbian reply and thus win a diplomatic victory at the price of renouncing military operations and recognizing Serbia's right to exist. Or Vienna could reject the Serbian answer and opt instead for military operations at the risk of triggering a European war. A diplomatic victory might have offered the advantages of establishing Austria-Hungary's right to limited intervention into Serbian affairs and even of extracting a European guarantee of Austro-Hungarian existence against Serbia in exchange for an equivalent Austro-Hungarian promise to Serbia. But such a diplomatic victory implied the disadvantage that Europe rather than Austria-Hungary would resolve the Serbian problem, and experience had taught Vienna to expect little satisfaction from the other powers. Above all a compromise solution assumed that Austro-Serbian coexistence was possible, whereas Austro-Hungarian statesmen assumed it was not. In short, the logic of early July still seemed to pertain in late July. Since they were determined to preserve the empire, the statesmen in Vienna perceived no choice but to reject the Serbian reply and solve the Serbian problem themselves, even at the risk of European war.[73]

The Austro-Hungarian decision confronted the continental powers with the implications of their policies. The issue was now whether they would abide by their previous decisions at the risk of war or alter their decisions at the risk of their great-power status. German leaders may have yielded briefly to the temptation of escaping this choice by finding a compromise solution.[74] But a compromise solution necessitated a fundamental change of German policy which was never seriously considered. On the contrary, Berlin encouraged Vienna to begin military operations quickly in order to force a Russian choice between diplomatic defeat and war.[75] Berlin made this choice clearer with its own localization argument that Russian intervention into the Austro-Serbian dispute would constitute aggression against Austria-Hungary.[76] The Russians altered these choices, however. They substituted Europeanization for localization with the assertion that the Austro-Serbian problem was European rather than strictly Austro-Hungarian.[77] This formula constituted diplomatic victory for Russia and diplomatic defeat for Austria-Hungary since it would institutionalize Serbian independence and thus Austro-Hungarian insecurity. Meanwhile Russia rejected a diplomatic defeat as implied in the Austro-Hungarian declaration of war on Serbia. Russian leaders demonstrated that they preferred war to diplomatic defeat by announcing mobilization first against Austria-Hungary and then Germany.[78] They thereby presented Germany with the choice between diplomatic defeat and war. The Germans rejected the Russian pressure and replied with their own threat of mobilization.[79] But the German counterthreat was rejected in turn by the Russians.[80] Threats of war had therefore failed to make Serbia, Austria-Hungary, Russia, or Germany accept diplomatic defeat.

Diplomatic defeat might have been accepted only if a threat of war had been credible, but none could have been credible. A threat can be credible only if it implies immediate defeat which assumes concentration of forces. None of these powers, however, concentrated against any of the others. Austria-Hungary did not against Serbia, nor did Russia against either Austria-Hungary or Germany, nor did Germany against Russia. None concentrated because doing so would have contradicted its basic strategic and diplomatic assumptions. Austria-Hungary did not concentrate against Serbia because it assumed that it would be unnecessary if Russia renounced Serbia and impossible if Russia supported Serbia. Russia did not concentrate against Austria-Hungary or Germany because it assumed that it would be necessary to fight both or neither; if it fought both, it preferred to divide its forces. Germany did not concentrate against Russia because it too assumed that it would have to fight both France and Russia or neither; if it fought both, it preferred to concentrate on France. Thus none of these threats succeeded because none was coordinated with basic strategic and diplomatic assumptions. They might have succeeded only if these assumptions had proven fallacious. But the threats were necessary only if the assumptions were valid. Thus the threats of war could have succeeded only if they had been unnecessary and failed when they were necessary. The threats, however, had to succeed if war were to be avoided. Therefore war could not be avoided by Austro-Hungarian, Russian, or German threats against one another.

War might be avoided, however, if France accepted diplomatic defeat.

France might accept diplomatic defeat if a German threat were credible, namely, if it threatened France with immediate military defeat by concentrating against it. In fact, German strategists did plan a concentration against France precisely because they believed it could be defeated quickly (whereas Russia could not) and because doing so corresponded with their basic strategic and diplomatic assumptions.[81] German leaders assumed Germany would have to fight both Russia and France or neither. Since Russia would presumably opt for war only if supported by France, French decisions rather than German threats would determine Russian policy. French behavior could be affected only by a German threat to France. It was therefore appropriate that this was the only threat German strategists prepared. It was also the only threat during the crisis which coordinated military strategy with diplomatic policy in the sense of confronting France with the possibility of immediate defeat. Like the previous threats, it did not necessitate war since it offered France the alternative of diplomatic defeat.[82] But French rejection implied that the German threat was not credible.[83] Perhaps no threat would have been credible if diplomatic defeat were inconceivable because it required renouncing Russia and thus French great-power status. The French refusal confronted Germany with a hypothetical choice between diplomatic defeat and war. Berlin might have chosen diplomatic defeat if it had felt that the war could not be won or that the price would be too high, i.e., if the long-run Franco-Russian threat had been credible. But diplomatic defeat implied renunciation of Austria-Hungary and thus possibly German great-power status. The Germans therefore opted for war instead of diplomatic defeat.[84] The French and German decisions demonstrated that no military threat was sufficiently credible to make the continental powers accept a diplomatic defeat which jeopardized their great-power status. But, since war was avoidable only if a credible threat of war made diplomatic defeat preferable, war was unavoidable.

One alternative to this logic seemed to be British mediation. British mediation could succeed only as long as the balance of power was accepted by all the powers.[85] The balance of power was accepted by the powers as long as they believed it was unnecessary to change it in order to preserve their great-power status. British mediation might therefore have succeeded before the assassination. Before the assassination it, however, seemed unnecessary. It seemed necessary only after the assassination, in fact, only after the ultimatum. But the ultimatum indicated that the balance of power was no longer accepted by all the continental powers. Austria-Hungary and Germany had committed themselves to alter it by destroying Serbian independence in order to preserve their own great-power status. Yet France and Russia had committed themselves to defend Serbian independence in order to preserve their great-

power status. These two positions were irreconcilable and British mediation could have succeeded only if one side had accepted diplomatic
defeat. But neither would do so since both equated diplomatic defeat
with loss of great-power status. British mediation could therefore not
succeed after the ultimatum or even after the assassination and was
caught in a contradiction. It could succeed when it seemed unnecessary
but could not succeed when it seemed necessary. The fact that it was tried
is frequently interpreted as proof that it was practical but failed because
of British mistakes.[86] This criticism is, however, unjustified and misleading. British mediatory efforts were not a case of losing peace by mistake but of mistaken efforts to save peace when it was already lost.

The only remaining possibility for preserving peace seemed a threat of
British intervention against Germany.[87] Such a threat could succeed
only if it kept Germany from committing itself to change the balance of
power. Germany might not have done so if it believed British intervention could preclude victory. A threat of British intervention might therefore have succeeded before the assassination, but then it seemed unnecessary; it appeared necessary only after mediation had failed. The failure of
mediation indicated, however, that Germany had committed itself to
change the balance of power. The threat of British intervention could
then have succeeded only if Germany had been willing to accept diplomatic defeat. Germany would have accepted diplomatic defeat if it believed British intervention would preclude victory. Although German
leaders believed British intervention would reduce their chances (and
therefore sought to keep Britain neutral), they did not expect it to preclude victory.[88] The British threat thereby proved no more credible than
the other threats. Perhaps none could have been credible since German
leaders equated diplomatic defeat with renunciation of great-power status. In short British intervention could not succeed after mediation had
failed or even after the assassination. Thus, like British mediation, it was
caught in the syndrome that it could succeed when it seemed unnecessary but could not when it seemed necessary. The fact that it was tested is
frequently interpreted as proof that it was practical but failed because of
British mistakes.[89] As in the case of mediation, this criticism is unjustified and misleading. The British threat of intervention was not an instance of losing peace by mistake but of a mistaken attempt to save peace
when it was already lost.

THE IRRELEVANT PUBLIC: DIPLOMATIC
POLICY AND DOMESTIC POLITICS DURING THE CRISIS

The primarily diplomatic interpretation of the July crisis which has
been offered above is incomplete unless the role of domestic politics and
public opinion is minimized. It is sometimes suggested that public

opinion influenced the fundamental decisions of governments and thus the course of the crisis. European society has been described as anxious for violence.[90] To the extent that this consideration influenced the crisis, governments presumably went to war to satisfy these impluses. There is little evidence to demonstrate that governments sought to please the masses in this fashion, although it may have been a subconscious but therefore undocumentable consideration. Conversely, it was asserted that European society was decadent and in need of revitalization through violence, but there is little evidence that this was a critical consideration during the July crisis.[91] There is much evidence that the declaration of war caused hysterically jubilant response from the masses.[92] Although European statesmen were violent in the sense that they pursued power by the threat of war and eventually war itself, their decisions were influenced by policy, not by popular or psychic considerations. It has been suggested that governments opted for war to solve social problems and even to avoid revolution.[93] There is some evidence to support this contention.[94] But there is much which contradicts it. In May or early June of 1914 Jagow had rejected Moltke's suggestion of a preventive war in part because he felt it would jeopardize German prosperity.[95] Grey believed war would destroy the whole European economy.[96] German businessmen and bankers also opposed war.[97] Bismarck, Grey, and Lenin agreed with Bethmann's prediction that war would precipitate not prevent revolution.[98] Many members of the public were opposed to war during the crisis itself.[99] Thus the options which rulers and ruling classes in general perceived were not yet civil war and international peace versus civil peace and international war; instead, they envisaged the choice as civil and international peace versus civil and international war.

Circumstantial evidence also argues against the contention that politics and public opinion significantly affected policy. Few politicians were consulted by the German government on fundamental decisions, as indeed few outside of government were consulted by any government. The German Reichstag was not in session and no parliament was even informed until war was inevitable.[100] Domestic political questions delayed diplomatic decisions in some cases and distracted attention in others but did not alter policy.[101] By the time the public became aware that a diplomatic crisis was brewing—namely, with the presentation of the Austro-Hungarian ultimatum to Serbia—the critical diplomatic decisions had already been taken.[102] Nonetheless radical politicians sought to arouse public opinion against war and thereby influence governmental policy. Some German Social Democratic leaders succeeded in causing street demonstrations against the Austro-Hungarian rejection of the

Serbian reply.[103] These demonstrations, however, did not fundamentally alter the German government's policy and, to the extent that they expressed public opinion, these demonstrations indicated not the significance but the German people's ineffectuality during the crisis. It has been asserted that nationalism affected the outbreak of war.[104] There were some demonstrations in favor of war during the crisis, though very few; most occurred after war had been declared.[105] It can therefore be argued that war was popular but not that these demonstrations affected the course of the crisis. Except possibly for the cases of Austria-Hungary and Serbia, all demonstrations during the crisis occurred after the fundamental government decisions had been made, i.e., after the Austro-Hungarian ultimatum.[106] In fact demonstrations in favor of war were not only unimportant in governmental decisions but even sometimes unwelcome to governments for tactical reasons.[107] The press has been blamed for causing war, but during the crisis it played an insignificant role in influencing governmental decisions except possibly in Austria-Hungary and Serbia.[108] The radical German press sought to arouse anti-war sentiment but did not alter the government's decisions.[109] Rather than being determined by public opinion, the German government sought to determine opinion and prepare it for war.[110] Thus, when politics and public opinion differed from policy, they were overridden; when they agreed with policy, they were exploited.

Although politics and public opinion did not affect fundamental policy decisions, they did alter tactics and timing. When the German government decided that war was likely or even inevitable (around 26 July), its primary concern became maximization of the prospects of military victory. Its two major concerns in this connection were to improve the chances of British neutrality and to insure unanimous support from the German people.[111] Neither consideration permitted the German government to declare openly that it was fighting what amounted to a preventive war in order to preserve its great-power status.[112] Instead both objectives seemed to necessitate placing responsibility for war on Russia.[113] The German government attempted to produce this impression by a combination of tactics. It sought to avoid the appearance of being aggressive itself. Consequently, Bethmann discouraged moves which might seem to favor war.[114] He tried to give the impression of favoring British mediatory proposals.[115] The German government propagated in the German press the idea that it favored peace.[116] Bethmann and the kaiser traded fairly successfully on their reputations of favoring peace.[117] Above all, Bethmann sought to postpone German mobilization until Russian mobilization had been proclaimed.[118] Despite pressure from Moltke and several false alarms, he was ultimately successful.[119] Thus the German government continued to proclaim the localization formula which implied that Russia was anxious to start a European war by supporting Serbian aspirations to destroy Austria-Hungary.[120] This tactic was epitomized and summarized in the *White Book* which the government prepared during the crisis in order to put its case to the world. Although presented by Bethmann as an objective record of events, the book's main concern was not historical truth but persuasion of the British government and German public.[121]

Of the two concerns, the German public was both the more important and the more promising. Like all governments, German leaders could not be certain of their public's reaction to war.[122] Demonstrations for and against war occurred.[123] The major question mark was the Social Democrats. Supported by the radical Socialist press, the radical leaders favored opposition to war and called for mass protests critical of Vienna.[124] But, fearing such opposition would cause reprisal, two moderate Socialist leaders (Ebert and Braun) removed the party's treasury to Switzerland at the behest of the party's praesidium.[125] These fears were not without justification. Plans to incarcerate Social Democratic leaders had fallen into their hands and been published in 1910.[126] There were many military and civilian leaders (including the kaiser), as well as bourgeois politicians (including Erzberger), who favored the use of force against the Social Democrats.[127] Bethmann and Falkenhayn opted for a different tactic in arguing that the Social Democratic leaders be allowed the option of renouncing violence as a condition for not having the government move against them. In short, the goal was the same but the means were different: like his policy toward Russia, Bethmann's tactics toward the Social Democrats sought to place the onus of responsibility for force on them. His objective in doing so was to bring the German nation into war as unanimously and enthusiastically as possible.[128] In this kind of move, Bethmann had frequently been eminently successful.[129] The government exploited the inverted logic of crisis to make opposition to war appear as provocation, and support of the government seem a service to peace. He also discouraged criticism by perpetuating the myth of his being the victim of a war party within the government. The Social Democratic leaders decided (on 28 July) to renounce opposition to war, and Südekum gave Bethmann an assurance to this effect (on 29 July).[130] Bethmann and Falkenhayn seem to have taken the assurance at face value and opposed any moves against the Social Democrats.[131] In fact the Social Democratic leaders advised their press against antiwar propaganda.[132]

Renunciation of open opposition to war, however, was not equivalent to enthusiastic support. The question still remained whether the Social

Democratic Reichstag members would vote for war credits. Their overwhelming attitude seems to have been one of paralytic indecision and
ambivalence.[133] Some of the more radical leaders spoke out against war
despite the party leadership's warning.[134] There were, however, fundamental reasons for supporting the government. Previous experience
(such as the second Moroccan crisis and the vote for military expansion
in 1913) had demonstrated that the radicals could not win over the party
to opposition when the nation seemed in danger. The Social Democrats
had been much too thoroughly integrated into the state and expected too
many advantages as the result of this integration to risk opposition. The
trade unions which tended to be the politically most conservative elements in the party refused to risk the economic gains of their members by
opposition.[135] The font of international socialist pacifism, the International, failed completely to give leadership in opposition to war.[136] It
was possible that these impulses would have been sufficient to persuade
the Social Democratic Reichstag members to vote war credits. Russian
mobilization made it a virtual certainty. German public opinion reacted
so unanimously and angrily to the threat of Russian invasion that Social
Democratic leaders believed themselves faced with the choice between
following public opinion and supporting war or completely losing
public support and possibly arousing popular antipathy.[137] When the
Social Democratic Reichstag faction finally voted for war credits, it gave
the Russian threat as its primary consideration.[138]

German public opinion therefore seems to have fluctuated. Between
the assassination and Austro-Hungarian ultimatum, it may have been
anti-Serbian. Between the ultimatum and Russian mobilization, some
left wing elements at least shifted toward criticism of Austria-Hungary.
Russian mobilization caused German opinion to swing radically and
rapidly toward war. Bethmann's tactic had been successful. Yet perhaps
it had been irrelevant. As Social Democratic leader Kautsky had predicted, the threat of invasion was likely to unite the nation in any case.[139] In
this sense Russian rather than German policy determined German public opinion.

It was appropriate and not illogical or exceptional that public opinion should have been excluded by policymakers during the crisis. Despite considerable democratization of domestic politics before 1914, governments defined in the narrowest sense still determined policy. Indeed
great-power diplomacy during the July crisis would have been unfeasible if the public had been involved. Austro-Hungarian and German policies in particular were based on the element of surprise which would
have been jeopardized if public opinion had been consulted. But even
more than a matter of tactic, the exclusion of public opinion was essen-

tial to the objectives of all the powers. Diplomatic victory for one power implied diplomatic defeat for another. Diplomatic defeat could be accepted by a great power only if the public were not involved and its prestige not overtly threatened. Thus, a diplomatic resolution of the July crisis (or any serious crisis between powers) was possible only if the public was excluded. Great-power diplomacy and democratic control of policy were incompatible.

STRATEGY CONFIRMS POLICY: THE RELATIONSHIP BETWEEN MILITARY STRATEGY AND DIPLOMATIC POLICY DURING THE JULY CRISIS

The transition from peace to war raised the question of the relationship between diplomatic policy and military strategy. It has frequently been argued that military considerations influenced or even determined the outcome of the crisis. In particular military strategy, mobilization schedules, and demands for preventive war are reputed to have encroached on policy.[140] These interpretations imply that a fundamental conflict existed between German policy and strategy. This criticism is misleading. Strategy confirmed rather than contradicted policy. Far from pursuing other objectives or making other assumptions, strategy conformed relatively well to Clausewitz's ideal of "policy by other means."

Interest in the question of preventive war stemmed directly from the interwar debate over responsibility. Evidence that a government sought a preventive war was assumed to be sufficient proof of its responsibility for war. It has generally been a less interesting question to interpretations of chance or inevitability. In fact, preventive war is proof of responsibility only if responsibility is loosely defined, whereas it is more consistent with the interpretation of inevitability. The concept of preventive war assumes that war is both inevitable and preferable sooner rather than later. If war is not assumed to be inevitable, the term "preventive" is deceptive; the war then becomes either "inventive" (i.e., the invention and therefore responsibility of the statesman who provokes it) or "accidental." If war is assumed to be inevitable, then the statesman perceives no choice as to whether war will occur. Likewise, if war can be won only sooner rather than later, then the statesman perceives no choice as to when it will be fought. But the concept of responsibility rigidly defined assumes that the statesman is not responsible unless he has a choice on whether and when war will occur. Although war seemed inconceivable after the 1914–18 experience had shown that it was disastrous, in 1914 preventive war *in all but name* seemed not only possible but necessary to all the great powers if their status were threatened. It therefore became a government's responsibility to seek war under the

most advantageous circumstances; indeed to do otherwise was irresponsible. Preventive war seemed a duty not a crime.

The question of whether the German government sought a preventive
war is consequently less useful in ascertaining its responsibility for war
than in understanding its attitude toward war and the international situation. Certainly many—perhaps most—German leaders regarded a European war as inevitable, even imminent, in the next couple years. Many
believed that Germany's chances in such a war would lessen with time.
All of these concerns seem to have intensified during the spring of 1914,
although this is difficult to demonstrate.[141] Thus all of the concommi-
tants of preventive war were present: some German leaders advocated it,
others demonstrated sympathy at certain times for it, and, like other
leaders, Bethmann and Jagow logically and indeed necessarily stipulat-
ed conditions which would require war.[142] But there is no evidence that
German leaders consciously sought what they themselves designated as
a preventive war and many specifically rejected doing so. Circumstantial
evidence also indicates that they did not plan war for August 1914. On
the contrary, during the July crisis no special military preparations were
made. Moltke and Falkenhayn continued their debate over expansion
for 1915–16 which a preventive war in August 1914 would have rendered
pointless. No exceptional economic or financial dispositions seem to
have been initiated during the crisis. More immediate military considerations and consultations with the military occurred only after the
Austro-Hungarian ultimatum had been presented.[143] Thus the German
government accepted the assumptions of preventive war but refused to
make the specific decision for preventive war which was implied by the
assumptions. If preventive war is defined as a conscious decision, there is
no evidence to date that the German government launched a preventive
war.

But this definition is too narrow and artificial to facilitate understanding of German policy. It assumes statesmen call what they do by the
right name and pursue the implications of their decisions to their logical
conclusions. Policy is more usefully defined in terms of its assumptions
and implications rather than the terminology used to describe it by its
makers. German leaders accepted the necessity for a preventive war.
They sought a diplomatic victory which would either make war unnecessary if they were successful or would make war successful if it proved
necessary. They thereby created circumstances which presented their
opponents with the choice between unacceptable diplomatic defeat and
immediate war. The goal of diplomatic victory was best served by neither consciously seeking nor preparing for war. Likewise, the alternative
of immediate war was best served by postponing preparations until the

last moment since German success in war depended on its advantage of rapid mobilization. Hence, the lack of a conscious decision for preventive war or preparations for war can be explained as a logical result of German policy assumptions; it was simply unnecessary for German leaders to call their policy preventive war.

Nonetheless German decisions precipitated a war which was in all essentials preventive. Some were aware of these implications of their policy.[144] Yet even this recognition does not prove responsibility since, considering their assumptions about the state system and their determination to preserve Germany's great-power status, German leaders made decisions necessitated by circumstances. In this sense, it was "fortuitous" that war broke out in August 1914, as Moltke commented. The contradiction was not in German assumptions or actual German policy which were completely consistent but in German claims. The German government sought to make Russia appear responsible for war both because it mobilized first and because of its prewar military buildup. These two assertions were, however, contradictory. If Russian mobilization caused war, then its prewar buildup did not make war necessary and was irrelevant; conversely, if the prewar buildup caused war by forcing Germany to seek a preventive war, then Russian mobilization was irrelevant. The buildup argument assumed Russia was planning war for 1916–17 but not before; the mobilization argument assumed Russia wanted war in 1914. The contradiction was inherent in Moltke's thinking and he could reconcile his assumptions with Russian behavior only by claiming Russia had made a mistake.[145] The German government actually acted on the assumption that the Russian prewar military buildup made a preventive war necessary for Germany. But it could not admit doing so because of political side effects on German public opinion and British policy. By alternately claiming that Bismarck's wars were not preventive but praising him for launching wars necessary to German development, German statesmen (including Bethmann and Jagow) revealed their ambivalence. Yet policy is defined by what states do, not by what their statesmen say or even admit to themselves that they do.

In pursuing but not admitting that they were opting for what was effectively a preventive war, German leaders were typical. All governments sought to prevent undesirable eventualities through recourse to war in 1914. Austria-Hungary chose war to avoid expected Balkan developments which were believed to threaten its survival. Russia opposed Austro-Hungarian domination over Serbia which would jeopardize Russian ambitions in the Balkans. France sought to retain its great-power status by preserving the alliance with Russia. Britain was anxious to prevent French decline and German presence on the Channel coast.

All had the hypothetical option of avoiding or at least postponing war but chose instead the alternative of war then rather than under what seemed less advantageous circumstances later. The Germans may have confronted the choice more consciously and desperately than their opponents but the logic was the same. Any dubious moral distinctions which are applied to the essentially amoral world of international politics are therefore questions of degree but not kind.

The relationship between German diplomacy and strategy is critical in evaluating German behavior during both the July crisis and the war. It is frequently asserted that military strategy intervened and fundamentally altered the course of the July crisis—if not, then the role of the soldiers during the crisis was irrelevant. This interpretation is usually suggested by the critics of German militarism who imply that there existed a fundamental difference of assumptions between good (peace-loving) civilians and bad (bellicose) soldiers and that the crisis might have ended peacefully if the soldiers had not taken over. This criticism of the German military is misleading. The implication that their assumptions were fundamentally different from those of the civilians is untrue. Both accepted the necessity of maintaining the great-power status of Austria-Hungary, assumed that France would support Russia in war, and regarded war as essential if Germany's great-power status were threatened. If the civilians effectively pursued a policy of preventive war, as argued above, war cannot be said to have been forced upon them by the soldiers but was the logical consequence of their assumptions. On the basis of these assumptions, peace not war would have been the departure. War was made inevitable less by a demand of the military than by the decision of the civilians to support Austria-Hungary.[146]

The implication that military considerations, particularly the mobilization timetable, intervened and cut short the possibility of mediation (thus a diplomatic solution) is also misleading. Mobilization became important only after a German diplomatic victory had become unlikely (i.e., when Russia refused to drop Serbia) and the German civilian leaders had themselves concluded that war was likely.[147] British mediation was not precluded by the German mobilization schedule but by German policy. In fact, although Moltke demanded rapid mobilization, Bethmann successfully delayed it until its political disadvantages were blunted, i.e., until Russia had ordered mobilization and France had refused the German ultimatum. The differences between Moltke and Bethmann were in tactics not fundamental assumptions. In the last resort, Moltke was probably correct in assuming that British neutrality could not be won by such diplomatic tactics. Likewise the German population would probably have rallied against a Russian invasion, regardless of whether Russia mobilized before or after Germany. Bethmann exploited the differences between himself and the military for his own political and perhaps psychological reasons: it was more useful and perhaps comfortable to claim that war had been decided upon by others.[148] Even though it became an important consideration only after war had become inevitable, mobilization is frequently presented as critical to the outcome of the July crisis. It is usually presented as a turning point, an irreversible step toward war when technology and timing controlled men, rather than the reverse. Germans and apologists for Germans are particularly prone to this interpretation since it served the German policy objective of fixing responsibility on Russia. This interpretation is, however, misleading. Like many decisions, mobilization was reversible if it was perceived to be reversible. Since mobilization had been ordered and then reversed on several previous occasions, it could have been in 1914 had it not been viewed as irreversible. Yet it was not mobilization which caused war but the decision for war which caused mobilization.[149]

German violation of Belgian neutrality is likewise frequently presented as the subordination of policy to strategy. It is presumed to have been critical to Britain's decision for war but this interpretation is debatable since Britain would probably have declared war in any case when Germany threatened France with defeat. But, like the Russian government's decision to mobilize before Germany, the German violation of Belgian neutrality was useful to the British government in arousing British public opinion to support the war. Like the German government's tactic of allowing Russia to mobilize first, the violation of Belgium was, however, probably not essential for the British government to win public support; the British public probably would have supported its government even if the Germans had not invaded Belgium. Since German civilian leaders knew that the violation of Belgium was essential to German military plans, their efforts to avoid it were not only irrelevant to British decisions but illogical in terms of their own aspirations; in effect they wanted a rapid victory over France while trying to avoid its precondition. The generals were more realistic and consistent in accepting the violation of Belgium as the price of such a quick victory over France.[150] Thus, in his advocacy of preventive war, demands for rapid mobilization, refusal to mobilize against Russia alone, and acceptance of the necessity of violating Belgian neutrality, Moltke was more consistent with their shared assumptions than Bethmann and the other civilians.

The soldiers did not cause war but confronted the statesmen with war as the consequence of the statesmen's decisions. In particular, the soldiers indicated that war against France, Russia, and Britain was the logical result of the civilians' failure to win a diplomatic victory during the

July crisis. Although German statesmen had accepted the risk of war at the beginning of the crisis, they did not desire war and sought to escape it as long as possible—an inconsistent and unrealistic but understandable response.[151] Interpreting German policy is therefore complicated by the mixed feelings, inconsistencies, and ambiguities of German leaders. The debate over whether German policy was dominated by arrogance or anxiety is particularly heated in connection with the July crisis.[152] Arrogance can be perceived in the pursuit of a diplomatic victory, the decision for preventive war, and the confidence in eventual economic domination over Europe, but these impulses fell short of a conscious plan for German hegemony, however much hegemony was implicit in a possible German military victory.[153] Anxiety can be represented in the fears of the future and in Moltke's doubts about military victory.[154] To argue that one attitude prevailed to the exclusion of the other is to oversimplify. German military and civilian leaders seem to have been both anxious and arrogant, not infrequently exhibiting both feelings within the same argument.[155] Both were important, if not essential, elements in the mentality which made German statesmen and soldiers decide on war.

Each power had done what seemed necessary to remain a power. War was the logical and inevitable result. No government had specifically sought war, and all had preferred diplomatic victory since it implied the fruits of war without the risks. But none could win a diplomatic victory precisely for the reasons that it was so desirable: no power could accept diplomatic defeat since it implied the price of defeat without the possibility of victory. That European statesmen could perceive war as preferable to diplomatic defeat was due in part to the prevailing view of war. It was expected to be compatible with the European state system, short and decisive, not a war to end war but merely the existing status quo. It would presumably produce the goals diplomacy had failed to achieve—in the German case, the dissolution of the Triple Entente. It was therefore not perceived as a departure from policy but policy by other means. Because war was conceivable and the alternative of diplomatic defeat was inconceivable, war became inevitable.

But the world war would in fact destroy the European power system. The powers went to war in pursuit of their interests and in defense of their independence, as they had to do if they were to remain great powers. Germany would seek to destroy the balance of power, the anti-German coalition would seek to defend it. By electing war in Europe, the powers risked and ultimately sacrificed their power superiority over the world. The war would therefore confront the powers with a fundamental choice. They could avoid exhaustion and maintain their power superiority over the world by allowing Germany hegemony and sacrificing the balance of power. Or they could risk exhaustion and world power superiority by resisting German hegemony to preserve the balance of power. The anti-German coalition elected to risk its world power superiority in order to preserve the European power balance. But either alternative would have destroyed the system since both were essential to it. Europe could have avoided the choice only by avoiding war. Preservation of both the European balance and world superiority required the preservation of peace. The prewar assumption was fallacious: war was not compatible with the system. Ultimately war would prove to be not an extension but an extinction of prewar policy. The war became a "war to end war" in part because otherwise war would end the system. But here the contradiction emerged. War was necessary to the great-power system, essential to the definition of a great power since it had to be able to defend its independence and pursue its interests by war as well as peace. If one power renounced war, it ceased to be a power and, if all renounced war, all ceased to be powers and the system ceased to be a power system. Thus war was both incompatible with but essential to the great-power system. Since its existence required the reconciliation of irreconcilables, the European great-power system was doomed to collapse regardless of whether it chose war or peace in 1914.

The great-power system of 1914 was therefore predicated on a great paradox. It could exist only as long as it was not tested. The greater the power accumulated by the great powers, the less powerful they became. The more power they had, the less they could use it against one another or one another's protégés because war became more likely to destroy the system. Their power could be used only where it did not affect the system, namely in some parts of the colonial world. A system based on power can function only if power is limited and war possible. When war becomes impossible, power becomes irrelevant. Power and perpetual peace are irreconcilable.

NOTES

1 For an elegant analysis of the prevailing attitudes toward state relations, see James Joll, *1914: The Unspoken Assumptions* (London, 1968).

2 Kaiser to Bethmann, 8 June 1914, quoted by Fischer, *Griff*, pp. 57–58.

3 Albertini, *Origins*, 1:488–539; Fay, *Origins*, 1:438–57; May, *Monarchy*, pp. 459–75.

4 Fay, *Origins*, 2:53–135; Albertini, *Origins*, 2:22–88; Joachim Remak, *Sarajevo* (London, 1959), pp. 43–57.

5   Fay, *Origins*, 2:140–46; Remak, *Sarajevo*, pp. 182–229; Albertini, *Origins*, 2:89–111; Taylor, *Struggle*, p. 521.

6   Fay, *Origins*, 2:43–52, 140–66, 330–35.

7   For the view that Austro-Serbian coexistence was impossible, see G. L. Dickenson, *The International Anarchy, 1904–1914* (London, 1926), pp. 401, 412, and Oscar Jaszi, *The Dissolution of the Habsburg Monarchy* (Chicago, 1964), p. 422. This view is espoused particularly by apologists for the Central Powers: see Harry Elmer Barnes, Leopold Berchtold, Alexander Hoyos, Friedrich Wiesner, Gottlieb Jagow, "Did Germany Incite Austria in 1914?" *Current History*, July 1928, pp. 620–35.

8   Conrad, *Dienstzeit*, 4:31–32; Ritter, *Staatskunst*, 2:381; *Outbreak of the World War*, German documents coll. by Karl Kautsky, ed. by Max Montgelas and Walter Schüking (New York, 1924), 13–14, 29 (hereafter KD); Redlich, *Tagebuch*, 1:238; Barnes, "Germany," pp. 626–30.

9   Jaszi, *Dissolution*, pp. 298–378; May, *Monarchy*, pp. 476–92; Peter F. Sugar, "The Nature of the Non-Germanic Societies Under Habsburg Rule," *Slavic Review*, March 1963, pp. 1–30.

10 KD, 13–14. For the development of this program during the spring of 1914, see Fay, *Origins*, 2:188–98.

11 Conrad, *Dienstzeit*, 4:31–32; *OU*, 8:10118; *BD*, 11:50, 56.

12 *OU*, 8:10118, 10146, 10215; Ritter, *Staatskunst*, 2:379; Conrad, *Dienstzeit*, 4:36–37; Redlich, *Tagebuch*, 1:237–38.

13 Conrad, *Dienstzeit*, 4:31; Ritter, *Staatskunst*, 2:282–97; *OU*, 8:10118.

14 Fay, *Origins*, 2:198, 223–60, 550–52; Fischer, *Griff*, p. 94; Albertini, *Origins*, 2:125–26, 133; Jaszi, *Dissolution*, p. 429; Taylor, *Struggle*, pp. 520–21, 523, 527; Joachim Remak, "The Healthy Invalid: How Doomed the Habsburg Empire?" *Journal of Modern History*, June 1969, pp. 127–43; David Lloyd George, *War Memoirs* (London, 1933), 1:34; Camille Bloch, *The Causes of the World War* (London, 1935), p. 183. The kaiser shared this view (KD, 401).

15 See especially Berchtold's resistance to the pressures of his ambassadors and advisers during the spring of 1914 (*OU*, 8:32–202, passim).

16 See note 12 above and KD, 65, 87. A. Hoyos, *Der deutsch-englische Gegensatz und sein Einfluss auf die Balkanpolitik Österreich-Ungarns* (Berlin, Leipzig, 1922), p. 78; *OU*, 8:10393, 10437; *Das Wiener Kabinette und die Entstehung des Weltkrieges*, ed. R. Gooss (Vienna, 1919), p. 114.

17 Fay, *Origins*, 2:241; KD, 49.

18 Expressions indicating a sense of determinism and lack of choice run through the discussions between Austro-Hungarian leaders (see notes 16 and 17 above).

19 For evidence that German leaders were aware of their "dilemma," see: Erdmann, "Beurteilung," p. 536; KD, 72; Jarausch, "Illusion," pp. 48, 52–60. For Austro-Hungarian requests for German support, see: *OU*, 8:9966, 9984, 10006, 10039; KD, 7, 11; *Julikrise*, 1:10; *Deutsche Gesandtschaftsberichte zum Kriegsausbruch 1914*, ed. A. Bach (Berlin, 1937), pp. 2, 3.

20 Erdmann, "Beurteilung," p. 536; KD, 48, 72, 87, supplement 4:2.

21 *OU*, 8:9966, 10038, 10058; Bach, *Gesandtschaftsberichte*, p. 2; Erdmann, "Beurteilung," p. 536; KD, 36, 67, 72, 80, 82, 98.

22 KD, 62.

23 Erdmann, "Beurteilung," p. 536.

24 Ritter, *Staatskunst*, 2:306–7, 311.

25   KD, 72.

26   KD, 7; *OU*, 8:10039; Albertini, *Origins*, 2:137–40.

27   Fischer, *Griff*, pp. 57–59; Conrad, *Dienstzeit*, 3:668–73; Ritter, *Staatskunst*, 2:311; *Kriegsrüstung*, 1:206–10, 349; Zechlin, "Motive," pp. 92–93; House, *Papers*, 1:261–62; Tirpitz, *Erinnerungen*, p. 195; Naumann, *Profile*, p. 58; Schulthess, *Geschichtskalender*, pp. 281–84; *Bayr. Dok.*, p. 1; *BD*, 10:550–51, part 2; *GP*, 36:14611; and *GP*, 39:15674, 15861, 15883.

28   For Rumania, see: *OU*, 7:931–1095, passim; *OU*, 8:1–15, passim; *GP*, 36:569–788, passim; *GP*, 39:333–515, passim; Conrad, *Dienstzeit*, 3:633–38, 647, 669, 671, 781. For Italy, see: *OU*, 8:62–207, passim; *GP*, 36:647–717, passim.

29   KD, 7, 16.

30   KD, 56, 72, supplement 4:35; Erdmann, "Beurteilung," pp. 535–36.

31   See note 20 above. Evidence that Berlin gave Vienna unqualified support comes mostly from Austro-Hungarian sources: *OU*, 8:9966, 10038, 10058, 10076, 10215, 10448. German sources indicate that Berlin gave genuine although not specifically unqualified support: KD, 16, 26, supplement 4:2. In fact the distinction was practically insignificant since German leaders had decided early in the crisis that they could not revoke support: KD, 72; Erdmann, "Beurteilung," p. 536.

32   *OU*, 8:10058, 10215; Bach, *Gesandtschaftsberichte*, p. 3; KD, 72, supplement 4:2; Fay, *Origins*, 2:211; Erdmann, "Beurteilung," p. 536.

33   See note 30 above; KD, 58.

34   The evidence on German expectations regarding England is somewhat contradictory. Evidence of greatest German confidence that England would remain neutral comes from Austro-Hungarian sources: *OU*, 8:9966, 10215; Conrad, *Dienstzeit*, 4:157–58. Less confidence but still hope appears in German sources: KD, 36, 48, 52, 56, 61, 72, 120, supplement 4:2. But there is also considerable evidence that German leaders did not expect English neutrality: KD, 30, 43, 52, 55, 62, 72, 401, supplement 4:2.

35   See note 26 above; Conrad, *Dienstzeit*, 1:165; KD, 94.

36   Erdmann, "Beurteilung," p. 536; KD, 58, 72.

37   See note 21 above.

38   See notes 26 and 27 above.

39   For Anglo-German exchanges over the rumored Anglo-Russian naval agreement, see: *GP*, 39:617–33, passim; *BD*, 10:791–97, 802–4, part 2, passim. For Anglo-Russian negotiations, see: *BD*, 10:745–46, 776–77, 797–813, part 2, passim; *GP*, 39:632, 634–36.

40   For German deliberations, see: Fay, *Origins*, 2:203–23; Albertini, *Origins*, 2:137–45.

41   For the perception of some form of German stupidity, see: Fay, *Origins*, 2:207–9, 219–23; G. P. Gooch, *Germany* (London, 1926), pp. 110–12. For the view that Germany was motivated by aggressiveness, see: Fischer, *Griff*, pp. 103–8; Fritz Fischer, *Weltmacht oder Niedergang: Deutschland im ersten Weltkrieg* (Frankfurt am Main, 1965), pp. 51–60; Fritz Fischer, "Vom Zaun gebrochen—nicht hineingeschlittert: Deutschlands Schuld am Ausbruch des ersten Weltkrieges," *Zeit*, September 3, 1965.

42   For expressions by German leaders of compulsion and lack of choice, see: Erdmann, "Beurteilung," pp. 527, 536, passim; KD, 48, 72, 401.

43   The debate over German motives can be divided into the arguments of anxiety and arrogance. For the argument of anxiety, see: Hans Herzfeld, *Welt*, August 1, 1964; Gerhard Ritter, "Eine neue Kriegsschuldthese? Zu Fritz Fischers Buch 'Griff nach der Weltmacht,' "*Historische Zeitschrift*, 191:646–68, passim; Ritter, *Staatskunst*, 2:

309, 314; Rosenberg, *Birth*, p. 66. For evidence of anxiety, see: notes 27–30 above; Bethmann, *Betrachtungen*, 1:99–101; Ritter, *Staatskunst*, 2:314, 329, 335; Helmut Moltke, *Erinnerungen*, pp. 21–23. For arguments of arrogance, see: note 41 above; Pierre Renouvin, *The Immediate Origins of the War* (New Haven, 1928), p. 106. For evidence of arrogance, see: note 36 above; KD, 74, supplement 4:32; Conrad, *Dienstzeit*, 4:152; Zechlin, "Motive," pp. 92–93; Max M. Warburg, *Aus meinen Aufzeichnungen* (Glückstadt, 1952), p. 29. Not infrequently anxiety and arrogance occur in the same conversation or statement: Erdmann, "Beurteilung," p. 536; Jarausch, "Illusion," pp. 57–59; KD, 72, 401; Fischer, *Griff*, p. 65; Friedrich Thimme, ed., *Front wider Bülow* (Munich, 1931), p. 219.

44   See notes 30–31 above; KD, 3.

45   For evidence that Berlin knew the general outline of the Austro-Hungarian ultimatum, see: KD, 18, 19, 29, 40, 41a, 49, 50, 68, 87, supplement 4:2; Fischer, *Griff*, p. 68. For evidence that Berlin encouraged a hard line in Vienna, see: *OU*, 8:10127, 10145, 10215, 10393, 10448; KD, 62, 71, 87, supplement 4:2; Albertini, *Origins*, 2:137–55; Fischer, *Griff*, pp. 105–6; Hantsch, *Berchtold*, 2:589. For evidence that Berlin urged Vienna to present Europe with a *fait accompli*, see: *OU*, 8:10656; Erdmann, "Beurteilung," p. 536.

46   See note 30, chapter 7; KD, supplement 4:2, 4; Fischer, *Griff*, p. 74.

47   See notes 30–31, 45 above; KD, 36, 70, 100, 123, 127; *OU*, 8:10091.

48   KD, 36, 67, 70, 84, 91, 107, 126, 145, 153, supplement 4:2; House, *Papers*, 1:277; Fischer, *Griff*, p. 106.

49   KD, 56, 72, 100, 107, 123, supplement 4:2.

50   See notes 13, 16–17 above; Fay, *Origins*, 2:224–43.

51   *OU*, 8:10118, 10146, 10393.

52   For Berchtold's worries that Serbia might accept the ultimatum, see KD, 29, 87.

53   For Berchtold's efforts to make the ultimatum unacceptable, see: *OU*, 8:10118; KD, 29, 87, supplement 4:2. For Tisza's initial efforts to make the ultimatum acceptable, see *OU*, 8:10118, 10146.

54   This is essentially Tisza's initial argument (see *OU*, 8:10118, 10146).

55   For details on the preparation of the ultimatum, see: Fay, *Origins*, 2:224–54; Albertini, *Origins*, 2:164–78, 254–58. For German criticism of Austro-Hungarian delays, see note 45 above.

56   *IB*, 1:5, no. 47. For Austro-Hungarian and German awareness that Russian renunciation of Serbia would imply renunciation of great-power status, see Ritter, *Staatskunst*, 2:379.

57   The Russians were concerned about the state of the Entente. For French reassurances to Russia during Poincaré's visit to Russia, see Baron Schilling, *How the War Began in 1914* (London, 1925), pp. 113–4. For Russian concern about British intentions in an eventual war, see: Raymond Poincaré, *Les Origines de la guerre* (Paris, 1921), pp. 197–201; Maurice Paleologue, *La Russie des tsars pendant la grande guerre* (Paris, 1921), 1:2–3; *BD*, 11:60, 75, 164. For Russian efforts to win French support in persuading the British to resume conversations for a naval agreement and to resolve their differences in Persia, see: *BD*, 10:557–61, part 2, appendix 1; *BD*, 11:75, 164; Paleologue, *Russie*, 1:2–3; *Entente Diplomacy and the World War*, ed. G. A. Siebert-Schreiner (New York, 1921), p. 733.

58   Schilling, *War*, p. 31; *Les Pourparlers diplomatiques 16/29 juin 3/16 août* (Paris, 1914), p. 36; Serge Sazonov, *The Fateful Years, 1909–1916* (London, 1928), p. 177; *IB*, 5:25, 79; Albertini, *Origins*, 2:353.

59   Poincaré, *Origines*, pp. 197–201; Raymond Poincaré, *Au Service de la France* (Paris, 1928), 4:221–23; Paleologue, *Russie*, 1:6–7; *BD*, 10:101; *DD*, p. 39. For criticism of

this French "blank check" to Russia, see: Fay, *Origins*, 2:286; H. E. Barnes, *The Genesis of the War* (New York, 1926), pp. 315–28.

60   *DDF*, 10:15; Poincaré, *Service*, 4:288; *OU*, 8:10608; KD, 154.

61   For British concern about colonial complications with Russia, see: *BD*, 10:557–61, part 2, appendix 1; KD, 52.

62   For expressions of Grey's distaste for war between the great powers, see: BD, 11:68, 86; KD, 92; *OU*, 8:10537.

63   KD, 20, 30, 52, 72, 92, supplement 4:2.

64   For evidence that the British knew Russia and France would not accept diminution of Serbian independence, see *BD*, 11:40, 60. They made this clear to the Germans (KD, 30, 55) and Austro-Hungarians (*BD*, 11:56, 68, 86; *OU*, 8:10537). But this was precisely what Vienna (see notes 16–17 above) and Berlin (see notes 44–49 above) sought to do.

65   For Franco-Russian suggestions of British pressure on Vienna and Berlin, see *BD*, 11:76, 84.

66   For the British refusal, see minutes on *BD*, 11:76, 84.

67   For British suggestions of Austro-Russian conversations, see *BD*, 11:67, 86. For the French rejection, see *BD*, 11:76. For Russian unresponsiveness, see *BD*, 11:79.

68   For British efforts to avoid taking sides, see: *BD*, 11:40, 79; KD, 30, 43, 52, 62, 180. British diplomatic inactivity was also due in part to distraction by the Irish question: Herbert Henry Asquith, *Memories and Reflections, 1852–1927* (Boston, 1928), 2:5–8; Churchill, *Crisis*, pp. 181–93.

69   Measured in terms of official documents published per day of the crisis from 28 June to 4 August, the diplomatic activity of the powers was between ten and fifteen times as intense after 23 July as before.

70   For details on the presentation of the ultimatum, see: *OU*, 8:10518, 10536, 10526, 10521, 10540; Fay, *Origins*, 2:269–72; Albertini, *Origins*, 2:284–89.

71   For the argument that Serbian leaders may have considered unconditional acceptance of the ultimatum, see Albertini, *Origins*, 2:346–62, passim. For the Serbian answer, see: Fay, *Origins*, 2:343–48; Albertini, *Origins*, 2:364–72.

72   For the Russian reaction, see: *IB*, 5:25; Schilling, *War*, pp. 29–30; *OU*, 8:10616–19; *BD*, 11:125; S. K. Dobrorolski, *Die Mobilmachung der russischen Armee, 1914* (Berlin, 1922), pp. 17–18. For the British reaction, see: *BD*, 11:91, 99, 100, 102, 105, 118; KD, 157. For the French reaction, see *OU*, 8:10606. Even the kaiser regarded the Serbian reply as acceptable to Vienna (KD, 271).

73   For details of Austro-Hungarian rejection of the Serbian answer breaking off negotiations and declaration of partial mobilization against Serbia, see: Albertini, *Origins*, 2:372–89; Fay, *Origins*, 2:348–53. For evidence that Austro-Hungarian leaders had some second thoughts about forcing the issue with Serbia, see: Albertini, *Origins*, 2: 376–80, 387–89; Albertini, *Origins*, 3:526–27; *OU*, 8:10459; Conrad, *Dienstzeit*, 4: 148; Wladimir Giesl, *Zwei Jahrzehnte im Nahen Orient* (Berlin, 1927), p. 271; Albert Margutti, *La Tragédie des Habsbourg* (Vienna, 1919), pp. 116–18. But no serious consideration was given to a change of course and Austro-Hungarian statesmen reaffirmed their policy even when it became clear that it was leading to war (*OU*, 8: 11203).

74   The kaiser's reaction to the Serbian reply implied a compromise (KD, 271), as did his so-called "Halt-in-Belgrade" proposal (KD, 293). But even he rejected British mediation and refused to impose a solution on Vienna (KD, 157).

75   KD, 213, 257, 307; *OU*, 8:10656, 10792; *Bayr. Dok.*, p. 154.

76   KD, 100.

77 *IB*, 5:19, 23, 25; Schilling, *War*, pp. 28–29; *OU*, 8:10616–19; *BD*, 11:60, 125; KD, 160, 204, 217, 401, 412.

78 Dobrorolski, *Mobilmachung*, pp. 17–18, 23–26, 38; *IB*, 5:19, 23, 79, 167–69, 210, 224; KD, 230, 242, 343, 365, 370; *OU*, 8:11003, 11094; Paleologue, *Russie*, 1:38–41; *DDF*, 11:208; Fay, *Origins*, 2:446–50; Albertini, *Origins*, 2:292–94; Schilling, *War*, pp. 15–16, 49–50, 61.

79 KD, 219, 341, 342, 359, 378, 456, 479, 488, 490–91; *BD*, 11:677, 337.

80 *IB*, 1:5; Friedrich Pourtalès, *Meine letzten Verhandlungen in Sankt Petersburg* (Berlin, 1927), pp. 60–61.

81 For a discussion of German strategy (the Schlieffen plan), see: Albertini, *Origins*, 3: 236–42; Ritter, *Staatskunst*, 2:239–67; Ritter, *Schlieffenplan*, passim.

82 KD, 491; *DDF*, 11:438; Poincaré, *Service*, 4:448–53; Bethmann, *Betrachtungen*, 1: 165; Wilhelm Schoen, *The Memoirs of an Ambassador* (London, 1922), pp. 195–96.

83 KD, 528, 571; *DDF*, 11:417, 438, 505; René Viviani, *Réponse au Kaiser* (Paris, 1923), pp. 204–5.

84 For these reasons, Moltke regarded it as "very fortunate" that war had broken out in August 1914 (KD, supplement 4:35).

85 For the details of British mediatory efforts, see: Fay, *Origins*, 2:354–401; Albertini, *Origins*, 2:206–12, 334–40, 390–465, 637–50.

86 For typical criticism of Grey, see: Albertini, *Origins*, 2:307, 311, 331–33, 336–37, 417, 421, 425, 512–19, 642–43; Albertini, *Origins*, 3:479, 490.

87 For British warnings to Germany during the crisis, see: KD, 258, 265, 266, 368, 484; *BD*, 11:176, 188, 285, 286; *OU*, 8:10973. For the British ultimatum to Germany, see: *BD*, 11:563, 573, 576, 578, 580, 581, 584, 587, 593, 594, 612, 631, 671; KD, 662, 790, 810; *DDF*, 11:712; Churchill, *Crisis*, p. 220; Lloyd George, *Memoirs*, 1:73–74; Asquith, *Memories*, 2:10, 21; H. H. Asquith, *The Genesis of the War* (London, 1923), p. 215.

88 KD, supplement 4:35. Moltke had assumed long before the crisis that Britain would intervene in a Franco-German conflict: Ritter, *Staatskunst*, 2:268–72; Conrad, *Dienstzeit*, 2:151–53. For German rejection, see: *BD*, 11:671; Bethmann, *Betrachtungen*, 1:180.

89 For typical criticism, see: Albertini, *Origins*, 2:331–32, 421, 425, 512–19, 643–50; Albertini, *Origins*, 3:521–24.

90 Lafore, *Fuse*, pp. 186, 188, 191, 193–94; Churchill, *Crisis*, p. 188; Michael Howard, "Lest We Forget," *Encounter*, January 1964, pp. 63–65; Harold George Nicolson, *Portrait of a Diplomatist* (New York, 1930), p. 412.

91 Bethmann to Riezler, 29 July 1911, quoted by Erdmann, "Beurteilung," p. 534.

92 For Austro-Hungarian response, see: Lafore, *Fuse*, p. 236; Taylor, *Fall*, p. 210. For German response, see: Crown Prince William, *My War Experiences* (London, 1922), p. 5; André Hallays, *L'Opinion allemande pendant la guerre, 1914–1918* (Paris, 1919), p. 27; Alistair Horne, *The Price of Glory: Verdun 1916* (New York, 1962), p. 17; Walther Hubatsch, *Der Weltkrieg, 1914–1918* (Constance, 1955), pp. 8–9; Ludwig Reiners, *In Europa gehen die Lichter aus* (Munich, 1955), p. 297; Fritz Ernst, *The Germans and Their Modern History* (New York, 1966), p. 22; Ludwig Dehio, *Germany and World Politics in the Twentieth Century* (London, 1959), p. 19; Barrie Pitt, *1918: The Last Act* (New York, 1963), p. 1. For Evidence of German sentiment against war, see Hanssen, *Empire*, pp. 13, 19. For Belgian sentiment, see Tuchman, *Guns*, p. 125. For French sentiment, see Tuchman, *Guns*, p. 126. For British sentiment, see Lloyd George, *Memoirs*, 1:39–42. For Russian sentiment, see Paleologue, *Russie*, 1:48–49. The assertion of Franco-German historians that the French and German people did not want war in 1914 (James A. Corbett, "France and Germany Agree—on the Past," *HB*, 28 (March 1955), p. 158) is true in the sense that none of the governments specifically sought war, but it is misleading insofar as it implies that the declarations of war were not popular.

93 Lafore, *Fuse*, p. 190; Taylor, *Struggle*, p. 529; Konne Zilliacus, *Mirror of the Past* (New York, 1946), p. 149; Arno J. Mayer, *Domestic Causes of the First World War* (Garden City, 1967), pp. 286–300.

94 This was the basic consideration for Austro-Hungarian leaders and one of the major considerations for German leaders in supporting Vienna (see second section of this chapter). Some Austro-Hungarian and German soldiers regretted that Serbian acceptance of the ultimatum made internal reform seem unavoidable (Ritter, *Staatskunst*, 2:312). Jagow makes an enigmatic comment in a telegram to Lichnowsky that the preservation of Austria-Hungary was a necessity for Germany "both for internal and external reasons" but gives no elucidation (KD, 72).

95 Zechlin, "Motive," pp. 92–93.

96 *OU*, 8:10537.

97 Warburg, *Aufzeichnungen*, p. 29; Gwinner, quoted in *Politische Dokumente*, ed. by Alfred von Tirpitz (Berlin, 1926), 2:67; Stinnes, quoted by Class, *Strom*, p. 217.

98 Bethmann (*Bayr. Dok.*, pp. 111–13; Erdmann, "Beurteilung," p. 536); Bismarck (Rosenberg, *Birth*, p. 71); Grey (*OU*, 8:10537; *BD*, 11:86); Lenin (Taylor, *Fall*, p. 20).

99 L. L. Farrar, Jr., "Reluctant Warriors: Public Opinion on War During the July Crisis 1914," *East European Quarterly*, 1981.

100 Rosenberg, *Birth*, p. 42. Of the three Austro-Hungarian legislative bodies, only the Hungarian Diet was in session (Fay, *Origins*, 2:245).

101 Tisza's opposition to war against Serbia was based in part on domestic political considerations which were eventually subordinated to policy. The Irish problem distracted the attention of British leaders during the early phase of the crisis but would also be subordinated to policy.

102 See pp. 159–67 above.

103 See note 121 below.

104 Bethman, quoted by Zechlin, "Deutschland," p. 453; Fay, *Origins*, 1:44; Pierre Renouvin, *Histoire des relations internationales* (Paris, 1955), 6:384; Renouvin, *Crise*, pp. 131–32; Jagow, *Ursachen*, pp. 190–91.

105 See note 92 above.

106 Austro-Hungarian and Serbian demonstrations and press battles (see note 108 below) may have reinforced decisions already taken by these two governments but probably did not alter them.

107 Bethmann found patriotic demonstrations awkward since he was seeking to appear pacific during the several days after the Austro-Hungarian ultimatum had been delivered (see notes 112–15 below).

108 Dickenson, *Anarchy*, pp. 411–12; Fay, *Origins*, 2:47–49, 183, 199, 322, 331, 364; Theodor Goebel, *Deutsche Pressestimmen in der Julikrise 1914* (Stuttgart, 1939), pp. 129–30.

109 See following paragraph.

110 KD, 61, 83.

111 For German efforts to secure British neutrality, see pp. 167, 171 above.

112 For a discussion of preventive war, see pp. 176–81 above.

113 The need to make Russia appear responsible in order to win popular support for war had long been a consideration of German leaders.

114 Bethmann sought to discourage the kaiser's return to Berlin in a way likely to precipitate demonstrations in favor of war (Egmont Zechlin, "Bethmann Hollweg, Kriegs-

risiko und SPD 1914," *Monat*, January 1966, p. 23). Bethmann persuaded the kaiser to order the crown prince not to make bellicose statements (KD, 84, 105, 132). Bethmann sought unsuccessfully to discourage the early return of the fleet (KD, 182, 221, 231).

115 See pp. 167–71 above; note 121, this chapter; KD 323, 441.

116 Curt Schön, *Der Vorwärts und die Kriegserklärung* (Berlin, 1929), p. 40.

117 Jürgen Kuczynski, *Der Ausbruch des ersten Weltkrieges und die deutsche Sozialdemokratie* (Berlin, 1957), p. 53; Carl Grünberg, *Die Internationale und der Weltkrieg* (Leipzig, 1916), 1:60–61; Bethmann's speech of 31 July printed in *Kriegsreden Bethmann Hollwegs*, ed. by Friedrich Thimme (Berlin, 1919), p. 1.

118 Zechlin, "Bethmann," p. 32; KD, 323, 441.

119 Bethmann to Moltke, Jagow and Falkenhayn, 29 July, quoted by Hans Zwehl, *Erich von Falkenhayn, General der infanterie: eine biographische Studie* (Berlin, 1926), p. 57.

120 KD, 234, 423.

121 KD, 308, 335, 408.

122 Wayne C. Thompson, *In the Eye of the Storm* (Iowa City, Iowa, 1980), pp. 83–84. Other governments also had lists of persons suspected of provoking resistance to war. For a discussion of the French government's *Carnet B* and its fears of revolution, see Jean-Jacques Becker, *Le carnet B: Les pouvoirs publics et l'antimilitarisme avant la guerre de-1914* (Paris, 1973).

123 See notes 92, 101, 108, 122 above.

124 Schön, *Vorwärts*, p. 42; Heinz Wohlgemuth, *Burgkrieg, nicht Burgfriede!* (Berlin, 1963), p. 46–47.

125 *Das Werk des Untersuchungsausschusses der Verfassungsgebenden Nationalversammlung und des Deutschen Reichstags 1919 bis 1928*, Fourth Series, Die Ursachen des Deutschen Zusammenbruchs im Jahre 1918, vol. 1, ed. by Erich O. Volkmann (Berlin 1929), p. 277. (*UA*). Georg Kotowski, *Friedrich Ebert: Ein politische Biographie* (Wiesbaden, 1963), 1:21; Scheidemann, *Memoiren*, 1:245.

126 Schellenberg, "Herausbildung," p. 30.

127 KD, 332; Erzberger, in *Der Tag*, 28 July, quoted by Scheidemann, *Memoiren*, 1:246.

128 Schellenberg, "Herausbildung," pp. 33–34; Wohlgemuth, *Burgkrieg*, p. 49.

129 Bethmann's tactics in winning passage of the military budget a year before had been perhaps the best example (see chapter 3).

130 Kuczynski, *Ausbruch*, pp. 70, 78.

131 KD, 456.

132 Wohlgemuth, *Burgkrieg*, p. 49.

133 Karl Kautsky, *Sozialisten und Krieg* (Prague, 1937), p. 443.

134 Schön, *Vorwärts*, p. 67; Kuczynski, *Ausbruch*, p. 71.

135 Schorske, *Democracy*, pp. 288–89, 291; Zechlin, "Bethmann," p. 29; Grünberg, *Internationale*, 1:73.

136 Zechlin, "Bethmann," p. 29; Grünberg, *Internationale*, p. 73.

137 Zechlin, "Bethmann," pp. 29–30; Schorske, *Democracy*, pp. 289–90; Wohlgemuth, *Burgkrieg*, p. 56.

138 Haase speech, 4 August, quoted in Schulthess, *Geschichtskalender, 1914*, p. 386.

139 Kautsky statement in 1911, quoted by Kuczynski, *Ausbruch*, pp. 139–40.

140 For this view in general, see: Albertini, *Origins*, 2:479–80, 518, 579; Albertini, *Origins*, 3:60, 106, 224; Fay, *Origins*, 1:40–42; Tuchman, *Guns*, p. 72; Taylor, *History*, pp. 12–13; B. H. Liddell Hart, *The Real War 1914–1918* (Boston and Toronto, 1930), pp. 28–35; René Albrecht-Carrié, *The Meaning of the First World War* (Englewood Cliffs, 1965), p. 40; Dickenson, *Anarchy*, pp. 432–33. For this view of German strategy, see: Lafore, *Fuse*, p. 251–53; Jarausch, "Illusion," p. 70; Craig, *Politics*, pp. 291–95. Ritter is contradictory; he sometimes sees the military as not particularly responsible (*Staatskunst*, 2:308–15) but at other times as responsible (Ibid., pp. 329–42). For this view of Russian policy, see: Lafore, *Fuse*, pp. 254–56; Turner, "Mobilization," p. 87; Fay, *Origins*, 2:479–81, 555. Ritter is again contradictory; he sometimes sees the military as not particularly responsible (*Staatskunst*, 2:112–14) but at others as responsible (Ibid., p. 320). For this view of Austro-Hungarian strategy, see: Fay, *Origins*, 2:242; Ritter, *Staatskunst*, 2:308–28. For the debate over whether Germany launched a preventive war, see: Schäfer, "Präventivkrieg," pp. 543–61; Lutz, "Moltke," pp. 1107–20; Schmitt, *Coming*, 2:58; Albertini, *Origins*, 2:299–300, 486–87; Hart, *War*, p. 46; Rosenberg, *Birth*, p. 66; Brandenburg, *Bismarck*, p. 433; Bethmann, *Betrachtungen*, 1:102; Ritter, *Staatskunst*, 2:309–12; Craig, *Politics*, p. 291; Fischer, *Griff*, pp. 103–8; Fischer, *Krieg*, pp. 663–82. See note 33, chapter 6.

141 See notes 25, 31, 35, chapter 6, and 27, chapter 7.

142 For pre-crisis discussions of a preventive war among German leaders, see note 33, chapter 6. For sympathy toward the logic of a preventive war during the crisis, see, for Moltke: KD, supplement 4:35; Conrad, *Dienstzeit*, 4:152; Albertini, *Origins*, 2:491; for Jagow: KD, 72; for Zimmermann: KD, supplement 4:2. For pre-crisis discussions of the conditions under which war would be necessary, see note 34, chapter 6. German leaders perceived these conditions at the end of the crisis: e.g., Moltke (Schulthess, *Geschichtskalender*, pp. 996–97) and Bethmann (Jarausch, "Illusion," p. 71). Most German leaders believed Germany had to support the efforts of Austria-Hungary to preserve its great-power status (see note 31, chapter 7).

143 For pre-crisis rejection of a preventive war, see note 33, chapter 6. Jagow rejected it specifically during the crisis (KD, 72). For subsequent denials, see: Bethmann, *Betrachtungen*, 1:102; Brandenburg, *Bismarck*, p. 433; Rosenberg, *Birth*, p. 66; Fay, *Origins*, 2:168–69. For evidence that no special military preparations were made, see: Fay, *Origins*, 2:212–13; Julikrise, 1:23a–b; Albertini, *Origins*, 2:634. For evidence that some preparations were made, see: KD, 74 and supplement 8; Albertini, *Origins*, 2:490. For evidence that Germany was prepared for war and therefore did not need to make special preparations, see: KD, 74; Fischer, *Griff*, pp. 64–65. For the Moltke-Falkenhayn discussions, see *Kriegsrüstung*, pp. 208–10. For evidence that German soldiers did not expect the crisis to eventuate in war, see Moltke, *Erinnerungen*, pp. 380, 385. For evidence of the lack of exceptional financial or economic preparations, see Fay, *Origins*, 2:173–74; for evidence to the contrary, see KD, 80. For evidence that German leaders felt no special economic or financial measures were necessary for war, see: KD, supplement 4:13; Delbrück, *Mobilmachung*, p. 96. For evidence of lack of special military preparations until after the ultimatum, see: Fay, *Origins*, 2:405, 407; Albertini, *Origins*, 2:673. For evidence of lack of special diplomatic preparations for war, see the German rejection of an alliance with Turkey until 23 July: KD, 45, 71, 117, 149.

144 Bethmann: Jarausch, "Illusion," pp. 48, 76; Zechlin, "Deutschland," pp. 451–58; Erdmann, "Beurteilung," p. 536; Steglich, *Friedenspolitik*, 1:418; Theodor Wolff, *The Eve of the War* (London, 1935), pp. 442–43. Hoffmann: Max Hoffmann, *Die Aufzeichnungen des Generalmajors Max Hoffmann*, ed. by K.F. Novak (Berlin, 1929), 1:155. Jagow: KD, 72; Fischer, *Krieg*, pp. 670–71.

145 KD, supplement 4:35.

146 For the view that strategy altered policy, see note 145 above. For the agreement among German leaders to support Austria-Hungary, see note 31 above. For agreement among German leaders that they would probably have to confront France and Russia in war, see notes 31, chapter 6 and 30, chapter 7; for Moltke: KD, 349; for Bethmann: Bethmann, *Betrachtungen*, 1:156. For their agreement that Germany

would have to fight if its great-power status were threatened, see note 148 below. For evidence that the civilians made their decision to support Austria-Hungary without pressure from the soldiers, see Ritter, *Staatskunst*, 2:308–9, 312.

147   For evidence that Bethmann began to prepare public opinion for war and to place the responsibility for a war on Russia before Moltke had decided that war was inevitable, see: Fischer, *Griff*, pp. 59–60; Klaus Epstein, "German Aims in the First World War," *WP*, October, 1962, p. 181.

148   For Bethmann: Albertini, *Origins*, 2:496; Bethmann, *Betrachtungen*, 2:156–57; Steglich, *Friedenspolitik*, 1:418. For Zimmermann: *DDF*, 11:339; Albertini, *Origins*, 3:473.

149   For the argument that Russian mobilization made war inevitable, see: Fay, *Origins*, 2:479–81, 555; Barnes, *Genesis*, pp. 308–80; Brandenburg, *Bismarck*, pp. 441–44; Max Montgelas, *The Case for the Central Powers* (London, 1925), pp. 201–3. Mobilization was ordered halted twice during the crisis, once by the kaiser (Albertini, *Origins*, 3:171–81) and once by the tsar (Albertini, *Origins*, 2:557–58); the kaiser asserted that mobilization did not necessarily mean war (KD, 401). Mobilization had been ordered and then called off by the Austro-Hungarians and Russians during the Bosnian and Balkan crises.

150   The German violation of Belgian neutrality is generally regarded as a blunder: Ritter, *Staatskunst*, 2:338–43; Albertini, *Origins*, 3:243–44. German civilian leaders sought to lay the blame for violating Belgium on the military: Bethmann (Jarausch, "Illusion," p. 71); Zimmermann (Albertini, *Origins*, 3:473); Schoen (*Memoirs*, pp. 248–49). But the civilian leaders had already accepted the necessity of violating Belgium: see note 6 above; Ritter, *Staatskunst*, 2:332; Zimmermann, "Plan," pp. 368–69; Albertini, *Origins*, 3:473.

151   For evidence that German leaders perceived a choice between war and diplomatic defeat equivalent to renunciation of great-power status, see: Bethmann (Jarausch, "Illusion," p. 71); Moltke (Schulthess, *Geschichtskalender*, pp. 996–97). For statements of distaste toward war, see: Bethmann (KD, 456; *BD*, 11:671); the kaiser (KD, 401); Moltke (KD, 349).

152   For arguments that German policy during the crisis was dominated by anxiety, see: Herzfeld, *Welt*, August 1, 1964; Ritter, "Kriegsschuldthese," pp. 763–67; Ritter, *Staatskunst*, 2:309, 314; Rosenberg, *Birth*, p. 66; Karl Heinz Janssen, *Zeit*, March 21, 1969; Mommsen, "Factors," p. 41; Karl Deitrich Erdmann, *Zeit*, August 28, 1964. For arguments that German policy was dominated by aggressiveness, see: Fischer, *Griff*, pp. 104–8; Fischer, *Krieg*, pp. 663–82; Fischer, *Weltmacht*, pp. 51–53, 55; Fischer, *Zeit*, September 3, 1965; Fischer in Gooch, *Germany*, p. v; Renouvin, *Origins*, p. 106.

153   For the discussion of preventive war, see notes 142–43 above. For confidence on the part of German soldiers about military success, see: KD, 74, supplement 4:32; Conrad, *Dienstzeit*, 4:152. For German hopes to split the Entente, see note 36, chapter 7. For confidence in the Germany economy, see: Warburg, *Aufzeichnungen*, p. 29; Zechlin, "Motive," pp. 92–93. Fischer argues that the German economy and imperialism were in a crisis during the spring of 1914 ("Weltpolitik," pp. 308–22; *Krieg*, pp. 413–80, 516–41) which runs counter to his argument of aggressiveness (*Weltmacht*, p. 52; *Krieg*, pp. 679–82).

154   For the discussions of preventive war, see: notes 142–43 above. For evidence of lack of confidence and anxiety, see: Ritter, *Staatskunst*, 2:314, 329, 335; Bethmann, *Betrachtungen*, 1:99–101; Moltke, *Erinnerungen*, pp. 21–23.

155   For Bethmann, see: Erdmann, "Beurteilung," p. 536; Jarausch, "Illusion," pp. 57–59; Stern, "Bethmann," pp. 263–68. For the kaiser, see: KD, 401; Fischer, *Griff*, p. 65. For Jagow, see: F. Thimme, *Front*, p. 219.

CONCLUSIONS

World War I is explicable only in terms of the system in which it occurred. Completely understandable considering its horror and futility, the indignation caused by the war was misleading in that it implied war was a complete departure from normalcy. The First World War was in fact a departure in size and duration from recent experience, as well as in launching an era which would end European history in the old sense. But the fact of war was normal—in the sense of being normative behavior—for the European system. Indeed, since the system was adjusted by violent means on the average of once every half century, World War I was "due." This phenomenon of recurring war was not a statistical coincidence but a fundamental characteristic of the system which was consistent with its general behavior.

The system was based on power. The salient characteristic of European civilization was the division of power among states which were defined by their ability to preserve themselves. Thus the objective of the state in practice was power. The power system was logically dominated by the most powerful, the great powers, which were defined not only in terms of their ability to defend but also to expand their power. For them, the distinction between defensive and offensive impulses was blurred if not erased. A system dominated by states which were defined in aggressive terms was logically aggressive. Power was consequently seen as the ability of a state to pursue what it perceived as its own interests. It pursued these interests by war and diplomacy. Diplomacy was never designed as a permanent substitute for war but only as an alternative means to pursue national interest. Peace is sometimes mistakenly regarded as the objective of diplomacy which is believed to have failed when war breaks out. Although some wars have occurred because of poor communication—i.e., because diplomacy "failed"—the significant wars took place because of basic conflicts of interest. Diplomacy, like war, is a facet of the state system based on power. Only when perpetual peace is established and states wither away will there be no diplomats or soldiers but only bureaucrats and policemen.

The division of power among independent states was challenged periodically by individual states which sought to destroy the system by centralizing power. These attempts were always unsuccessful because the other states were willing to pay the price of war in order to maintain their independence. Hence war was the cost of maintaining the states and thus the system. War was also the price of European vitality since it was a result of the competition between the states to develop power. This competition and the consequent continual change became notable characteristics of European civilization. Change caused fluctuations and shifts of power within the system which required periodic adjustments. It was logical that these adjustments should be made by war in a system based on power. Such adjustments occurred about once every half century during the existence of the state system since the beginning of the sixteenth century.

Europe's vitality also caused it to generate sufficient power first to defend and then to dominate the rest of the world. Involvement with the rest of the world not only increased Europe's power but redounded on the system by altering power relationships and creating causes of conflict. Indeed the system and the non-European world became increasingly involved such that peace in Europe eventually became the prerequisite for power outside.

The distribution of power within the system was also critical for its functioning. From the sixteenth to the nineteenth centuries power gravitated toward the periphery and left the center weak. This configuration not only gave the system flexibility but also provided a perennial area of conflict. More important, it left the second largest single group—the Germans—as objects of, rather than operators in, the system.

Europe's vitality also caused it to generate increasing power. Yet even such augmentations as caused by commercialism and mobilization of the French masses during the revolution had proven compatible with the system. In fact the French Revolution was an exception in its involvement of the masses in state relations. For most of the system's existence, state policy had been controlled by a narrow group which had not mobilized great mass or material power. Relations had been characterized by high control over power compatible with the system. Hence war was not an aberration but normal, and the operative question was not whether but when war would occur.

During the second half of the nineteenth century and first decade of the twentieth century, certain elements of the system changed or developed in ways which made war virtually inevitable. With the unification of Germany and Italy, central European weakness disappeared, and the traditional pattern of conflicts between peripheral powers over the center was thereby broken. Austro-French, Russo-French, Austro-Prussian, and Anglo-French wars which had characterized European relations for almost four centuries would not occur again since the object of their conflict—central Europe—was no longer vulnerable. Instead a new pattern of conflict between center and periphery would characterize the system during its final phase, namely, from 1870 to 1945. The unification of Germany also had the effect of incorporating into the system the second largest single national group and thus shifting power relationships. The industrialization of central and eastern Europe caused a second radical change in power relations, as a result of which the rank order of the powers virtually reversed: Britain and France were replaced by Germany and Russia as the greatest powers.

The radical increase in power had the characteristic effect of altering German policy. After a period of political consolidation and economic growth, German policymakers revolted against the restraints placed on German policy by Bismarck and began pursuing a policy consistent with German primacy. German policy became assertive and revisionist rather than conservative, while Germany military and naval strategy became offensive rather than defensive. Although German policymakers did not plan a hegemonic war, their power and assertiveness constituted a potential threat to the system if they were not restrained. Since they were determined to preserve their own existence and therefore the system, the other powers responded to the German threat and demonstrated in a series of crises that they would probably cooperate to contain it. Consequently a balance had been established by 1912 within the system at the cost of increased tensions and rigidity.

The maintenance of this precarious balance depended on its acceptance by Germany, the persistence of the anti-German alliance, and the continued existence of Austria-Hungary. A combination of German hopes for greater power and fear of other powers (particularly Russia) made the status quo unacceptable to Germany. Despite Entente frictions and German efforts, the Entente survived. More than anything else, however, it was the threat to Austria-Hungary's existence which jeopardized the status quo. The survival of both the Habsburg and Ottoman Empires was rendered more precarious by the Balkan wars which created the prospect of a radical shift in power between the alliances and a power vacuum. Accordingly the relative strength of the great powers had significantly changed since the mid-nineteenth century. Increased German power, Russian potential power, British and French relative decline, and potential Austro-Hungarian dissolution created tensions which had traditionally been resolved by war.

Power had not only shifted but had also sharply increased due to industrialization and population growth. This rise in total European power had paradoxical effects. Europe's superiority and actual domination over the unindustrialized world had become greater than ever even while its primacy was being challenged by American and Japanese industrialization. Its power and domination had consequently increased but its superiority and security had decreased.

The radical rise in Europe's total power also had ironic effects inside Europe. The general standard of living was improved and demands were made (notably by liberals, democrats, and socialists) that the state should use industrial power to increase living standards rather than state power. But these ideologies of happiness (liberalism, democracy, and socialism) were nullified by nationalism which reinforced the view that the state's purpose was power. In any case, despite considerable democratization of domestic politics, foreign policy remained under the control of narrow, traditional groups. In short, the conduct of state relations and the basic assumptions of the system remained unaltered.

The state and therefore the system were still based on power which implied periodic wars. A generation of peace before 1914 had caused many people to assume that peace was normal despite mass armies.and diplomatic crises. The peaceful resolution of crises gave the deceptive impression that good will and good diplomacy could resolve all conflicts. Yet the powers had not placed peace above their own interests. War did not occur because it did not seem in the interest of the powers involved to opt for war; when it appeared to their advantage, they would. The advantages of European civilization were also its disadvantages. Its quest for power allowed it to dominate the world, increase its standard of living, and remain vital. This power, however, had not only made war integral to the system but it had also increased by 1914 to a point where it could destroy the system.

These circumstances caused war in 1914. A great debate developed over its causes, an appropriate response since it was a significant historical event, a large amount of documents are available, and most of the classic historical questions are involved. The debate, in fact, became a historical phenomenon itself in that it reflected the attitudes, assumptions, moods, and official policies of the interwar and post–World War II periods. Because the debate was naturally confused and contradictory, it contributes to our understanding only if the points of view are isolated and simplified. The interpretations can be placed under the rubrics of responsibility, chance, lim ted choice, and multiple explanation. Depending on the definition issigned, each of these views can be argued convincingly and support 1 with ample evidence.

The explanation which provides the most insights and seems most consistent with the circumstances in 1914 is limited choice. The problems and practices prevailing within the system were incompatible with peace. Either the practice had to be changed and the power system renounced if peace was to be maintained, or peace had to be renounced and the problems resolved by war if the practice were to be maintained. Peace could have been maintained only if one or more of the great powers of 1914 had renounced the behavior that was normal to it as a great power.

This was hypothetically possible but so unlikely as to be historically impossible. None of the great powers did renounce its status, and all acted as they should have, i.e., to defend their interests at all costs. Austria-Hungary had to preserve itself as a great power against the perceived threat of South Slav nationalism. Germany had to preserve Austria-Hungary since it seemed essential to German offensive-defensive interests. Russia had to pursue its offensive-defensive aspirations in the Balkans. France had to support Russia in order to maintain its existence as a great power. Britain had to preserve French great-power status in order to defend the balance of power and thus its own interests. Hence diplomacy did not fail to keep the peace by error, inefficiency, or evil design but merely revealed that peace was not possible under the circumstances.

The conditions which made war unavoidable also made the end of the system virtually inevitable. Previously war had been possible because power had been limited and problems which had proven unsusceptible to diplomatic solution could be resolved by war. This remained the assumption of the statesmen of 1914 since none opted for war genuinely believing that it meant his society's destruction. As Bismarck commented, no one commits suicide because he is afraid of death. Despite their anxieties and regrets that it was necessary, all statesmen chose war on the assumption that it was preferable to peace. But war was no longer compatible with the system and would result either in stalemate or total victory. If a stalemate occurred, then the powers would dissipate their power until the system was exhausted. European power had increased radically enough as a result of industrialization to destroy itself. War could thereby jeopardize Europe's domination over the underdeveloped world and even its independence of outside domination, i.e., by the United States. Since European superiority over the underdeveloped world and, independence were essential qualities of the system, the system would thereby be revolutionized. Yet, the total victory of one side would also shatter the system. If Germany won, the balance of power would be destroyed; the individual states would either lose their independence (as in the case of Austria-Hungary and France) or be excluded (as in the case of Russia and Britain); the system would be unified under German hegemony and thus be destroyed. If Germany lost, the other powers would probably have to remain committed with all their power in Europe and thus have to renounce domination over the rest of the world. They might even need the United States to contain Germany and thereby make the system dependent on an outside factor. Either eventuality would destroy the system since European domination over the world and independence of outside power were essential qualities.

Only by avoiding war permanently could Europe perhaps maintain its dominion over the underdeveloped world and independence of the United States. War was, however, an essential part of the power system. If war were renounced, power would become irrelevant; the system would be based on peace rather than power and thereby revolutionized. Consequently the European system was destined for revolution whether war or peace resulted from the July crisis, whether the war was long or short, deadlocked or decisive. The issue was no longer whether Europe would be revolutionized but how and when.

The German experience from 1848 to 1914 (and indeed before and after) provides a case study in the effects of power on a state's policy. Like other states in the European system, Germany sought to use and expand its power. The other states assumed that Germany would do so and therefore tried to anticipate it. German policy became more assertive and active as its power increased. Policy is consequently determined largely by the basic fact of power.

The role of personality in policymaking is conditioned by this relationship between power and policy. If policy is determined largely by power, the policymaker's choices are limited. This constraint defines the distinction between good and bad statecraft. The wise statesman understands the power situation for what it is—he listens for the rustle of God's garment, as Bismarck observed—whereas the unwise statesman either does not understand or accept these realities. In these terms Bismarck's policy of reorganizing central Europe in the 1860s was possible because of the power relationships among Prussia, Austria-Hungary, and France. His policy of consolidating his gains and renouncing further expansion after 1870 was likewise consistent with German power. But his policy was no longer appropriate after 1890 because of the increase in German power. Either a new policy or a new policymaker was required. William II and German policy after 1890 were consistent with German power. The importance of personality is therefore severely limited.

The magnitude of German power and the distribution of power within the European state system at the turn of the century affected the attitudes of German statesmen toward power. Had Germany remained weak, German leaders would probably have been more consistently anxious. Had Germany become dominant and removed all serious rivals (as the Romans and Americans did during periods of their history), they might have become more consistently confident or even arrogant. German power, however, fell between these extremes. Although the strongest European power in 1914, Germany had only about a third of Europe's power. Furthermore much greater actual power already had been achieved by the United States and potential power existed in Russia and Japan. The attitudes of German leaders reflected this ambivalence in their oscillating arrogance and anxiety. What appear to be contradictory qualities turn out to have been corollaries and perhaps even preconditions for each other. Arrogance and anxiety reinforced one another and created a syndrome. Arrogance encouraged aspirations and aggressive policies which caused reactions from the other powers. These rebuffs fostered German anxieties which made Germans want security implying removal of rivals and tantamount to European hegemony. Although this circle was particularly vicious in the German case, it was not unique with the Germans. The power of all the European great powers fell between the extremes of servility and supremacy. Hence the anxiety-arrogance syndrome applied in varying degrees to all the great powers.

The view of German policy as determined by German power defines the relationship between diplomatic policy and military strategy. These two activities are traditionally seen as essentially different and sometimes even conflicting. Frequently diplomacy is identified with a desire for peace and strategy with a desire for war. The interpretation offered here suggests that this distinction is misleading. Diplomacy and strategy are perceived as essentially complementary and consistent. Both were determined by a state's power and the distribution of power within the system. In the German case, military and naval strategies were consistent with diplomatic policy of greater assertiveness which in turn reflected Germany's growing power. The outbreak of war in 1914 was therefore not caused by an intervention of the soldiers and military consideration extraneous to diplomacy, as is frequently asserted. It was due instead to assumptions and aspirations which soldiers and statesmen shared. This view of the relationship between statecraft and strategy implicates the relations between statesmen and strategists. They are often seen to constitute two distinct and disagreeing groups, sometimes regarded as peace and war parties. This view had particular appeal to historians seeking to distribute responsibility for the war. The interpretation applied here suggests on the contrary that the military-civilian conflict was essentially superficial. Although personal antipathies, struggles for authority, and different methods of formulating problems emerged, they neither altered German policy nor indicated fundamentally different views of Germany's international position.

This general interpretation likewise implicates the relationship between diplomatic policy on the one hand and domestic politics and public opinion on the other. Like strategy and policy, politics and policy are frequently seen as conflicting. Traditionally diplomacy was believed to have overridden or deceived opinion, whereas more recently diplomacy has been seen as determined by aggressive opinion or domestic political considerations such as the fear of revolution. Although bitter disagreements certainly existed among articulate Germans over the timing and tactics of German foreign policy, their very bitterness obscured the basic agreement among most Germans on their country's international role. To a large extent these disputes can be attributed to Germany's ambiguous power position which made an ascertainment of its proper policy difficult; many of these disagreements took the form of oscillations between arrogance and anxiety which characterized the views of German leaders. Domestic political problems had certainly caused many conservatives to fear a revolution from the bottom or to advocate one from the top. These concerns were shared by many in government, most of whom were conservatives themselves. But few advocated war as a solution for domestic political problems and some explicitly opposed it. German diplomacy during the July crisis is notably free of concern either for aggressive public opinion or domestic political problems. Public opinion and domestic politicians were uninvolved in the decision for war, not because government and people were in conflict but because such consultation was neither normal nor necessary. Diplomacy was (and still is) seldom conducted on the basis of broad consultation. But such consultation was unnecessary because governments and peoples shared general views of what national interests were, and no government seriously considered sacrificing these concerns to preserve peace. In short, diplomatic policy and domestic politics were generally complementary and consistent rather than conflicting.

Finally, the argument that power determines policy affects the efficacy of diplomacy. Traditionally diplomatic historians have paid great attention to the policies, aspirations, and idiosyncracies of statesmen and diplomats. They did so on the assumption that diplomacy mattered, i.e., altered the course of state relations. The interpretation applied here suggests instead that policymakers have limited choices and can alter international events only marginally. Relations between states and indeed the policies of individual states are largely determined by power, namely, factors which leaders are virtually powerless to alter. Their role in this view becomes one of discovering what these factors are and accommodating themselves to them. Thus to a great extent foreign policy registers rather than alters the basic elements of international relations. Like the geologist who can perhaps measure but cannot manipulate an earthquake, the statesman can ascertain and accommodate but seldom fundamentally affects. This is hardly an optimistic prospect for rational control over human events and perhaps suggests that diplomatic history should take over from economics the role of dismal science. It seems a realistic conclusion, however, as long as states seek power and resolve their differences by war.

BIBLIOGRAPHY

Albertini, Luigi. *The Origins of the War of 1914*. Vols. 1–3. London, New York, Toronto, 1952–57.

Albrecht, Carrié, René. *The Meaning of the First World War*. Énglewood Cliffs, New Jersey, 1965.

Anderson, E. N. *The First Moroccan Crisis*. New York, 1930.

Andrassy, J. *Diplomacy and the War*. London, 1921.

Andrew, Christopher. "German World Policy and the Reshaping of the Dual Alliance." *Journal of Contemporary History*, 1:137–51.

Angell, Norman. *The Great Illusion*. New York, 1910.

Aron, Raymond. *The Century of Total War*. Boston, 1966.

Art, Robert J. *The Influence of Foreign Policy on Seapower: New Weapons and Weltpolitik in Wilhelminian Germany*. Los Angeles, 1978.

Askew, William C. "The Austro-Italian Antagonism, 1896–1914." In *Power, Public Opinion and Diplomacy*, essays in honor of E.M. Carroll, pp. 105–30. Durham, 1959.

Asquith, Herbert Henry. *Memories and Reflections, 1852–1927*. Vols. 1–2. Boston, 1928.

_____. *The Genesis of the War*. London, 1923.

Bach, August. "Die englisch-russische Verhandlungen." *Preussiche Jahrbücher*, 1924, pp. 183–200.

Bach, August, ed. *Deutsche Gesandtschaftsberichte zum Kriegsausbruch 1914*. Berlin, 1937.

Bachem, Karl. *Vorgeschichte, Geschichte und Politik der Deutschen Zentrumspartei*. Vol. 4. Cologne, 1928.

Baernreither, Josef M. *Dem Weltbrand entgegen*. Berlin, 1928.

Barlow, I. C. *The Agadir Crisis*. Chapel Hill, 1940.

Barnes, Harry Elmer. *The Genesis of the War: An Introduction to the Problem of War Guilt*. New York, 1926.

Barnes, Harry Elmer; Berchtold, L.; Hoyos, A.; Weisner, F.; and Jagow, G. "Did Germany Incite Austria in 1914?" *Current History*, July 1928, pp. 620–35.

Barthels, Walter. *Die Linken in der Sozialdemokratie im Kampf gegen Militarismus und Krieg*. Berlin, 1958.

Bayerische Dokumente zum Kriegsausbruch und zum Versailler Schuldspruch. Edited by Pius Dirr. Munich and Berlin, 1925. (*Bayr. Dok.*)

Becker, J.-J. *Le Carnet B: Les Pouvoirs publics et l'antimilitarisme avant la guerre de 1914*. Paris, 1973.

_____. *1914: Comment les Français sont entrés dans la guerre*. Paris, 1977.

Berghahn, Volcker R. "Zu den Zielen des deutschen Flottenbaus unter Wilhelm II." *Historische Zeitschrift*, February 1970, pp. 34–100.

———. *Der Tirpitz-Plan: Genesis und Verfall einer innenpolitischen Krisenstrategie unter Wilhelm II.* Düsseldorf, 1971.

———. *Rüstung und Machtpolitik: Zur Anatomie des "Kalten Krieges" vor 1914.* Düsseldorf, 1973.

———. *Germany and the Approach of War in 1914.* London, 1973.

———, and Deist, Wilhelm. "Kaiserliche Marine und Kriegsausbruch 1914." *Militärgeschichtliche Mitteilungen*, January 1970, pp. 37–58.

Bergsträsser, Ludwig. *Geschichte der politischen Parteien in Deutschland.* Munich, 1965.

Bernstorff, Johann H. *My Three Years in America.* London, 1920.

———. *Erinnerungen und Briefe.* Zurich, 1936.

Bethmann Hollweg, Theobald. *Betrachtungen zum Weltkriege.* Vol. 1. Berlin, 1919.

Beyens, Baron. *L'Allemagne avant la guerre: Les Causes et les responsibilités.* Brussels, Paris, 1915.

———. *Deux années à Berlin, 1912–1914.* Vols. 1–2. Paris, 1931.

Bloch, Camille. *The Causes of the World War.* London, 1935.

———. "Les Socialistes allemandes pendant la crise de juillet 1914." *Revue d'Histoire de la Guerre Mondiale*, October 1933, pp. 150–71.

Böhme, Helmut. *Deutschlands Weg zur Grossmacht.* Cologne, Berlin, 1966.

———. *Deutsche Handelspolitik 1848–81: Studien zur Verhältnis von Wirtschaft und Staat während der Reichsgrundungszeit.* Cologne, 1967.

Bonnefous, Georges. *Histoire politique de la troisième république.* Vol. 2. Paris, 1957.

Born, Karl Erich. "Deutschland als Kaiserreich (1871–1918)." In *Handbuch der Europäischen Geschichte.* Stuttgart, 1968.

———. *Staat und Sozialpolitik seit Bismarcks Sturz, 1890–1914.* Wiesbaden, 1957.

Bourgeois, E. and Pages, G. *Les Origines et les responsibilités de la guerre.* Paris, 1922.

Bracher, Karl Deitrich. Review of Fischer's *Griff nach der Weltmacht. Neue Politische Literatur*, 1962, pp. 471–82.

———. *The German Dilemma: The Throes of Political Emancipation.* London, 1974.

Brandenburg, Erich. *Von Bismarck zum Weltkriege: Die deutsche Politik in den Jahrzehnten vor dem Kriege.* Berlin, 1925.

British Documents on the Origins of the War, 1898–1914. Edited by G.P. Gooch and Harold Temperley. Vols. 10–11. London, 1936–38. (*BD*)

Buchanan, George. *My Mission to Russia and Other Diplomatic Memories.* Vol. 1. Boston, 1923.

Bülow, B.H.M.K. *Denkwürdigkeiten.* Vols. 1–2. Berlin, 1931.

Burchardt, Lothar. *Friedenswirtschaft und Kriegsvorsage: Deutschlands Wirtschaftliche Rüstungsbestrebungen vor 1914.* Boppard, 1968.

Buse, D.K. "Ebert and the Coming of the War." *International Review of Social History*, 1968, pp. 33–45.

Calleo, David. *The German Problem Reconsidered*. Cambridge, England, 1978.

Callwell, C.E. *Field Marshall Sir Henry Wilson: His Life and Diaries*. Vol. 1. London, 1927.

Cambon, Paul. *Correspondance, 1870–1924*. Vols. 1–2. Paris, 1946.

Carroll, E.M. *Germany and the Great Powers: A Study in Public Opinion and Foreign Policy*. New York, 1938.

Carsten, F.L. "Living with the Past: What German Historians Are Saying." *Encounter*, 127 (April 1964):100–110.

Cecil, Lamar. *Albert Ballin: Business and Politics in Imperial Germany, 1888–1918*. Princeton, 1967.

Chickering, Roger. *Imperial Germany and a World Without War*. Princeton, 1975.

Choucri, Nazli and North, Robert C. *Nations In Conflict: Domestic Growth and International Violence*. San Francisco, 1975.

Churchill, W.S. *The World Crisis, 1911–1914*. London, 1923.

Class, Heinrich. *Wenn ich der Kaiser wäre*. Berlin, 191?.

――――. *Wider den Strom: Vom Werden und Wachsen der nationalen Opposition im alten Reich*. Leipzig, 1932.

Conrad von Hötzendorf, Franz. *Aus meiner Dienstzeit*. Vols. 1–4. Vienna, Leipzig, Munich, 1921–25.

Cooper, J.M. *Causes and Consequences of World War I*. New York, 1972.

Corbett, James A. "France and Germany Agree—on the Past." *Historical Bulletin*, 28 (March 1955):158–62.

Craig, Gordon A. *The Politics of the Prussian Army, 1640–1945*. Oxford, 1955.

――――. "Relations Between Civil and Military Authorities in the Second German Empire: Chancellor and Chief of Staff, 1871–1918." In *War, Politics and Diplomacy*, pp. 121–33. New York, 1966.

――――. *From Bismarck to Adenauer: Aspects of German Statecraft*. New York, 1965.

――――. *Germany, 1866–1945*. Oxford, 1978.

Dahrendorf, Ralf. *Society and Democracy in Germany*. New York, 1967.

Dedijer, Vladimir. *The Road to Sarajevo*. New York, 1966.

Dehio, Ludwig. *Germany and World Politics in the Twentieth Century*. London, 1959.

――――. *The Precarious Balance*. New York, 1962.

Deuerlein, Ernst. *Die Bundesratsausschuss für auswärtige Angelegenheiten 1870 bis 1918*. Regensburg, 1955.

Devlehouwer, R. *Les Belges et le danger de guerre*. Liège, 1958.

Dickenson, G.L. *The International Anarchy, 1904–1914*. London, 1926.

Diplomatischer Schriftwechsel Alexander Graf von Benckendorff. Edited by B. Siebert. Berlin, Leipzig, 1928.

Der diplomatische Schriftwechsel Iswolskis, 1911–1914. Edited by Friedrich Stieve. Vols. 1–4. Berlin, 1926.

Dobrorolski, Sergie Kostantinovich. *Die Mobilmachung der russischen Armee, 1914.* Berlin, 1922.

Documents diplomatiques Français (1871–1914). Edited by Commission de publication des documents relatifs aux origines de la guerre de 1914, series 3 (1911–14). Vols. 1–2. Paris, 1929. *(DDF)*

Documents diplomatiques, 1914. La Guerre européenne, Ministère des affaires étrangères. Paris, 1914. *(DD)*

Drachkovitch, Milord M. *Les Socialismes francais et allemand et le problème de la guerre, 1870–1914.* Geneva, 1953.

Ebert, Friedrich. *Schriften, Aufzeichnungen, Reden.* Dresden, 1926.

Eltzbacher, Paul. *Die Presse als Werkzeug der auswärtigen Politik.* Jena, 1918.

Ensor, R.C.K. *England, 1870–1914.* Oxford, 1936.

Entente Diplomacy and the World War. Edited by G.A. Siebert-Schreiner. New York, 1921.

Epstein, Fritz T. "Ost-Mitteleuropa als Spannungsfeld zwischen Ost und West um die Jahrhundertwende bis Ende des ersten Weltkrieges." *Welt als Geschichte,* 1956, pp. 64–123.

Epstein, Klaus. *Matthias Erzberger and the Dilemma of German Democracy.* Princeton, 1959.

———. "German Aims in the First World War," *World Politics,* October 1962, pp. 163–85.

Erdmann, Karl Dietrich. "Zur Beurteilung Bethmann Hollwegs. *Geschichte in Wissenschaft und Unterricht,* September 1964, pp. 525–40.

———. "Der Kanzler und der Krieg." *Die Zeit,* 28 August 1962.

———. "Bethmann Hollweg, Augstein und die Historikerzunft." *Die Zeit,* 25 September 1964.

Ernst, Fritz. *The Germans and Their Modern History.* New York, 1966.

Eubank, Keith. *Paul Cambon: Master Diplomatist.* Norman, Okla., 1960.

Evans, R.J., ed. *Society and Politics in Wilhelmine Germany.* New York, 1978.

Eyck, Erich. *Das persönliche Regiment Wilhelms II.* Zurich, 1948.

Fainsod, Merle. *International Socialism and the World War.* Cambridge, Mass., 1935.

Farrar, L.L., Jr. "The Limits of Choice: July 1914 Reconsidered." *Journal of Conflict Resolution,* March 1972, pp. 1–23.

———. "Cycles of War: Historical Speculation on Future International Violence." *International Interactions,* 3 (1977): 161–80.

———, ed. *War: A Historical, Political, and Social Study.* Santa Barbara and Oxford, 1978.

———. "Reluctant Warriors: Public Opinion on War During the July Crisis 1914." *East European Quarterly,* 1981.

Fay, Sidney Bradshaw. *The Origins of the World War*. Vols. 1–2. New York, 1966.

———. *The Influence of the Pre-War Press in Europe*. Boston, 1932.

Feldman, Gerald D. *Army, Industry and Labor in Germany, 1914–1918*. Princeton, 1966.

Fellner, Fritz. *Der Dreibund: Europäischer Diplomatie vor dem ersten Weltkrieg*. Munich, 1960.

Fischer, Fritz. *Griff nach der Weltmacht: Die Kriegszeilpolitik des kaiserlichen Deutschland 1914–18*. Düsseldorf, 1964.

———. "Die Schuld am ersten Weltkrieg: Eine Stellungnahme von Professor Fritz Fischer." *Zeit*, 24 September 1961.

———. "Deutsche Kriegsziele, Revolutionierung und Separatfrieden im Osten, 1914–1918." *Historische Zeitschrift*, 88:249–310.

———. "Kontinuität des Irrtums: Zum Problem der deutschen Kriegszielpolitik im ersten Weltkrieg." *Historische Zeitschrift*, 191:83–100.

———. "Weltpolitik, Weltmachtstreben und deutsche Kriegsziele." *Historische Zeitschrift*, 199:265–346.

———. "Vom Zaun gebrochen-nicht hineingeschlittert: Deutschlands Schuld am Ausbruch des ersten Weltkrieges." *Zeit*, 3 September 1965.

———. *Weltmacht oder Niedergang: Deutschland im ersten Weltkrieg*. Frankfurt am Main, 1965.

———. *Krieg der Illusionen, Die deutsche Politik von 1911 bis 1914*. Düsseldorf, 1969.

Fisher, H.A.L. Introduction to *Germany*, by George Peabody Gooch. London, 1926.

Foerster, Wolfgang. *Graf Schlieffen und der Weltkrieg*. Berlin, 1925.

———. *Aus der Gedankenwerkstatt des deutschen Generalstabes*. Berlin, 1931.

Frantz, G. *Russland auf dem Wege zur Katastrophe*. Berlin, 1926.

French, Field Marshal. *1914*. London, 1919.

Freund, Michael. "Bethmann-Hollweg, der Hitler des Jahres 1914?" *Frankfurter Allgemeine Zeitung*, 28 March 1964.

Fuller, J.V. *Bismarck's Diplomacy At its Zenith*. Cambridge, Mass., 1922.

Fussell, Paul. *The Great War and Modern Memory*. New York and London, 1975.

Gasser, Adolf. "Deutschlands Entschluss zum Präventivkrieg." In *Festschrift für E. Bonjour*. Basel, 1946.

———. "Der deutsche Hegemonialkrieg von 1914." In *Deutschland in der Weltpolitik des 19 und 20 Jahrhunderts*. Edited by I. Geiss and B.-J. Wendt, pp. 305–40. Düsseldorf, 1973.

Gay, Peter. *The Dilemma of Democratic Socialism*. New York, 1952.

Geiss, Imanuel. *German Foreign Policy, 1871–1914*. London, 1976.

———, and Strandmann, Hartmut Pogge von. *Der Erforderlichkeit des Unmöglichen: Deutschland am Vorabend des ersten Weltkrieges*. Frankfurt, 1965.

———, and Wendt, B.-J., eds. *Deutschland in der Weltpolitik des 19 und 20 Jahrhunderts*. Düsseldorf, 1973.

Giesl, Wladimir. *Zwei Jahrzehnte im Nahen Orient*. Berlin, 1927.

Gilbert, Felix. *The End of the European Era, 1890 to the Present*. New York, 1970.

Goebel, Theodor. *Deutsche Pressestimmen in der Julikrise 1914*. Stuttgart, 1939.

Göhring, M. *Bismarcks Erben 1890–1945*. Wiesbaden, 1958.

Gooch, George Peabody. *Before the War*. Vol. 2. London, 1938.

————. *Germany*. London, 1926.

————. *Franco-German Relations, 1871–1914*. London, 1923.

Gordon, Michael R. "Domestic Conflict and the Origins of the First World War: The British and the German Cases." *Journal of Modern History*, June 1974, pp. 191–227.

Grelling, H. *La Campagne innocentiste en Allemagne*. Paris, 1925.

Grey, Edward. *Twenty-Five Years, 1892–1916*. Vols. 1–2. New York, 1925.

Groener, Wilhelm. *Lebenserinnerungen*. Göttingen, 1957.

Groener-Geyer, Dorothea. *General Groener: Soldat und Staatsmann*. Frankfurt am Main, 1953.

Groh, D. "The 'Unpatriotic Socialists' and the State." *Journal of Contemporary History*, 1 (1966):166–80.

————. *Negative Integration und revolutionären Attentismus*. Frankfurt, 1973.

Die Grosse Politik der Europäischen Kabinette, 1871–1914. Sammlung der Diplomatischen Akten des Auswärtigen Amtes. Edited by Johannes, Lepsius, Albrecht Mendelssohn-Bartholdy, Friedrich Thimme. Vols. 33–39. Berlin, 1924–27. (*GP*)

Grünberg, Carl. *Die Internationale und der Weltkrieg*. Leipzig, 1916.

Hale, Oron J. *Publicity and Diplomacy with Special Reference to England and Germany, 1890–1914*. New York, 1940.

————. *The Great Illusion, 1900–1914*. New York, 1971.

Hall, A. *Scandal, Sensation and Social Democracy: The SPD Press and Wilhelmine Germany, 1890–1914*. Cambridge, England, 1977.

Hallays, André. *L'Opinion allemande pendant la guerre, 1914–1918*. Paris, 1919.

Hallgarten, G.W.F. *Imperialismus vor 1914*. Vols. 1–2. Munich, 1951.

Hamerow, Theodore. *Restoration, Revolution and Reaction*. Princeton, 1958.

————. *The Social Foundations of German Unification, 1856–1871, Ideas and Institutions*. Princeton, 1969.

Hammann, Otto. *Bilder aus der letzten Kaiserzeit*. Berlin, 1922.

Hanssen, H.P. *Diary of a Dying Empire*. Edited by R.H. Lutz. Bloomington, Indiana, 1955.

Hantsch, Hugo. *Leopold Graf Berchtold: Grandseigneur und Staatsmann*. Vols. 1–2. Graz, 1963.

Haupt, G. *Socialism and the Great War*. Oxford, 1972.

Haussmann, Conrad. *Schlaglichter: Reichstagsbriefe und Aufzeichnungen*. Edited by U. Zeller. Frankfurt am Main, 1924.

Heide, Walther. *Diplomatie und Presse*. Cologne, 1930.

Heidorn, Günther. *Monopole-Presse-Krieg: Die Rolle der Presse bie der Vorbereitung des ersten Weltkrieges. Studien zur deutschen Aussenpolitik in der Periode von 1902 bis 1912*. Berlin, 1960.

Helfferich, Karl. *Der Weltkrieg*. Vol. 1. Berlin, 1919.

Helmreich, Ernst Christian. *The Diplomacy of the Balkan Wars 1912–1913*. Cambridge, Mass., 1938.

Henderson, W.O. *The Rise of German Industrial Power, 1834–1914*. New York, 1976.

Hermann, Charles F. and Margaret G. "An Attempt to Simulate the Outbreak of World War I." *American Political Science Review*, June 1967, pp. 400–16.

Herre, Paul. *Weltgeschichte der neuesten Zeit 1890–1925*. Vol. 1. Berlin, 1925.

_____. *Kronprinz Wilhelm: Seine Rolle in der Politik*. Munich, 1954.

Herwig, Holger H. *The German Naval Officer Corps: A Social and Political History, 1890–1918*. Oxford, 1973.

_____. *"Luxury Fleet": The Imperial German Navy, 1888–1918*. New York, 1980.

Herzfeld, Hans. *Die deutsche Rüstungspolitik vor dem Weltkriege*. Bonn and Leipzig, 1923.

_____. *Die Welt*, 1 August 1964.

Heuss, Theodor. *Friedrich Naumann, der Mann, das Werk, die Zeit*. Stuttgart and Berlin, 1937.

Hillgruber, Andreas. *Kontinuität und Diskontinuität in der deutschen Aussenpolitik von Bismarck bis Hitler*. Düsseldorf, 1970.

Hoffmann, Max. *Die Aufzeichungen des Generalmajors Max Hoffmann*. Edited by K. F. Novak. Berlin, 1929.

Holborn, Hajo. *A History of Modern Germany, 1840–1945*. New York, 1970.

Holstein, F. *Die geheimen Papiere F. von Holsteins*. Edited by W. Frauendienst. Vols. 1–3. Göttingen, 1961.

Holsti, Ole. *Crisis Escalation War*. Montreal, 1972.

Hölzle, Erwin. *Die Selbstentmachtung Europas: Die Experiment des Friedens vor und im Ersten Weltkrieg*. Göttingen, 1975.

Horne. Alistair. *The Price of Glory: Verdun 1916*. New York, 1962.

House, Edward. *The Intimate Papers of Colonel House*. Edited by C. Seymour. Vol. 1. London, 1926.

Howard, Michael. "Lest We Forget." *Encounter*, January 1964, pp. 61–66.

Hoyos, A. *Der deutsch-englische Gegensatz und sein Einfluss auf die Balkanpolitik Österreich-Ungarns*. Berlin, Leipzig, 1922.

Hubatsch, Walther. *Die Ära Tirpitz: Studien zur deutschen Marinepolitik, 1890–1918*. Göttingen, 1955.

_____. *Der Weltkrieg, 1914–1918*. Constance, 1955.

Huldermann, Bernhard. *Albert Ballin*. Oldenburg, Berlin, 1922.

Die Internationalen Beziehungen im Zeitalter des Imperialismus. Dokumente aus den Archiven der Zarischen und Provisorischen Regierung. Edited by Kommission beim Zentralexekutivkomitee der Sowjetregierung unter dem Vorsitz von M.N. Prokowski. German edition edited by Otto Hoetzsch, series 1. Vols. 1–5. Berlin, 1931–40. *(IB)*

Jäckh, Ernst. *Kiderlen-Wächter: Der Staatsmann und der Mensch*, Vols. 1–2. Berlin and Leipzig, 1925.

Janssen, Karl Heinz. *Zeit*, 21 March 1964.

Jagow, Gottfried. *England und der Kriegsausbruch.* Berlin, 1925.

———. *Ursachen und Ausbruch des Weltkrieges.* Berlin, 1919.

Jarausch, Konrad H. "The Illusion of Limited War: Chancellor Bethmann Hollweg's Calculated Risk, July 1914." *Central European History*, March 1969, pp. 48–76.

———. *The Enigmatic Chancellor: Bethmann Hollweg and the Hubris of Imperial Germany.* New Haven, 1973.

Jaszi, Oscar. *The Dissolution of the Habsburg Monarchy.* Chicago, 1964.

Joffre, Joseph J.C. *Memoirs.* Vol. 1. New York, 1932.

Joll, James. *The Second International.* London, 1955.

———. "The 1914 Controversy Continued," *Past and Present*, July 1966, pp. 100–13.

———. *1914: The Unspoken Assumptions.* London, 1968.

———. "War Guilt 1914: A Continuing Controversy." In *Aspekte der deutschbritischen Beziehungen.* Edited by P. Kluke and P. Alter, pp. 60–80. Stuttgart, 1978.

Julikrise und Kriegsausbruch 1914. Edited by Imanuel Geiss. Vols. 1–2. Hanover, 1963, 1964.

Jux, Anton. *Kriegsschrecken. Die Kriegsschrecken des Frühjahrs 1914 in der europäischen Presse.* Berlin, 1929.

Kaelble, Hartmut. *Industrielle Interessenpolitik in der Wilhelminischen Gesellschaft: Centralverband Deutscher Industrieller, 1895–1914.* Berlin, 1967.

Kahler, Miles. "Rumors of War: The 1914 Analogy." *Foreign Affairs*, December 1979, pp. 374–96.

Kautsky, Karl. *Sozialisten und Krieg.* Prague, 1937.

———. *Outbreak of the World War.* German Documents collected by Karl Kautsky. Edited by Max Montgelas and Walther Schücking. New York, 1924. (KD)

Kehr, Eckart. *Der Primat der Innenpolitik. Gesammelte Aufsätze.* Berlin, 1965.

Kennan, George F. *The Decline of Bismarck's European Order: Franco-Russian Relations, 1875–1890.* Princeton, 1979.

Kennedy, Paul R., ed. *The War Plans of the Great Powers.* London, 1979.

Kitchen, Martin. *The German Officer Corps, 1890–1914.* Oxford, 1968.

———. *The Political Economy of Germany, 1815–1914.* London, 1978.

Klein, Fritz. *Deutschland von 1897–98 bis 1917.* Berlin, 1961.

———. "Die Rivalität zwischen Deutschland und Österreich-Ungarn in der Türkei am

Vorabend des ersten Weltkrieges." In *Politik im Krieg 1914–1918*. Edited by F. Klein, pp. 1–22. Berlin, 1964.

———. *Warum nach Sarajevo Kreig?* Berlin, 1964.

———, ed. *Österreich-Ungarn in der Weltpolitik, 1900–1918*. Berlin, 1965.

Kloster, Walter. *Der deutsche Generalstab und die Präventivkriegsgedanke*. Stuttgart, 1932.

Koch, H.W., ed. *The Origins of the First World War: Great Power Rivalry and German War Aims*. London, 1972.

Koschnitzke, R. *Die Innenpolitik des Reichskanzlers Bethmann Hollweg im Weltkrieg*. Ph.D. dissertation, University of Kiel, 1951.

Koszyk, Kurt. *Zwischen Kaiserreich und Diktatur: Die Sozialdemokratische Presse von 1914 bis 1933*. Heidelberg, 1958.

Kotowski, Georg. *Friedrich Ebert: Ein politische Biographie*. Vol. 1. Wiesbaden, 1963.

Kriegsreden Bethmann Hollwegs. Edited by Friedrich Thimme. Berlin, 1919.

Kriegsrüstung. Der Weltkrieg 1914–1918: Kriegsrüstung und Kriegswirtschaft. Vol. 1. Berlin: Reichsarchiv, 1930.

Kuczynski, Jürgen. *Der Ausbruch des ersten Weltkrieges und die Sozialdemokratie*. Berlin, 1957.

Kühlmann, Richard. *Erinnerungen*. Heidelberg, 1948.

Lafore, Laurence. *The Long Fuse*. New York, 1965.

Lancken-Wakenitz, O. *Meine 30 Dienstjahre 1888–1918, Potsdam/Paris/Brussels*. Berlin, 1931.

Langer, William L. *European Alliances and Alignments, 1871–1890*. New York, 1950.

———. *The Diplomacy of Imperialism, 1890–1902*. Vols. 1–2. New York, 1950.

Leed, Eric J. *No Man's Land: Combat & Identity in World War I*. Cambridge, England. 1979.

Lichnowsky, Prince. *Heading for the Abyss*. London, 1928.

Liddell Hart, B.H. *The Real War 1914–1918*. Boston and Toronto, 1930.

Lloyd George, David. *War Memoirs*. Vol. 1. London, 1933.

Loewenberg, Peter. "Arno Mayer's 'Internal Causes and Purposes of War in Europe, 1870–1956,' An Inadequate Model of Human Behavior, National Conflict and Historical Change." *Journal of Modern History*, December 1970, pp. 628–36.

Lutz, Hermann. "Generaloberst von Moltke und der Präventivkrieg." *Kriegsschuldfrage*, 5:1107–20.

———. *Die europäische Politik in der Julikrise 1914. Gutachten*. Berlin, 1930.

Mansergh, Nicholas. *The Coming of the First World War: A Study In European Balance, 1878–1914*. London, New York, Toronto, 1949.

Marder, Arthur J. *The Anatomy of British Sea Power, 1880–1905*. New York, 1940.

———. *From Dreadnought to Scapa Flow: The Road to War*. Vol. 1. London, 1961.

Margutti, Albert. *La Tragédie des Habsbourgs*. Vienna, 1919.

May, Arthur J. *The Hapsburg Monarchy, 1867–1914*. New York, 1968.

Mayer, Arno J. "Domestic Causes of the First World War." In *Responsibility of Power*, pp. 286–300. Garden City, 1967.

Mehring, Franz. *Die Arbeiterklasse und der Weltkrieg: Sozialdemokratische Korrespondenz vom 30 Juli 1914. Krieg und Politik*. Vol. 1. Berlin, 1959.

Meinecke, Friedrich. *Strassburg, Freiburg, Berlin, 1901–1919: Erinnerungen*. Stuttgart, 1949.

_____. *Politische Schriften und Reden*. Darmstadt, 1958.

Messerschmidt, Manfred. *Militär und Politik in der Bismarckzeit und im Wilhelminschen Deutschland*. Darmstadt, 1975.

Meyer, Henry Cord. *Mitteleuropa in German Thought and Action, 1815–1945*. Hague, 1955.

Michon, Georges. *The Franco-Russian Alliance, 1891–1917*. London, 1929.

Molt, Peter. *Der Reichstag vor der improvisierten Revolution*. Cologne, Opladen, 1963.

Moltke, Helmut. *Erinnerungen, Briefe, Dokumente, 1877–1916*. Edited by E. Moltke. Stuttgart, 1922.

Mommsen, Wolfgang J. *Max Weber und die deutsche Politik*. Munich, 1959.

_____. *Zeitalter des Imperialismus*. Frankfurt, 1968.

_____. "Die deutsche 'Weltpolitik' und der Erste Weltkrieg." *Neue Politische Literatur*, March 1971, pp. 23–45.

_____. "Domestic Factors in German Foreign Policy before 1914." *Central European History*, March 1973, pp. 3–43.

Montgelas, Max. *The Case for the Central Powers*. London, 1925.

Morley, John Viscount. *Memorandum on Resignation, August, 1914*. London, 1928.

Moses, J.A., ed. *The Politics of Illusion: The Fischer Controversy in German Historiography*. New York, 1975.

Mühlmann, Carl. *Deutschland und die Türkei, 1913–1914*. Berlin, 1929.

Müller, G.A. *Der Kaiser . . . Aufzeichnungen des Chefs des Marinekabinetts Admiral Georg Alexander von Müller über die Ära Wilhelms II*. Edited by W. Görlitz. Göttingen, 1965.

Müller, K.A. *Mars und Venus: Erinnerungen, 1914–1918*. Stuttgart, 1954.

_____. *Aus dem Garten der Vergangenheit*. Munich, 1952.

Müller-Link, Horst. *Industrialisierung und Aussenpolitik*. Göttingen, 1977.

Musilin, Alexander. *Das Haus am Ballplatz*. Munich, 1924.

Naumann, Victor. *Profile*. Munich, 1925.

_____. *Dokumente und Argumente*. Berlin, 1928.

Nichols, J. Alden. *Germany After Bismarck: The Caprivi Era, 1890–1894*. Cambridge, England, 1958.

Nicolson, Harold George. *Portrait of a Diplomatist*. New York, 1930.

Nomikos, Eugenia V. and North, Robert C. *International Crisis: The Outbreak of World War I*. Montreal and London, 1976.

North, Robert C. "Perception and Action in the 1914 Crisis." *Journal of International Affairs*, 21 (1967):103–22.

_____, and Choucri, Nazli. *Nations in Conflict: Domestic Growth and International Violence*. San Francisco, 1975.

Oman, Charles W.C. *The Outbreak of the War of 1914–18*. London, 1919.

Oncken, Hermann. *Das deutsche Reich und die Vorgeschichte des Weltkrieges*. Vols. 1–2. Berlin, 1933.

Österreich-Ungarns Aussenpolitik von der bosnischen Krise 1908 bis zum Kriegsausbruch 1914. Diplomatische Aktenstücke des Österreich-Ungarischen Ministeriums des Äussern. Edited by L. Bittner, A.F. Pribram, H. Srbik, H. Uebersberger. Vols. 7–8. Vienna and Leipzig, 1930.

Österreich-Ungarns letzter Krieg 1914–1918. Edited by E. von Glaise-Horstenau. Vols. 1–2. Vienna: Österreiches Bundesministerium für Heerwesen und Kriegsarchiv, 1931–38.

Page, Walter H. *The Life and Letters of Walter H. Page*. Vols. 1–3. New York, 1925.

Paleologue, Maurice. *La Russie des tsars pendant la grande guerre*. Vol. 1. Paris, 1921.

_____. *Journal intime de Nicolas III*. Paris, 1934.

Payer, Friedrich. *Von Bethmann Hollweg bis Ebert: Erinnerungen und Bilder*. Frankfurt, 1923.

Petrie, Charles. *The Drift to World War, 1900–1914*. London, 1968.

Pitt, Barrie. *1918: The Last Act*. New York, 1963.

Poidevin, Raymond. *Les Relations économiques et financières entre la France et l'Allemagne de 1898 à 1914*. Paris, 1969.

Poincaré, Raymond. *Au Service de la France: Neuf années de souvenirs*. Vols. 1–5. Paris, 1928.

_____. *Les Origines de la guerre*. Paris, 1921.

Politische Dokumente. Edited by Alfred von Tirpitz. Vols. 1–2. Berlin, 1924, 1926.

Poll, Bernhard. *Deutsches Schicksal*. Berlin, 1937.

Potiemkine, Vladimir. *Histoire de la diplomatie*. Paris, 1935.

Les Pourparlers diplomatiques 16/29 juin–3/16 août. Paris, 1914. (PD)

Pourtales, Friedrich. *Meine letzten Verhandlungen in Sankt Petersburg*. Berlin, 1927.

Pribram, A.F. *Austrian Foreign Policy, 1908–1918*. London, 1923.

Puhle, Hans-Jürgen. *Agrarische Interessenpolitik und Preussischer Konservatismus im Wilhelminischen Reich*. Hanover, 1966.

Rachfahl, F. *Deutschland und die Weltpolitik*. Stuttgart, 1923.

Rassow, Peter. "Schlieffen und Holstein." *Historische Zeitschrift*, 173:297–313.

Rathenau, Walther. *Briefe.* Vol. 1. Dresden, 1926.

———. *Walther Rathenau-ein preussischer Europäer.* Edited by M. Eynern. Berlin, 1955.

———. *Tagebuch 1907–1922.* Edited by H. Pogge von Strandmann. Düsseldorf, 1967.

Rathmann, Lothar. "Zur Legende vom 'anti-kolonialen' Charakter der Bagdadbahnpolitik in der wilhelminischen Aera der Monopolkapitalismus." *Zeitschrift für Geschichtswissenschaft,* 9 (1961):465–77.

———. *Berlin-Bagdad.* Berlin, 1962.

Recouly, Raymond. *Les Heures tragiques d'avant-guerre.* Paris, 1922.

Redlich, Joseph. *Das politische Tagebuch Joseph Redlichs: Schicksalsjahre Österreichs 1908–1919.* Edited by Fritz Fellner. Vols. 1–2. Graz, Cologne, 1953.

Stenographische Berichte der Verhandlungen des Deutschen Reichstags Vol. 289. (RT).

Reiners, Ludwig. *In Europa gehen die Lichter aus.* Munich, 1955.

Remak, Joachim. *Sarajevo: The Story of a Political Murder.* London, 1959.

———. *The Origins of World War I, 1871–1914.* New York, 1975.

———. "The Healthy Invalid: How Doomed the Habsburg Empire?" *Journal of Modern History,* June 1969, pp. 127–43.

———. "1914—The Third Balkan War: Origins Reconsidered." *Journal of Modern History,* September 1971, pp. 353–66.

Renouvin, Pierre. *The Immediate Origins of the War.* New Haven, 1928.

———. *Histoire des relations internationales.* Vol. 6. Paris, 1955.

———. *La Crise européenne et la première guerre mondiale.* Paris, 1962.

Rich, N. *Friedrich von Holstein: Politics and Diplomacy in the Era of Bismarck and William II.* Vol. 1. Cambridge, Mass., 1965.

Riezler, Kurt, *Tagebücher, Aufsätze, Dokumente.* Edited by Karl Dietrich Erdmann. Göttingen, 1972.

Ritter, Gerhard. *The Corrupting Influence of Power.* Hadleigh, Essex, 1952.

———. "Die Zusammenarbeit der Generalstäbe Deutschlands und Österreich-Ungarns vor dem ersten Weltkrieg." *Historische Zeitschrift,* 190:401–25.

———. *Staatskunst und Kriegshandwerk. Das Problem des "Militarismus" in Deutschland.* Vol. 2. Munich, 1960.

———. "Eine neue Kriegsschuldthese? Zu Fritz Fischers Buch 'Griff nach der Weltmacht.' " *Historische Zeitschrift,* 191:646–68.

———. "Zur Fischer-Kontraverse." *Historische Zeitschrift,* 200:763–67.

———. *Der erste Weltkrieg. Studien zum deutschen Geschichtsbild.* Publications of the Federal Center for Political Education. Number 65. Bonn, 1964.

———. *Der Schlieffenplan: Kritik eines Mythos.* Munich, 1956.

———. *Das deutsche Problem.* Oldenburg, Munich, 1962.

Roberts, Penfield. *The Quest for Security, 1715–1740.* New York, 1947.

Roesler, Konrad. *Finanzpolitik des Deutschen Reiches.* Berlin, 1967.

Röhl, J.C.G. *Germany Without Bismarck: The Crisis of Government in the Second Reich, 1890–1900.* Berkeley, 1967.

———. "Admiral von Müller and the Approach of War." *Historical Journal,* December 1969, pp. 25–49.

———. *1914—Delusion or Design?* London, 1973.

Ropponen, Risto. *Die russische Gefahr.* Helsinki, 1976.

Rosenberg, Arthur. *The Birth of the German Republic, 1871–1918.* New York, 1931.

Rothfels, Hans. "Die englische-russischen Marineverhandlungen." *Berliner Monatshefte,* 1934, pp. 365–90.

———. *Zeitgeschichtliche Betrachtungen.* Göttingen, 1963.

Sazonov, Serge. *The Fateful Years, 1909–1916.* London, 1928.

Schäfer, Theobold. "Generaloberst von Moltke in den Tagen vor der Mobilmachung und seine Einwirkung auf Österreich." *Kriegsschuldfrage,* August 1926, pp. 514–49.

———. "Wollte Generaloberst von Moltke den Präventivkrieg?" *Kriegsschuldfrage,* June 1927, pp. 543–61.

Scheidemann, Philipp. *Memoiren eines Sozialdemokraten.* Vol. 1. Dresden, 1928.

Schenk, Willy. *Die deutsch-englische Rivalität vor dem ersten Weltkrieg in der Sicht deutscher Historiker.* Aarau, 1967.

Schellenberg, Johanna. "Die Heransbildung der Militärdiktatur in den ersten Jahren des Krieges." In *Politik im Krieg 1914–1918.* Edited by F. Klein, pp. 22–49. Berlin, 1964.

Schieder, Wolfgang, ed. *Erster Weltkrieg: Ursachen, Entstehung und Kriegsziele.* Cologne, Berlin, 1969.

Schilling, Baron. *How the War Began in 1914.* Diary of the Russian F.O. from 3 to 20 July 1914 (Russian Calendar). London, 1925.

Schmitt, Bernadette. "Triple Alliance and Triple Entente, 1902–1914." *American Historical Review,* April 1924, pp. 449–73.

———. *The Coming of the War, 1914.* Vols. 1–2. New York, 1930.

———. *The Annexation of Bosnia.* Cambridge, England, 1937.

Schoen, Wilhelm. *The Memoirs of an Ambassador.* London, 1922.

Schön, Curt. *Der "Vorwärts" und die Kriegserklärung.* Berlin, 1929.

Schorske, Carl E. *German Social Democracy, 1905–1917: The Development of the Great Schism.* Cambridge, Mass., 1955.

Schroeder, Paul W. "World War I as Galloping Gertie." *Journal of Modern History,* September 1972, pp. 319–45.

Schroeter, Alfred. *Krieg-Staat-Monopol 1914 bis 1918.* Berlin, 1965.

Schulthess. *Europäischer Geschichtskalender, 1912–14.* Munich, 1915–17.

Schüssler, Wilhelm, ed. *Weltmachtstreben und Flottenbau.* Witten, 1956.

Scott, J.F. *Five Weeks: The Surge of Public Opinion on the Eve of the Great War.* New York, 1927.

Seton-Watson, R.W. *Sarajevo: A Study into the Origins of the Great War.* London, 1925.

Sheehan, James J. *German Liberalism in the Nineteenth Century*. Chicago, 1978.

———. *German Imperialism*. New York, 1976.

Singer, L. *Ottokar Graf Czernin: Staatsmann einer Zeitwende*. Graz, 1965.

Snell, John L. *The Democratic Movement in Germany, 1789–1914*. Chapel Hill, 1976.

Sola Poole, I. and Kessler, A. "The Kaiser, the Tsar and the Computer: Information Processing in a Crisis." *American Behavioral Scientist*, 8 (1965):31–38.

Spender, J.A. and Asquith, Cyril. *Life of Herbert Henry Asquith, Lord Oxford and Asquith*. Vols. 1–2. London, 1932.

Spring-Rice, C. *Letters and Friendships of Sir Cecil Spring-Rice*. Vol. 2. London, 1929.

Stadelmann, R. "Der neue Kurs in Deutschland." *Geschichte in Wissenschaft und Unterricht*, 1953, pp. 150–72.

Steglich, Wolfgang. *Die Friedenspolitik der Mittelmächte 1917/18*. Vol. 1. Wiesbaden, 1964.

Stegmann, Dirk. *Die Erben Bismarcks: Parteien und Verbände in der Spätphase des Wilhelminischen Deutschlands, Sammlungspolitik, 1897–1918*. Cologne, 1970.

Steinberg, Jonathan. *Yesterday's Deterrent: Tirpitz and the Birth of the German Battle Fleet*. New York, 1965.

Steiner, Barry. *Arms Races, Diplomacy and Recurring Behavior: Lessons from Two Cases*. Los Angeles, 1977.

Steiner, Zara. *Britain and the Outbreak of the First World War*. London, 1977.

Stengers, Jean. "July 1914: Some Reflections." *L'Annuaire de l'institut de philologie et d'histoire orientales et slavs*, pp. 105–48. Brussels, 1963–1965.

Stenkewitz, Kurt. *Gegen Bajonette und Dividende: Die politische Krise in Deutschland am Vorabend des ersten Weltkrieges*. Berlin, 1960.

Stern, Fritz. "Bethmann Hollweg and the War: The Limits of Responsibility." In *Responsibility of Power*, pp. 252–85. Garden City, 1967.

———. *The Failure of Illiberalism: Essays on the Political Culture of Modern Germany*. New York, 1971.

Stieve, Friedrich. *Die Tragödie der Bundesgenossen Deutschland und Österreich-Ungarn, 1908–1914*. Munich, 1930.

Stolper, Gustav. *German Economy, 1870–1940*. New York, 1940.

Stone, Norman. "Moltke-Conrad: Relations Between the Austro-Hungarian and German General Staffs, 1909–1914." *Historical Journal*, January 1966, pp. 71–90.

Strandmann, Hartmut Pogge von and Geiss, Imanuel. *Die Erforderlichkeit des Unmöglichen: Deutschland am Vorabend des ersten Weltkrieges*. Frankfurt am Main, 1965.

Stürmer, M., ed. *Das kaiserlichen Deutschland*. Düsseldorf, 1970.

Suchomlinov, W.A. *Erinnerungen*. Berlin, 1924.

———. *Die russische Mobilmachung im Lichte amtlicher Urkunden und der Enthüllungen des Prozesses*. Bern, 1917.

Sugar, Peter F. "The Nature of the Non-Germanic Societies Under Habsburg Rule." *Slavic Review*, March 1963, pp. 1–30.

Taylor, A.J.P. *The Course of German History*. New York, 1962.

———. *A History of the First World War*. New York, 1966.

———. *From Sarajevo to Potsdam*. New York, 1967.

———. *The Struggle for Mastery in Europe, 1848–1918*. Oxford, 1960.

———. *The Habsburg Monarchy, 1809–1918: A History of the Austrian Empire and Austria-Hungary*. New York, 1965.

———. "What Else Indeed?" *New York Review of Books*, 5 August 1965, pp. 9–10.

———. *English History, 1914–1945*. Oxford, 1965.

———. *War By Timetable*. London, 1969.

———. "Fritz Fischer and His School." *Journal of Modern History*, March 1975, pp. 120–24.

Taylor, Edmond. *The Fall of the Dynasties: The Collapse of the Old Order, 1905–1922*. Garden City, 1963.

Thaden, Edward C. *Russia and the Balkan Alliance of 1912*. Philadelphia, 1965.

Thompson, Wayne C. *In the Eye of the Storm. Kurt Riezler and the Crisis of Modern Germany*. Iowa City, Iowa, 1980.

Thimme, A. *Hans Delbrück als Kritiker der Wilhelminischen Epoche*. Düsseldorf, 1956.

Thimme, Friedrich, ed. *Front wider Bülow*. Munich, 1931.

Tirpitz, Alfred. *Erinnerungen*. Leipzig, 1919.

———. *Der Aufbau der deutsche Weltmacht*. Berlin, 1924.

Tuchman, Barbara W. *The Guns of August*. New York, 1962.

Turner, L.C.F. "The Russian Mobilization in 1914." *Journal of Contemporary History*, 1968, pp. 65–68.

———. *Origins of the First World War*. New York, 1970.

Uebersberger, H. *Oesterreich-Ungarn zwischen Russland und Serbien*. Cologne, 1958.

Untersuchungsausschuss. Das Werk des Untersuchungsausschusses der Nationalversammlung und des Deutschen Reichstags 1919 bis 1928. Fourth series, Die Ursachen des Deutschen Zussamenbruchs im Jahre 1918. Vol. 1. Edited by Erich O. Volkmann. Berlin, 1929. *(UA)*

Valentin, Viet. *Deutschlands Aussenpolitik von Bismarcks Abgang bis zum Ende des Weltkrieges*. Berlin, 1921.

Valentini, R. *Kaiser und Kabinettschef: Nach eigenen Aufzeichnungen und dem Briefwechsel des Wirklichen Geheimen Rats R. von Valentini*. Edited by B. Schwertfeger. Oldenburg, 1931.

Vietsch, Eberhard. *Wilhelm Solf: Botschafter zwischen den Zeiten*. Tübingen, 1961.

———. "Der Kriegsausbruch 1914 im Lichte der neuesten Forschung." *Geschichte in Wissenschaft und Unterricht*, August 1964, pp. 472–86.

Viviani, René. *Réponse au Kaiser*. Paris, 1923.

Vogel, Barbara. *Deutsche Russlandpolitik: Das Scheitern der deutschen Weltpolitik unter Bülow, 1900–1906*. Gütersloh, 1973.

Waldersee, Graf. "Der deutsche Generalstab und die Kriegsschuld." *Deutsche Offizier Bund*, 1926, pp. 1–21.

Warburg, Max M. *Aus meinen Aufzeichnungen*. Glückstadt, 1952.

Weber, Max. *Gesammelte politische Schriften*. Munich, 1921.

Wedel, O. *Austro-German Diplomatic Relations, 1908–1914*. Stanford, 1932.

Wehler, H.U. "Der Fall Zabern." *Welt als Geschichte*, 1963, pp. 34–56.

———. *Das Deutsche Kaiserreich, 1871–1918*. Göttingen, 1973.

Der Weltkrieg 1914–1918. Vol. 1. Berlin: Reichsarchiv, 1925. (*Weltkrieg*)

Wernecke, Klaus. *Der Wille zur Weltgeltung: Aussenpolitik und Öffentlichkeit im Kaiserreich am Vorabend des ersten Weltkrieges*. Düsseldorf, 1970.

Werner, Lothar. *Der Alldeutsche Verband, 1890–1918: Ein Beitrag zur Geschichte der öffentlichen Meinung in Deutschland*. Berlin, 1935.

Westarp, Kuno. *Konservative Politik im letzten Jahrzehnt des Kaiserreiches*. Vol. 1. Berlin, 1935.

Das Wiener Kabinette und die Entstehung des Weltkrieges. Edited by Roderich Gooss. Vienna, 1919.

William, Crown Prince. *My War Experiences*. London, 1922.

Williamson, Samuel R. *The Politics of Grand Strategy: Britain and France Prepare for War, 1904–1914*. Cambridge, Mass., 1969.

Witt, Peter-Christian. *Die Finanzpolitik des Deutschen Reiches 1903–1913*. Lübeck, Hamburg, 1969.

Wohlgemuth, Heinz, *Burgkrieg, nicht Burgfriede!* Berlin, 1963.

Wolff, Theodor. *The Eve of War*. London, 1935.

———. *Der Marsch durch zwei Jahrzente*. Amsterdam, 1936.

Woodward, E.L. *Great Britain and the German Navy*. Oxford, 1935.

Young, Harry F. *Prince Lichnowsky and the Great War*. Athens, Ga., 1978.

Zechlin, Egmont. *Staatsstreichpläne Bismarcks und Wilhelms II, 1890 bis 1894*. Stuttgart, 1929.

———. *Bismarck und die Grundlegung der deutschen Grossmacht*. Stuttgart, 1930.

———. "Probleme des Kriegskalküls und der Kriegsbeendigung im Ersten Weltkrieg." *Geschichte in Wissenschaft und Unterricht*, September 1963, pp. 69–88.

———. "Die Illusion vom begrenzten Krieg: Berlins Fehlkalkulation im Sommer 1914." *Zeit*, 17 September 1965.

———. Letter to the Editor of *Der Spiegel*, 30 May 1966.

———. "Bethmann Hollweg, Kriegsrisiko und SPD 1914." *Monat*, January 1966, pp. 17–32.

———. "Motive und Taktik der Reichsleitung 1914: ein Nachtrag." *Monat*, February 1966, pp. 91–95.

———. "Deutschland zwischen Kabinettskrieg und Wirtschaftskrieg," *Historische Zeitschrift*, 199:347–458.

_____. "Friedensbestrebungen und Revolutionierungsversuche: Deutsche Bemühungen zur Ausschaltung Russlands im ersten Weltkrieg." Supplements to *Das Parlament, Aus Politik und Zeitgeschichte*, 17 May 1961, 14 June 1961, 21 June 1961, 15 May 1963.

Ziebura, G. *Die deutsche Frage in der öffentlichen Meinung Frankreichs von 1911 bis 1914.* Berlin, 1955.

_____, ed. *Grundfragen der deutschen Aussenpolitik seit 1871.* Darmstadt, 1975.

Zilliacus, Konne. *Mirror of the Past: A History of Secret Diplomacy.* New York, 1946.

Zimmermann, E. "Um Schlieffens Plan." *Süddeutsche Monatshefte*, 1921, pp. 73–98.

Zmarzlik, Hans Günther. *Bethmann Hollweg als Reichskanzler 1904–1914: Studien zu Möglichkeiten und Grenzen seiner innerpolitischen Machtstellung.* Düsseldorf, 1957.

Zorn, Wolfgang. "Wirtschaft und Politik im deutschen Imperialismus." In *Festschrift für F. Lütge*, pp. 301–30. Stuttgart, 1966.

Zwehl, Hans. *Erich von Falkenhayn, General der Infanterie: eine biographische Studie.* Berlin, 1926.

INDEX